T0319414

FISCAL ADJUSTMENT AND
ECONOMIC DEVELOPMENT

This study is an attempt to find a solution to the problem of fiscal adjustment between a province or a state and its municipalities–a pressing problem throughout Canada and the United States and in many other countries in view of the great disparities in the revenue-raising capacity of municipalities, their limited tax bases, and the pressure on them to provide higher levels of public services. The principles developed are of general applicability, but their use is illustrated by using Nova Scotia as a case study.

The first of the series "Atlantic Provinces Studies" was established by the Social Science Research Council of Canada to encourage research on the economic and social problems of the Atlantic Provinces.

JOHN F. GRAHAM is Fred C. Manning Professor of Economics and Head of the Department of Economics and Sociology at Dalhousie University. Dr. Graham is General Editor of the Atlantic Provinces Studies which this book inaugurates.

LABRADOR

QUEBEC

ST. LAWRENCE RIVER

ANTICOSTI I.

QUEBEC

GULF OF
ST. LAWRENCE

DALHOUSIE
CAMPBELLTON
CHALEUR BAY
CARAQUET
SHIPPEGAN
BATHURST

EDMUNDSTON

ST. LEONARD
GRAND FALLS

MAGDALEN
ISLANDS

CABOT

NEWCASTLE CHATHAM

TIGNISH

C. NORT

NEW
BRUNSWICK

HARTLAND

WOODSTOCK

P.E.I.

CAP

SUMMERSIDE

U.S.A.

FREDERICTON MARYSVILLE
OROMOCTO

SHEDIAC
MONCTON
DIEPPE
PORT ELGIN
SACKVILLE

BORDEN

CHARLOTTETOWN

INVERNESS

SYDNEY MINES
NORTH SYDNEY

NEW
DO
SYDN

NORTHUMBERLAND STRAIT

SUSSEX

AMHERST
OXFORD
SPRINGHILL

PICTOU
NEW GLASGOW
WESTVILLE TRENTON
STELLARTON

ANTIGONISH

PORT HAWKESBURY
MULGRAVE

LO

ROTHESAY
ST. STEPHEN SAINT JOHN
MILLTOWN
ST. ANDREWS ST. GEORGE LANCASTER

PARRSBORO

TRURO

CANSO

KENTVILLE WOLFVILLE
BERWICK HANTSPORT
MIDDLETON WINDSOR
ANNAPOLIS ROYAL BRIDGETOWN

STEWIACKE

NOVA SCOTIA

BAY OF FUNDY

DIGBY

HALIFAX DARTMOUTH

MAHONE BAY
BRIDGEWATER LUNENBURG

SABLE ISLAND

LIVERPOOL

YARMOUTH

SHELBURNE
LOCKEPORT
CLARK'S HARBOUR CAPE SABLE

ATLANTIC PROVINCES

SCALE • 1:5,000,000

0   20   40   60   80
MILES

70°

50°

70°

45°

65°

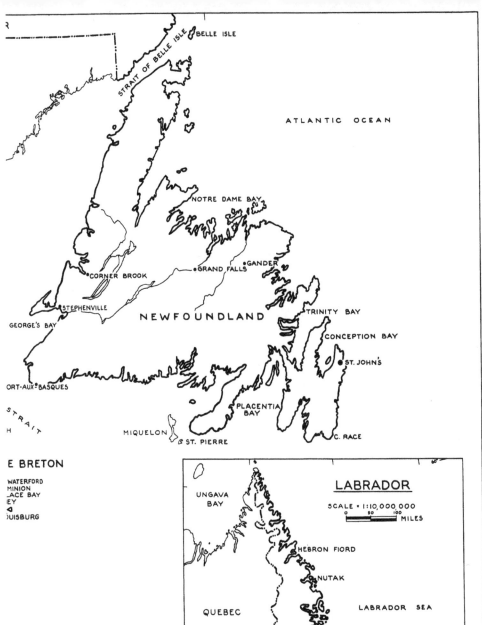

BELLE ISLE

STRAIT OF BELLE ISLE

ATLANTIC OCEAN

NOTRE DAME BAY

CORNER BROOK

GRAND FALLS GANDER

STEPHENVILLE

GEORGE'S BAY

NEWFOUNDLAND

TRINITY BAY

CONCEPTION BAY

ST. JOHN'S

ORT-AUX-BASQUES

STRAIT

H

MIQUELON

ST. PIERRE

PLACENTIA BAY

C. RACE

E BRETON

WATERFORD
MINION
ACE BAY
EY
UISBURG

ATLANTIC
OCEAN

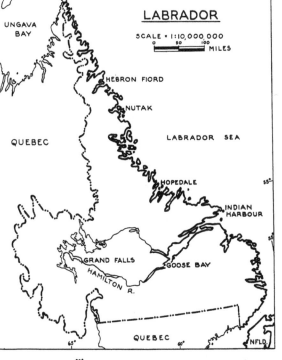

UNGAVA BAY

LABRADOR

SCALE = 1:10,000,000

0   50   100
MILES

HEBRON FIORD

NUTAK

QUEBEC

LABRADOR SEA

HOPEDALE

INDIAN HARBOUR

GRAND FALLS   GOOSE BAY

HAMILTON R.

QUEBEC

NFLD.

60°

55°

55°

65°   60°

55°

ATLANTIC PROVINCES STUDIES

A series of studies, edited by John F. Graham, sponsored by the Social Science Research Council of Canada, and published with financial assistance from the Canada Council.

1. *Fiscal Adjustment and Economic Development: A Case Study of Nova Scotia.* By JOHN F. GRAHAM

FISCAL
ADJUSTMENT
AND ECONOMIC
DEVELOPMENT

A Case Study of
Nova Scotia

~

JOHN F. GRAHAM

~

University of Toronto Press

© UNIVERSITY OF TORONTO PRESS 1963

Printed in Canada

Reprinted 2017

ISBN 978-1-4875-9919-5 (paper)

TO HAZEL MARIE GRAHAM

Preface

A SUBSTANTIAL SECTION of the literature of public finance deals with fiscal adjustment in a federal country between the federal government and the state or provincial governments. Little has been written on fiscal adjustment between state or provincial governments and municipal governments. This study was undertaken in an effort to fill part of this gap. It was also prompted by the general concern over the present fiscal plight of the municipalities in Nova Scotia and elsewhere in North America. The fact that Nova Scotia, like the other three Atlantic Provinces, is economically retarded in comparison with the rest of the country suggested the desirability of relating the treatment of provincial-municipal fiscal adjustment to that province's problems of economic development. Consequently, an attempt has been made to develop general principles of provincial-municipal fiscal adjustment which are consistent with optimum allocation of resources and to apply them to Nova Scotia.

I have drawn heavily on the writings of Professor J. M. Buchanan on the subject of federal fiscal adjustment and on a journal debate between him and Professor A. D. Scott on the effects of federal grants on resource allocation. My intellectual debt to both men is considerable. I am indebted to Professor J. N. Wolfe who first suggested to me the general line of approach that has been followed. The idea of integrating the treatment of fiscal adjustment and economic development in a low-income province was suggested by Professor Carl S. Shoup who sponsored the dissertation on which this book is based and gave generously of his time and energy in the course of its preparation. His stimulating questions, trenchant criticisms, and patience are in large measure responsible for any merit this study may have.

Most of the writing was done while I was on leave at Columbia University in the academic year 1958-9 where I had the privilege of participating in the Public Finance Workshop sponsored by the Ford Foundation and directed by Professor Shoup, the members of which read and criticized a preliminary draft of the study. This final version was prepared mainly in the summer of 1961, when I had the capable assistance of Miss Joyce Wyman in revising the statistical and other empirical material and in typing and checking the manuscript. As with previous drafts, I had the expert help of Mrs. Parker Hamilton with the typing of part of the manuscript. On very short notice, Mrs. Helen J. Stein of the Nova Scotia Research Foundation kindly drew the map for the endpapers.

Professor J. H. Aitchison, my friend and colleague, gave continual and vital encouragement and painstakingly read the whole of the preliminary draft from the point of view of a political scientist and suggested numerous improvements in style and content, at a time when his energies were already severely taxed by other tasks. Professor N. H. Morse read chapter II and made valuable suggestions for its revision. Professor W. R. Maxwell, while my department head, gave his full support and postponed his own much deserved leave of absence and bore the burden of extra students so that I could have the necessary leave to finish the original version of this study.

The generous assistance of numerous public servants and others consulted was invaluable. Unfortunately , I cannot name them because of the controversial nature of some of the views expressed here. It is not to be assumed that they would agree with these views. On at least two occasions, the Canadian Tax Foundation came to the rescue with information which was not readily available elsewhere.

Grateful acknowledgment of financial assistance is made to the Nova Scotia Research Foundation for supporting research on investment in Nova Scotia which eventually led me into this field of study, to the Canada Council for a fellowship and grant which made it possible for me to take a year's leave and for financial assistance in publishing this book, to the Public Finance Workshop at Columbia University for a fellowship and grant, and to the Social Science Research Council of Canada for a grant for typing expenses and a grant from its Atlantic Provinces Studies project for Miss Wyman's assistance.

I had the pleasure and good fortune to have Mrs. A. M. Magee, of the editorial department of the University of Toronto Press, edit the manuscript and see the book through the press.

My wife bore the real brunt of the writing of this book and performed many tiresome chores such as proofreading and checking. Without her support and encouragement, I could not have written it.

This book is the first in the series of Atlantic Provinces Studies, which was established by the Social Science Research Council of Canada in August, 1959, following a request by the Atlantic Provinces Economic Council that it consider ways of furthering research on the Atlantic Provinces. The purposes of the project are to give assistance to scholars, in the Atlantic Provinces and elsewhere, who are interested in undertaking fundamental studies of their own choosing on the economic, social, and political conditions and problems of the Atlantic Provinces; to publish in the Atlantic Provinces Series those studies appropriate for publication; and in so doing to help provide a favourable environment for research in the social sciences in the Atlantic Provinces. It is hoped that the studies will shed light on the economic and social problems of the Atlantic Provinces and help in the formulation of policies for their solution. Most of the financial support for the programme has been generously provided by the Atlantic Provinces Research Board and the Canada Council. The programme has benefited considerably from the continuous co-operation of the Atlantic Provinces Economic Council.

JOHN F. GRAHAM

Halifax, Nova Scotia
March 6, 1963

Contents

Tables and Figures

FIGURES

FISCAL ADJUSTMENT AND
ECONOMIC DEVELOPMENT

Introduction

IT IS THE PURPOSE of this study to determine principles of provincial-municipal, or state-municipal, fiscal adjustment consistent with sound economic development, that is with optimum allocation of resources, and to apply these principles in a case study of Nova Scotia. Most of the theoretical discussion is relevant to any province or state in a federal country, and much of it to fiscal adjustment between any two levels of government, whether a country has a federal or unitary form of government.

Ordinarily the theoretical argument would come at the beginning of a combined theoretical and empirical study; but, as an examination of the relation of fiscal adjustment to economic development in Nova Scotia required the introduction of much material on the economic and fiscal structure of the province before discussing provincial-municipal fiscal adjustment, the most satisfactory arrangement seemed to be that followed here of placing the theoretical discussion after this background material but before the empirical chapters on fiscal adjustment in Nova Scotia.

Nova Scotia is a low-income province. Over the five-year period, 1956–60, its average annual personal income per capita was $1,077, compared with $1,451 for Canada, and $1,721 for Ontario and $1,727 for British Columbia, the richest provinces. The amount for Nova Scotia was only 74.2 per cent of that for Canada, 62.6 per cent of that for Ontario, and 62.4 per cent of that for British Columbia.[1] Being a poor province, Nova Scotia cannot tolerate waste on a scale tolerable by Ontario or British Columbia. Of great importance to a rich province,

[1]Calculated from Dominion Bureau of Statistics (hereinafter D.B.S.), *National Accounts Income and Expenditure, 1960* (Ottawa: Queen's Printer, 1961), p. 40.

the best allocation of resources is, therefore, of even greater importance to a poor one like Nova Scotia. It is more urgent for a poor than for a rich province to find the optimum division between the public and the private sectors, for in a poor province the balance at the margin between public goods and private goods is at a point where marginal social benefit and marginal social burden are greater than in a wealthy province, assuming similar attitudes towards public and private goods in the two provinces;[2] and it is more urgent that the resources within both sectors be put to their most effective uses.

All four of the Atlantic Provinces (the term includes Newfoundland, which Maritime Provinces does not) are low-income provinces. Nova Scotia has the highest personal income per capita of the four. Their economies are sufficiently alike to make applicable to all some of the generalizations which can be made about Nova Scotia. But there are also important respects in which they differ and the discussion will be less equivocal if reference is made throughout only to Nova Scotia.

There are many determinants of the allocation of resources, some within the reach of democratic government and some not. It is one of the primary functions of government to determine the broad division between the public and private sectors, and there are many decisions of government that affect the allocation of resources within both sectors. Among the latter is the pattern of provincial-municipal fiscal relations. This pattern obviously affects the allocation of resources in the public sector. It also affects it in the private sector. The pattern of fiscal relations is by no means the most important determinant in the latter sector, but it is one which is under the control of government and one which a poor province cannot afford not to exploit to the full.[3] Improved allocation of resources resulting from fiscal adjustments would in turn have favourable fiscal consequences. Although it is unlikely that Nova Scotia, even if its resources were used as effectively as possible, could expect to have as high a per capita income as the more favourably endowed provinces, its fiscal capacity will nevertheless be greater with improved use of resources.

It is the concern of this study to explain why Nova Scotia is a low-income province and to consider what pattern of provincial-municipal fiscal relations would be most conducive to the best use of its resources. To achieve this purpose it will be necessary to determine and

---

[2]Compare A. C. Pigou, *A Study in Public Finance* (3rd edition, revised; London: Macmillan and Co., 1949), pp. 31–2.

[3]This study, then, is not primarily concerned with more direct ways of influencing economic development, such as subsidies and tax concessions to industries.

apply the principles of fiscal adjustment consistent with the best use of the province's resources; and also to discover the effects on resource allocation of particular kinds and levels of government services. Where they are relevant, the traditional norms of public finance, equity in particular, will also be brought into the discussion.

A consideration of provincial-municipal fiscal relations would appear to be timely, for it is becoming more and more evident that substantial changes in municipal finance in Canada, generally, are sorely needed. Property was possibly an adequate local tax base when financial demands on the municipalities were fairly modest; but as the demands of society for services have grown, and as what were once regarded as local services have come to be considered general services of wider interest, not only have local revenues become inadequate, but the appropriateness of municipal responsibility for providing many of these traditional services can be called into question. Therefore, in any consideration of adjustments in provincial-municipal fiscal relations, these problems must be dealt with.

Much of the treatment of fiscal adjustment will be related to the principle of fiscal equity developed by J. M. Buchanan.[4] This principle will be discussed at length later on; the following terse description is intended merely to give the reader an initial inkling of its meaning and significance. Buchanan argues that if the fiscal treatment of otherwise similarly situated taxpayers in different provinces[5] is not equal, there will be pressure on those less favourably treated to move themselves or their capital, or both, to where the treatment is more favourable. The pressure may take the form of heavier tax burdens, inferior services, or a combination of both. In a federal country like Canada or the United States, which is economically integrated on a national scale in that labour and capital are free to move throughout the country according to the marginal productivity rule, it is anomalous that differential fiscal pressures in the different provinces or states should cause factors to be located where their productivity is less than it would be elsewhere.

To eliminate differential fiscal pressures and their harmful effects on the allocation of resources, Buchanan proposes that transfers should be made from high-income to low-income provinces, either by means

[4]J. M. Buchanan, "The Pure Theory of Government Finance: A Suggested Approach," *Journal of Political Economy*, XLVII (December, 1949); and "Federalism and Fiscal Equity," *American Economic Review*, XL (September, 1950), *passim*.

[5]Buchanan, since he develops his arguments with regard to the United States, refers to "states," but "provinces" is more appropriate in this, Canadian, context.

of equalization grants from the federal government, or by means of differential federal tax rates in the different provinces, to make possible equal fiscal treatment of equals. Even with perfect allocation of resources throughout the nation, provinces would still differ in per capita income because of lack of uniformity in the distribution of natural resources and of high- and low-income occupations, and fiscal adjustment as just described would therefore still be necessary.

Although Buchanan developed these propositions with reference to fiscal adjustment at the federal-provincial level, they are also applicable at the provincial-municipal level. Indeed, for the principle of fiscal equity to be fully applied in a federal country it must be followed through at the provincial-municipal level. The federal government makes grants to provincial governments, not to individuals; whether the principle of fiscal equity is implemented or not depends upon the effects on individuals of the provinces' use of the grants. This point requires emphasis, for too often discussions in public finance stop with consideration of relations between governments of different levels or between governments and the people as a whole; whereas, ultimately, public policy of the type envisaged here can only be meaningfully assessed in terms of its effect on individual citizens. A provincial government has considerably more freedom to effect adjustment between itself and its municipalities, since they are its own creations, than has the federal government to effect adjustment between itself and the provinces, which possess a large amount of sovereignty in their own right.

Since the aim of this study is to arrive at a prescription for fiscal adjustment which will be conducive to optimum allocation of resources, it will be necessary to determine what economic adjustments are required to achieve, or at least approach, this optimum. Determining the desirable directions of economic development is no simple task. At many points empirical evidence is unavailable or inconclusive, and assumptions have had to be made unsupported by such evidence. However, in most cases these can be supported at least by the informed opinions of people of good judgment who are familiar with the problems of Nova Scotia. (These opinions have been solicited in confidential interviews conducted by the writer with about twenty such people.) Each person was chosen for his special knowledge about some particular aspect or aspects of the economy of the province. These interviews were valuable as sources of information and of judgments not available elsewhere and as checks on the soundness of the writer's own reasoning.

Some essential background material is introduced in chapters II, III, and IV. One cannot clearly understand the provinces's present economic problems without knowing something of its geography and its economic history, hence chapter II. Since the ability of a low-income province to effect adjustments relating to its municipalities is to a large extent determined by its relations with the Dominion, and since the degree to which optimum fiscal adjustment can be accomplished in the nation as a whole depends initially upon fiscal adjustment among the provinces, chapter III on federal-provincial relations in Canada has been included. Finally, in order to discuss adjustments in provincial-municipal relations it is necessary to know about municipal organization and finance in Nova Scotia and about provincial participation in the performance of municipal functions (chapter IV). These chapters and chapters V and VI, although integrated with the rest of the study, are written so that they can stand by themselves for the benefit of readers not concerned with the theory and problems of fiscal adjustment, which are the core of the study. Chapter VII on the principles of fiscal adjustment can also be read in isolation from the rest of the study, as this theoretical discussion is relevant to any province or state.

Inevitably much of the statistical data used will get out of date quickly; but it is hoped that they adequately serve their analytical and illustrative purposes and that their organization in this study will continue to be sufficiently relevant that the reader interested in doing so can readily bring them up to date himself.

Since chapter V is essentially a continuation of the discussion in chapter II, there would be some value in putting them next to one another; but, as this study is primarily concerned with public finance, it was decided to introduce the material in chapters III and IV at this early stage, rather than after chapter V. This arrangement has the further advantages that chapter VI develops directly from chapter V and that the main thread of the argument runs without interruption from chapter V to the end of the study. Even so, the reader may prefer to skim chapters III and IV for the present and examine them in more detail later, in conjunction with chapters VIII and IX.

$$\sim\!\sim \text{ II } \sim\!\sim$$

The Economy of Nova Scotia: A Geographical and Historical Perspective

THE GEOGRAPHY OF NOVA SCOTIA[1]

NOVA SCOTIA is a long narrow peninsula held by the continent at the middle and thrust out into the north Atlantic Ocean which has carved a heavily indented coastline along the whole of the part directly exposed to it. The province runs northeast to southwest for a total distance of 374 miles, of which Cape Breton Island, now joined to the mainland by a causeway, accounts for 106. The width ranges from 60 to 100 miles. Nova Scotia is 21,068 square miles in area. Like the other Maritime Provinces and the New England States, Nova Scotia is part of that ancient geological formation, the Appalachian Region. Although an upland extends like a backbone for the entire length of the province, the region is not really a single formation, but consists of five groups of highlands and as many lowlands.

The population of Nova Scotia was estimated in the 1961 census to be 730,007, about 4.0 per cent of that of Canada and about 38.8 per cent of that of the Atlantic Provinces. Halifax, the capital and largest city, accounted for 92,511 persons; Sydney for 33,617; and Dart-

[1]Much of the material in this section is based upon: S. A. Saunders, *Studies in the Economy of the Maritime Provinces* (Toronto: Macmillan Company of Canada, 1939), pp. 1–13; A. W. Currie, *Economic Geography of Canada* (Toronto: Macmillan Company of Canada, 1945), pp. 1–101; and James Wreford Watson, "The Geography," in *Canada*, edited by George W. Brown (Berkeley and Los Angeles: University of California Press, 1950), pp. 33–52.

mouth for 46,966; the thirty-nine incorporated towns, ranging from 800 to 24,186, for 172,573; and the rural areas, including villages, for the balance of 391,340.

Of the many rivers, the longest, the Mersey, is only about fifty miles long. Their shortness is determined by the smallness of the province and by the fact that most of them flow southeast or northwest, that is, in the short directions. Only a few of the rivers are useful for navigation, but they do provide some electric power, practically all of the potential of any significance having already been developed, and they are valuable to the fishing industry as spawning grounds and to the tourist industry for sport fishing, as are the numerous lakes. The largest lakes, the Bras d'Or Lakes, are really an inland arm of the sea and almost cut Cape Breton Island into two parts.

The continental influence on the climate of the prevailing winds from the west and northwest in the winter, and the south and southwest in the summer, is modified by the oceanic influences. The Gulf Stream is deflected eastward, away from the land, off Halifax, by the Labrador Current, which sweeps down around the eastern end of Labrador. The net result is in general a cool, humid, temperate climate, with pleasant but short summers and moderately cold winters. The variety of influences, however, produces considerable variation for the size of the province; the southwestern part, for example, comes more under the influence of the Gulf Stream and the northeastern part more under the influence of the Labrador Current. The average temperature at Halifax for the year around is 44° F., for February 23° F., and for July and August 64° F. The average annual precipitation at Halifax is about 55 inches distributed fairly evenly throughout the year, while that for the province as a whole is about 45 inches.

The soil, which is of the brown podsolic type, is in general " . . . thin, low in fertility and organic matter, and highly acid"[2] and so requires considerable fertilizer and lime. There is, however, great variation in the quality of soil over even very small areas, and some, such as that in the Annapolis Valley, is of much better than average quality. Fruit (mainly apples) is grown in the Annapolis Valley, and poultry farming, dairy farming, livestock raising, and mixed farming are carried on in most of the agricultural areas.

The climate and soil are generally suitable for forest growth. It has

[2]W. M. Drummond, W. Mackenzie, *et al.*, *Progress and Prospects of Canadian Agriculture* (A study for the Royal Commission on Canada's Economic Prospects; Ottawa: Queen's Printer, 1957), p. 146. The Royal Commission on Canada's Economic Prospects will sometimes be referred to hereafter as the Gordon Commission, after its chairman, W. L. Gordon.

recently been estimated that of the total land and fresh water area of 13,342,110 acres in the province, 9,378,518 (70.3 per cent of the total) are productive forest land and 1,453,378 (10.9 per cent of the total) are agricultural and other improved land.[3] Of this total area of productive forest, 55 per cent contains softwood, 39 per cent mixed wood, and the balance of 6 per cent hardwood.[4] Although lumber production has declined with the exhaustion of timber suitable for lumber, the forest industry, with proper management, has a fairly good long-run potential in the production of pulp.

The fisheries (both offshore and inshore) are probably the natural resource in which the province has the strongest natural advantage and the greatest long-run economic potential. The offshore fisheries on the various fishing banks off the Nova Scotian and Newfoundland coasts require fairly large vessels which can stay away from port for a number of days. They yield cod and haddock in the main, but also other varieties of groundfish (fish that feed on the bottom of the ocean), such as halibut and hake. The inshore fisheries, extending over most of the waters near the coast, especially on the Atlantic shore, require smaller, frequently one-man, boats which go out by the day after cod, haddock, pollock, herring, mackerel, salmon, swordfish, tuna, and shellfish (mainly scallops, clams, and the ubiquitous lobster, the largest single money-earner after cod). There are numerous small fishing villages and a few fishing towns all around the coast, especially on the very heavily indented Atlantic shore, where the ocean has carved out hundreds of coves with varying degrees of shelter and a number of fine big harbours.

The many varieties of rock formation, of minerals, and of geological ages represented in Nova Scotia make it a geologist's paradise. Yet though many a geologist has been known to wax enthusiastic about the minerals, economically exploitable deposits are found to consist chiefly of coal and industrial minerals such as salt, gypsum, and barytes. Coal deposits both on the mainland and on Cape Breton Island have long held a dominant place in the province's economy, but can now be mined only at high cost and marketed outside of the Maritime Provinces only with the assistance of large federal freight subventions. Extensive gypsum deposits found in several parts of the province, especially in Hants County, account for about 80 per cent

[3]Government of Nova Scotia, Department of Lands and Forests, *The Forest Resources of Nova Scotia* (1958), p. 28.

[4]*Ibid.*, p. 74. In the period 1952–6 the province produced an annual average of 340,488,171 f.b.m. of sawlog material and 354,876 cords of pulp wood and pit props, *ibid.*, p. 38.

of Canadian production.[5] Practically all of Nova Scotia's output is exported to the United States in raw form. Salt is mined at Pugwash on the Northumberland Shore and is also obtained at Nappan near the New Brunswick border. Barytes is obtained from an immense deposit at Walton near the southern shore of Minas Basin and shipped to the United States and South America. Limestone and building materials, quarried mainly for local use, account for most of the rest of production.

The manufacturing of the province is mainly what might be called primary manufacturing, as in the cases of fish and other food processing, the production of primary iron and steel, the milling of lumber, and the making of pulp and paper. Much of the secondary manufacturing industry is small and supplies only local markets, as in the case of bakery products. Some of the exceptions are the manufacture of railway rolling stock at Trenton as an adjunct of the primary steel industry, of some textiles (several firms supply national markets), of pleasure boats at Weymouth and other centres, which are sold in the United States and elsewhere, and of confectionery at Halifax. Defence is a very important factor in the manufacturing picture, especially in the Halifax area, which is the eastern headquarters for the Royal Canadian Navy. Shipbuilding and repairing, aircraft repairing, the production of electronic equipment, and oil refining are all heavily dependent on the naval installations.

The tourist industry is important to the province, although its value is difficult to measure. The main tourist attractions are the seacoast, both for its scenic beauty and for recreation, the summers which are pleasant compared with those of the large cities of central Canada and the eastern United States, the sport fishing and hunting, and the alleged leisurely pace of life. Since the province is not well endowed with natural resources in relation to population, the potential of the tourist industry should be fully explored and exploited, although the shortness of the season inhibits investment of capital and is unsatisfactory for those requiring year-around employment.

The Province is served with a variety of transportation facilities. Since the 1930's the government has vigorously pursued a policy of paving all trunk and other important highways. An extensive network of good roads is important both for the tourist industry and for the motor trucking industry, as well as for the general facilitation of

[5]John Davis, *Mining and Mineral Processing in Canada* (A study for the Royal Commission on Canada's Economic Prospects; Ottawa: Queen's Printer, 1957), p. 226.

commerce—especially since there are many small centres of industry connected with farming, fishing, and forestry.

The Dominion Atlantic Railway (a subsidiary of the Canadian Pacific Railway) runs from Halifax through the Annapolis Valley and on to Yarmouth, with a ferry operating between Digby and Saint John, New Brunswick, and connecting there with railway lines to Boston (freight only) and Montreal. The main line of the Canadian National Railways runs from Halifax across the province to Moncton, New Brunswick, and from there, west to Montreal and south to the United States. A branch line from Sydney, where there is a ferry connection with Newfoundland, meets the main line at Truro. Another line runs from Halifax to Yarmouth along the South Shore. There are also other less important lines of the two railroad systems in the province.

Trans-Canada Air Lines has flights connecting Halifax, Sydney, and Yarmouth with Montreal, Fredericton, Saint John, and Boston, and with points in Newfoundland and in Europe. A regional air line, Maritime Central Airways, links up a larger number of Maritime centres including some of the smaller ones.

Shipping by water is of course very important with a location like Nova Scotia's. Halifax, the main seaport, has a fine, well-serviced harbour which is ice-free the year around. Its busy season, like that of its rival, Saint John, New Brunswick, is in the winter when the St. Lawrence ports of Quebec and Montreal are icebound, making the longer rail haul between central and western Canada and the eastern seaports necessary. However, New York and other American ports get a large part of this traffic, to the continual annoyance of Maritimers. In addition to the traffic of tramp freighters, there are regular calls by liners connecting with European and American ports. There is now year-around ferry service between Yarmouth and Bar Harbour, Maine; Caribou (near Pictou) and Wood Islands, Prince Edward Island; Tormentine, New Brunswick, and Borden, Prince Edward Island; and Sydney and Port aux Basques, Newfoundland; as well as the service already mentioned between Digby and Saint John. There is also considerable movement of freight at other ports; for example, iron ore and limestone are brought into Sydney, and iron, steel, and coal are shipped from Sydney; also, gypsum is exported from Hantsport, apples from Port Williams (near Kentville), fish products from Lunenburg, and newsprint from Liverpool.

In spite of all these facilities, transportation remains a basic problem of the Nova Scotia economy, principally because the long distance from central Canada (over 800 miles to Montreal, and about 1,200 to Toronto from Halifax) imposes serious disadvantages upon Nova Scotian producers competing in the main Canadian market area there, but also because the heavily indented coasts of Nova Scotia and New Brunswick make land transportation circuitous and awkward.

THE ECONOMIC HISTORY OF NOVA SCOTIA[6]

The salient feature of Nova Scotia's economic history over the past century has been the failure of the province to adjust satisfactorily to the deterioration of a well-integrated, sea-oriented economy, for which its resources and location had been well suited, by switching to an inland-oriented economy, for which they were not well suited. As a result, Nova Scotia, like the other Maritime Provinces, has remained on the periphery of the transcontinental development of the Canadian nation. Even if resources and location had been well suited to an inland orientation towards central and western Canada, the fundamental changes required in the firmly established economic and social structure of the province would likely have been difficult to make and slow in coming. As it was, adjustment of the economic structure was impeded by the unsuitability of resources and location. The economic problems facing Nova Scotia today are largely of these same origins and it is therefore necessary to have some knowledge of the province's economic history to understand these problems clearly.

The great cod fisheries off the coasts of Newfoundland and Nova Scotia attracted Europeans to the region after Cabot's voyage of 1497 and continued to dominate the economy of what is now Nova Scotia for more than two centuries. The French controlled the mainland of Nova Scotia for most of the period until 1713 and Cape Breton Island until 1763, when the Treaty of Paris gave Britain all of France's Canadian possessions except the small islands of St. Pierre and Miquelon. In

[6]Much of the material in this section is based upon: Saunders, *Studies*; S. A. Saunders, *Economic History of the Maritime Provinces* (A research study prepared for the Royal Commission on Dominion-Provincial Relations; Ottawa: King's Printer, 1940); H. A. Innis, *The Cod Fisheries: The History of an International Economy* (revised edition; Toronto: University of Toronto Press, 1954); B. S. Keirstead, *The Theory of Economic Change* (Toronto: Macmillan Company of Canada, 1948); W. T. Easterbrook and Hugh G. J. Aitken, *Canadian Economic History* (Toronto: Macmillan of Canada, 1956); George W. Brown, ed., *Canada* (United Nations Series, edited by Robert J. Kerner; Berkeley and Los Angeles: University of California Press, 1950); and R. D. Howland, *Some Regional Aspects of Canada's Economic Development* (A study for the Royal Commission on Canada's Economic Prospects; Ottawa: Queen's Printer, 1958).

1763, Nova Scotia included all of what are now the three Maritime Provinces, but in 1769 Prince Edward Island and in 1784 New Brunswick and Cape Breton Island were made separate provinces. The present boundaries of Nova Scotia date from 1820 when Cape Breton Island was again made part of Nova Scotia.

In the last quarter of the eighteeenth century, fishing was still the main occupation, but forestry, shipbuilding, and trading, mostly with Great Britain, New England, and the West Indies, were developing rapidly. Farming, except in the Bay of Fundy region, developed more slowly and was mainly a subsistence occupation. It was at this time that, under the stimulus of British mercantile policy which provided protected markets in the British West Indies for Nova Scotia's cod and, during the Napoleonic wars, in Britain for its timber, the "Golden Age" of the wood-wind-water economy began. This was a period when the products of the forest and sea were carried in wind-propelled wooden ships, which sailed the seven seas. For Nova Scotia this era of prosperity lasted until the third quarter of the nineteenth century, and was shared by the other Maritime Provinces, especially New Brunswick, and also by New England. Extensive shipbuilding all along the coast of Nova Scotia was stimulated by the natural desire of the people to carry their own fish and lumber to markets and to bring needed agricultural commodities and manufactures back home. These developments were both accelerated by and conducive to the influx of large numbers of United Empire Loyalists after 1783 and of British settlers and British capital.

The shipbuilding and carrying trade, which had begun from natural roots to supply local needs, extended far beyond local demands. In fact the Maritimes became a major commercial maritime power. In the middle of the nineteenth century they stood fourth in the world in registered tonnage.[7] Then as now it was common for the same individual to engage in farming, fishing, and forestry activities, and not uncommon for him also to build his own ship and carry his own produce to market. Small manufactories developed in many centres, partly in response to local demand and partly to provide the seagoing traders with more diversified cargoes. Halifax was the most important commercial centre, but the activities described above were well distributed along the coast.

Throughout most of the first half of the nineteenth century the province depended upon imports for many of its foodstuffs. Agriculture continued to lag for a number of reasons: men tended to be drawn into

[7]*Report of the Royal Commission on Dominion-Provincial Relations* (Ottawa: King's Printer, 1940), I, 22.

the more lucrative and exciting fishing, forestry, and trading activities; farming technique was poor and good roads were lacking; food could be imported easily from places where the land was more fertile. Most of the local production consisted of livestock and dairy products, areas in which foreign competition was weaker.

The wave of immigration that came after the Napoleonic Wars reached its peak in the 1840's and virtually ceased in Nova Scotia by 1850, at which time its population stood at about 275,000. Although the province persisted in its efforts to attract settlers, there was to be no further substantial immigration.

Nova Scotians were greatly concerned at the admission of American ships to the British West Indies' hitherto protected market in 1830, and they feared economic disaster when this was accompanied by Britain's adoption of complete free trade in the early 1850's, with the consequent elimination of its preference for Maritime timber. In spite of these unfavourable developments, prosperity continued, in part as a result of the Reciprocity Treaty of 1854–66 with the United States, which provided for free trade in natural products between British North America and the United States. Although Nova Scotia came to attach great importance to reciprocity, the treaty was negotiated largely at the instigation of the central Canadian provinces over the protests of Nova Scotia against the concessions which gave the United States access to the Maritime inshore fisheries. The duration of the treaty coincided with a period of considerable growth in Nova Scotia's exports, especially of fish and coal, and of continued strength in shipbuilding and in the carrying trades.

It has long been argued that reciprocity was the main factor contributing to the prosperity of the period and that the abrogation of the treaty by the United States in 1866 was largely responsible for the ensuing decline in the economic fortunes of the Maritimes. S. A. Saunders has shown that while reciprocity was no doubt partly responsible for the increased trade with the United States, "the Reciprocity Treaty contributed less to the prosperity of this period than did the American Civil War [which generated increased demands for Maritime products], railway construction in Nova Scotia and New Brunswick, and those external forces that greatly stimulated the shipbuilding industry and carrying trade."[8]

The very favourable conjuncture of conditions during the period

[8]Saunders, *Studies*, p. 104. He supports this statement with extensive argument. He also argues convincingly that the gain in exports to the United States from reciprocity was much greater in the Canadian provinces than in the Maritimes. (Pp. 103–55.)

of the Reciprocity Treaty created an economic expansion, based directly upon indigenous resources, that has never been repeated in the province's history. The momentum of the forces at work during this era and the gold rushes in the 1850's which created a strong demand for fast wooden ships prolonged the period of prosperity until the third quarter of the nineteenth century. But adverse forces, more fundamental than the freeing of British trade, were to bring good times to an end. These forces had begun to operate even before prosperity had begun.

Nova Scotia entered Confederation in 1867, a year after the abrogation of the Reciprocity Treaty, with its economy still buoyant. The fact that its prosperous, well-integrated economy began to decline rapidly within a few years after both the abrogation of the treaty and Confederation, and that this decline was especially pronounced after the introduction of the federal government's National Policy in 1879, led many Nova Scotians to blame Confederation and federal policies (including the failure to negotiate a new reciprocity treaty) for the ensuing years of chronic depression in the province. Nova Scotia felt it had been dragooned into Confederation under unfavourable terms by an imperial government acting under pressure from the Province of Canada and out of concern about the fate of the western territories in North America and about the defence of British North America (concern intensified by the bad relations between the United States and Britain arising from the Civil War). These circumstances enhanced the belief of Nova Scotians that there was a direct connection between Confederation and their economic plight.[9]

The principal reason for Nova Scotia's economic decline was beyond doubt the gradual undermining of its wood-wind-water economy by the ever increasing use of steel and steam, that is, by technological change. Steel steamships replaced wooden sailing ships, bringing drastic reductions to Nova Scotia's carrying trade and, consequently, to her shipbuilding industry. The fact that the steamships had larger capacity and greater speed and were more expensive than sailing ships placed a premium on volume of cargo. Even Halifax was removed from the

---

[9]"From the very date of the union, there had been a widespread and burning conviction in Nova Scotia that it had been manœuvred into a bargain prejudicial to its vital interests. In the provincial elections held late in 1867 thirty-six out of the thirty-eight members elected to the legislature were anti-Confederates. The new Government tried desperately to extricate the Province from the bonds of the union. Although these efforts were unavailing, the sentiment against Confederation remained strong in Nova Scotia and was significant in New Brunswick." (*Report of the Royal Commission on Dominion-Provincial Relations*, I, 54.)

schedule of Cunard steamships in 1867 because of the smallness of its cargoes—an ironic development, for the Cunard company was started by a Halifax merchant, Samuel Cunard, in 1840. A large economic hinterland had become a necessity for a thriving port.

The attempt to develop such a hinterland required the building of railways focused on a larger port, with the consequent decline of the many once flourishing smaller ports, and of the shipbuilding and other local industries clustered around them. Such railways could be built and the social costs borne, but even so the problem would not be solved, for a more intractable difficulty stood in the way: the ideal of short rail hauls to a heavily populated hinterland was lacking in Nova Scotia and stood little chance of developing, even with respect to Halifax, because of the lack of resources rich enough to attract sufficient population. The long haul to central Canada failed to provide the hoped for markets, even after the Intercolonial Railway was completed by the federal government in 1876. Freight rates over that distance proved to be a serious hindrance to trade. The development of low-cost, large-scale manufacturing techniques gave further important advantages to firms located near large markets.

There were other unfavourable factors. The easily accessible forestry resources became depleted, and in the present century the forest industry met new competition resulting from the development of vast new resources elsewhere, especially on the west coast after the Panama Canal was opened in 1914. On the other hand, the pulp and paper industry provided new opportunities for using forestry resources that have been exploited successfully. Agriculture, never a strong part of the Nova Scotian economy, met overwhelming competition from western grain, even before the turn of the century, upon the completion of transcontinental railways and the extension of westward settlement in North America. The introduction of canning and refrigeration into the meat trade in the late nineteenth century not only encroached upon the traditional fish markets as a result of the ensuing competition of frozen and chilled meat but also brought competition into the local and export meat markets from western beef and other meats. Other developments further hurt the dried fish trade. The policies of the United States and of some European countries for stimulating domestic sugar beet production reduced the market for West Indies sugar and hence the purchasing power with which the islands could buy fish. Mediterranean markets failed to recover after the First World War, and, to make matters worse, there was increased competition in them from Iceland, Britain, and Norway. On the favourable side, a flourishing apple industry began to develop in the Annapolis Valley in the late nineteenth century to supply the British markets,[10] and the lobster and fresh fish trade came to more than make up for the decline in the dried fish trade.

As for coal, the loss of the markets in the United States was inevitable. The increase in these markets while the Reciprocity Treaty was in force was not due to reciprocity but to the delay in the opening of new, lower cost mines in the United States occasioned by the Civil War. Even in the Maritime and central Canadian markets Nova Scotian coal was meeting stiff competition from British coal returning at ballast rates in timber ships.[11]

Confederation and the National Policy are bound together in their impact on Nova Scotian development in that the National Policy, which was really a series of federal policies to develop a transcontinental economy, was a logical consequence of Confederation.[12] In brief, the National Policy was a three-pronged plan: to cement the west to the east by a transcontinental railway; to settle the west by immigration, both to consolidate the Dominion's claim to the west and to provide freight, especially wheat, to support the railways; and to erect protective tariffs on manufactured goods in order to encourage the development of Canadian secondary industry and strengthen the east-west flow of trade and in doing so utilize the excess capacity of the railroads. This well-integrated policy achieved its nation-building purpose, no doubt at some economic cost.

Nova Scotia shared in the development fostered by the National Policy mainly through its expanded coal, and iron and steel industries. The expectation that central Canada, once the railway link with it was made by the Intercolonial Railway, would provide a large and lucrative market for other Nova Scotian products was roundly disappointed. Coal production was stimulated by the Canadian tariff imposed in 1879, which made it easier for Nova Scotian coal to reach central Canadian markets, and by the growth of the iron and steel industry, which was protected by duties and further stimulated over the period 1900–11 by subsidies. Since 1928, freight subventions have been paid

[10]It has declined greatly since the end of World War II, mainly because of the loss of much of the United Kingdom market as a result of the dollar-saving import restrictions imposed by that country; but even earlier it was suffering from competition elsewhere, especially from British Columbia and Britain itself.

[11]Saunders, *Studies*, pp. 123–4.

[12]Strictly speaking the term "National Policy" denotes the protective tariff for Canadian industry introduced in 1879, but it is commonly used in the broader context as described here.

to make Nova Scotian coal competitive with American coal at least as far as Montreal.

The iron and steel industry was originally built up to sizable proportions in response to a demand for steel rails and railway cars in the great railway-building period in the first part of this century. In its early days in the nineteenth century the industry had been based on small local deposits of iron ore, on local limestone deposits, and, of course, on Nova Scotian coal. Since the turn of the century, however, practically all of the ore has come from the Wabana deposits on Bell Island, Newfoundland. Newfoundland is also the present source of the limestone used. Since 1930, control of the bulk of the iron, steel, and coal industry has been integrated in the hands of the Dominion Steel and Coal Company which has its head office in Montreal. Dosco, as the company is called, is Canada's third largest producer of primary iron and steel, and is now controlled by A. V. Roe of Canada, a subsidiary of the Hawker Siddeley group of England. The primary iron and steel operations are at Sydney, adjacent to the province's major coal supplies, while there is a railway car plant at Trenton and a shipyard at Halifax. With all of its operations near tide water, Dosco would appear to be very favourably situated both with regard to materials and to markets, but this advantage is at least partly outweighed by the high costs of extracting both the coal and the iron ore from submarine mines, and by metallurgical problems arising from the high phosphorous and silica content of the iron ore and the high sulphur content of the coal. The long distance to central Canadian markets and the freeze-up of the St. Lawrence in the winter put the company at a disadvantage, in relation to its competitors which have their plants located in Ontario, in supplying diversified products for secondary manufacturing to these major markets.

The industry was largely a product of the National Policy but, after the railroad construction it had been developed to service was completed, it was unable to find another secure base for its activities. Neither the coal industry nor the iron and steel industry has exhibited much economic health since 1913. Only in the two world wars, when costs were of secondary importance, have these industries done well. Their failure to prosper in peacetime is of considerable consequence to the provincial economy. In 1939 it was estimated that one-fifth of the population of Nova Scotia was dependent upon the coal industry and its subsidiaries.[13] The number dependent on the coal industry alone

[13]*Report of the Royal Commission on Dominion-Provincial Relations*, I, 188, n. 2. The figure of one-fifth apparently includes the steel manufacturing industry.

is smaller but still substantial. A few years ago, one estimate was 120,000 persons, another 90,000.[14] The number would be lower today with the contraction that has taken place in the industry.

It is ironic that these industries which were the major developments in Nova Scotia resulting from the National Policy should constitute two chronic economic problems (the iron and steel industries less than the coal) instead of providing a basis for sustained economic growth. Nevertheless, considerable investment has been made since the end of World War II in improving Dosco's steel plant and coal mines in Nova Scotia and its iron ore mine at Wabana, Newfoundland, so that it is likely that its operations there will continue into the foreseeable future, although perhaps at reduced levels.

It is probable that Nova Scotia's export industries were retarded to some extent by higher costs of capital equipment and possibly higher labour costs attributable to the tariff, and it is certain that the tariff has made the costs of manufactured consumer goods higher. There seems to be general agreement that since secondary manufacturing is concentrated in central Canada and since Nova Scotia has been a heavier per capita importer than the central Canadian provinces, it has, in relation to population, borne more of the burden and experienced less of the benefits of the tariff than they have.[15]

Nevertheless, Nova Scotia should not attach all of the blame to Confederation or the National Policy for its loss of secondary industry. The introduction of new large-scale techniques of production requiring expensive machinery favoured locations near heavy concentrations of population. With the tariff, central Canada was the culprit. If there had been no protective tariff, Nova Scotian industries would have been put out of business as a result of competition from the United States and other countries. The thin, scattered nature of the population of the Maritimes was unsuited to the development of large-scale secondary manufacturing based upon local markets.

In discussions of the economic problems of the Maritimes the harmful effects of federal government policy are frequently exaggerated and the relative lack of resource endowment ignored. The

[14]Urwick, Currie Limited, *The Nova Scotia Coal Industry* (A study for the Royal Commission on Canada's Economic Prospects; Ottawa: Queen's Printer, 1957), pp. 20, 32.

[15]See, for example, Government of Nova Scotia, *A Submission on Dominion-Provincial Relations and the Fiscal Disabilities of Nova Scotia within the Canadian Confederation* (A brief submitted by N. McL. Rogers to the Royal Commission: Provincial Economic Inquiry; [Halifax: King's Printer], 1934), pp. 88–104; and "Complementary Report of Dr. Harold A. Innis," *Report of the Royal Commission: Provincial Economic Inquiry* (Halifax: King's Printer, 1934), pp. 148–56.

western provinces grew up in the environment of the tariff, while the Maritime Provinces had the tariff imposed on existing patterns of development. Nevertheless, the western provinces have suffered from the same burdens of tariffs and long freight hauls as the Maritime Provinces and (especially British Columbia and Alberta) have forged ahead simply because they were richly endowed with economically exploitable resources, while the Maritimes have languished because they were not.

An extensive seacoast is generally thought to be an asset to commerce, and under the conditions of the "Golden Age" it was. But, as N. H. Morse has pointed out,[16] in the case of the Maritimes with their widely scattered population its great irregularity makes rapid communication by land difficult and so is conducive to many small-scale enterprises in lumbering, fish processing, and other types of primary manufacturing. Not only are there transportation problems in reaching the central Canadian market; there are problems of transportation within the Maritime region as well.

In spite of the fact that Nova Scotia and the other Maritime Provinces have remained on the periphery of the transcontinental development—partly, it must be allowed, because of the concentration of political power in central Canada where it was, to say the least, not going to be used to the economic disadvantage of that region—Nova Scotia is no doubt better off in Confederation than out of it. It obtains strength, or at least security, by being a part of a large and generally thriving economic unit.[17] A welfare-conscious country like Canada cannot easily let any of its regions lag very far behind the others in level of living, at least in those public services relating to education, health, and social welfare, which have continually been increasing in importance.[18] Although a great deal of economic adjustment should still be made in Nova Scotia, there is much more scope for such adjustment in a large country like Canada than there would be in a small one the

---

[16]Norman H. Morse, "Further Observations on the Economy of Nova Scotia" (A report for the Nova Scotia Research Foundation; Wolfville, 1956), p. 47.

[17]Morse has a very good discussion of the probable consequences of the Maritimes remaining on their own and of the political and economic strength they gained from Confederation, for which see *ibid.*

[18]There is no doubt that Nova Scotia has benefited in this respect from net transfers from the richer provinces. It is the general economic strength of the country that has made possible its scale of social security schemes, like family allowances, old age pensions, unemployment insurance, and the new National Health Plan; and the transfers in the form of tax equalization payments, the more recent special Atlantic Provinces Adjustment Grant, and the freight subventions on coal, to name only some of the types of payment.

size of the Maritime Provinces. Labour and capital and to some extent other resources are much freer to move into and out of the region. The fate of Newfoundland, which languished on its own for over fifty years and did not enter Confederation until 1949, suggests what might have happened to the Maritime Provinces if they had followed a similar course, even admitting their greater economic strength compared to Newfoundland.

THE RELATIVE SIZE AND GROWTH OF THE NOVA SCOTIAN ECONOMY

The following statistical description of the level and growth of the Nova Scotian economy in recent years in relation to the country as a whole is needed to complete this brief account of the province's economic history. This information is of special relevance to this study because of the greater significance of improvements in the use of resources in a poor province than in a rich province.

TABLE I

POPULATION GROWTH IN CANADA AND NOVA SCOTIA, 1851–1956

Census year	Pop., N.S. (in thousands)	Pop., Canada (in thousands)	N.S. % inc. over prev. cens.	Canada % inc. over prev. cens.	N.S. as % of Canada
1851	277	2,436			
1861	339	3,230	19.5	32.6	
1871	388	3,689	17.2	14.2	
1881	441	4,325	13.6	17.2	
1891	450	4,833	2.2	11.8	
1901[a]	460	5,371	2.0	11.1	8.6[a]
1911	492	7,207	7.1	34.2	6.8
1921	524	8,788	6.4	21.9	6.0
1931	513	10,377	−2.1	18.1	4.9
1941	578	11,507	12.7	10.9	5.0
1951	643	13,648	11.2	18.6	4.7
1956	695	15,666	8.1	14.8	4.4

SOURCE: D.B.S., *Ninth Census of Canada, 1951* (Ottawa: Queen's Printer, 1956), X, 11–12; and D.B.S., *National Accounts, Income and Expenditure, 1955–1957* (Ottawa: Queen's Printer, 1958), p. 10.

[a]From 1901, all of the present provinces and territories, except Newfoundland, are included in the Canadian figures; hence the populations of Nova Scotia and Canada are strictly comparable only over this period. Thus the ratio of Nova Scotian to Canadian population is given only for this period.

Table I shows Nova Scotia's population growth since 1851 compared with that of Canada. From 1881 the rate of growth in Nova Scotia was very small, even becoming negative in the decade 1921–31, in the first half of which Nova Scotia was particularly depressed. Since 1931 the growth has been substantial, and even exceeded that of

Canada in the decade 1931–41, during most of which the economy of
the whole country was depressed. Nova Scotia had, in large part, a
rural subsistence economy; it offered stability and security, if at a low
level of living, which the more highly industrialized areas of the
country did not. This attraction no doubt pulled home many unemployed Nova Scotians who had emigrated to other parts of the country.
Not even in recent years, however, has Nova Scotia held its natural
increase in population; its actual increase over the period 1941–51 was
only 62 per cent of the accumulated natural increase, compared with
109 per cent for Canada. The corresponding percentages for the period
1951–6 are 83 per cent for Nova Scotia and 141 per cent for Canada.[19]

TABLE II

COMPARISON OF PERSONAL INCOME PER CAPITA
FOR NOVA SCOTIA AND CANADA, 1926–59
(CURRENT DOLLARS)

	Nova Scotia	Canada	N.S. as % of Canada
Personal income per capita, 1926	$ 258	$ 425	61
Personal income per capita, 1959	$1,116	$1,487	75
Percentage increase, 1926–59	333%	250%	
Personal income per capita, 1946	$ 678	$ 791	86
Percentage increase, 1946–59	65%	88%	

SOURCE: Calculated from D.B.S., *National Accounts, Income and
Expenditure, 1926–1956* (Ottawa: Queen's Printer, 1958), pp. 364–5;
and *ibid.*, 1959 (Ottawa: Queen's Printer, 1960), p. 38.

Table II shows that over the whole period 1926–59, the rate of increase in personal income per capita was greater for Nova Scotia than
for Canada, although the amount of personal income per capita for
Nova Scotia was still considerably below the amount for Canada in
1959. It is necessary to allow for the fact that in 1926 Nova Scotia was
depressed, while other parts of the country were booming. A more
significant comparison is that of 1959 with 1946, in both of which years
Nova Scotia was closer to, although still short of, the level of employment of the rest of the country.[20] Over this period personal income
per capita for Canada increased by 88 per cent, and that for Nova
Scotia by only 65 per cent. It appears that in the postwar period,
although Nova Scotia has made considerable progress, her position
relative to the country as a whole has deteriorated.

[19]Calculated from D.B.S., *Canada Year Book, 1956* (Ottawa: Queen's Printer),
pp. 199, 201; and *Canada Year Book, 1957–58*, p. 120. Net migration from Nova
Scotia was 49,913 over the period 1941–56. (*Canada Year Book, 1957–58*, p.
120.)   [20]See Table XXIV.

Another good indicator of economic growth is capital expenditure per capita on new durable physical assets and, as Table III shows, Nova Scotia lagged far behind Canada in this respect. Only in the category "Institutions and Government Departments" does it even approach the Canadian amount.

TABLE III

CAPITAL EXPENDITURE PER CAPITA IN NOVA SCOTIA
OVER THE PERIOD 1949–56 COMPARED WITH THAT IN
CANADA (Canada = 100)

Primary and construction industries	52.8
Utilities	54.3
Manufacturing	36.9
Trade, finance, and commercial services	64.9
Housing	46.9
Institutions and government departments	96.9
TOTAL	58.8

SOURCE: R. D. Howland, *Some Regional Aspects of Canada's Economic Development* (A study for the Royal Commission on Canada's Economic Prospects; Ottawa: Queen's Printer, 1958), p. 113.

Comparisons of per capita measures of the Nova Scotia economy with those of the nation as a whole, or with those of a wealthier province, like Ontario, are informative, but must be used with caution. It must not be inferred from such comparisons that the objective should be to raise the Nova Scotian economy to the per capita level of the nation or some other province. While differences in income levels and other indices may in part be due to relatively poor resource use within Nova Scotia and therefore be subject to reduction, they are likely in large part due to better resource endowment and a consequently higher proportion of high-income occupations in other areas.

Table IV shows that per capita personal income and gross product for Nova Scotia as percentages of the amounts for Canada declined sharply from 1946 to 1948 and remained steady since 1948. As would be expected, since investment is generally a less stable element than personal income or gross product, new capital investment per capita for Nova Scotia as a percentage of the value for Canada has fluctuated more than the other two series, with if anything, a downward trend over the period. In all three series the values for Nova Scotia are much less than for Canada. The smaller difference between Nova Scotia and Canada in personal income per capita than in gross product per capita is at least in part a result of the levelling effect of federal transfer payments, which are included in personal income but not in gross product.

TABLE IV

COMPARISON OF NOVA SCOTIA AND CANADA WITH RESPECT TO PERSONAL INCOME, GROSS PRODUCT, AND NEW CAPITAL INVESTMENT PER CAPITA, 1946–56 (MILLIONS OF DOLLARS)

	Personal income per capita in current dollars			Gross product per capita in current dollars			New capital investment per capita, in constant (1949) dollars		
	N.S.	Canada	N.S. as % of Canada	N.S.	Canada	N.S. as % of Canada	N.S.	Canada	N.S. as % of Canada
1946	678	791	86	679	964	70			
1947	685	827	83	722	1,049	69			
1948	664	928	72	752	1,179	64			
1949	696	940	74	779	1,215	64	186	260	72
1950	726	979	74	835	1,313	64	162	266	61
1951	776	1,130	69	893	1,511	59	154	275	56
1952	847	1,203	70	954	1,660	57	167	300	56
1953	891	1,235	72	1,003	1,685	60	185	309	60
1954	902	1,205	75	1,018	1,627	63	184	293	63
1955	924	1,263	73	1,053	1,724	61	184	313	59
1956	999	1,365	73	1,142	1,872	61	180	357	50

SOURCE: Personal income and gross national product: D.B.S., *National Accounts, Income and Expenditure, 1926–1956*, pp. 33, 65. Gross provincial product for Nova Scotia (GPP): A. C. Parks, *The Economy of the Atlantic Provinces, 1940–1958* (Halifax: Atlantic Provinces Economic Council, 1960), p. 2. For the method of estimating GPP see *ibid.*, Appendix B. GPP cannot be measured in the same way as GNP as the data necessary for measuring some of the components are not available on a provincial basis. These estimates of GPP can therefore be used only to make rough comparisons. New capital investment per capita: Howland, *Some Regional Aspects of Canada's Economic Development*, pp. 95–7.

TABLE V

POSTWAR GROWTH OF THE NOVA SCOTIAN AND CANADIAN ECONOMIES
AS REFLECTED IN CONSTANT (1949) DOLLAR ESTIMATES OF
PERSONAL INCOME PER CAPITA, GROSS PRODUCT PER CAPITA,
AND NEW CAPITAL INVESTMENT PER CAPITA[a]

	Personal income per capita (1946 = 100)		Gross product per capita (1946 = 100)		New capital investment per capita (1949 = 100)	
	N.S.	Canada	N.S.	Canada	N.S.	Canada
1946	100	100	100	100		
1947	92	95	100	99		
1948	78	94	87	99		
1949	80	92	86	98	100	100
1950	81	93	90	103	87	102
1951	78	97	87	107	83	106
1952	83	101	89	112	90	115
1953	88	105	94	113	99	119
1954	89	101	95	106	99	113
1955	91	106	96	113	99	116
1956	97	113	102	118	97	137

SOURCE: Personal income and gross national product: D.B.S., *National Accounts, Income and Expenditure, 1926-1956*, pp. 35, 37, 64, 100. Constant dollar estimates of gross national expenditure were used in calculating per capita gross national product in constant dollars. The consumer price index for Canada (from D.B.S., *Prices and Price Indexes*, May, 1958 (Ottawa: Queen's Printer, 1958) p. 17) was used for deflating per capita personal income both for Canada and Nova Scotia. Gross provincial product: see source for Table IV. This series was deflated by the implicit deflators for the gross national expenditure (*National Accounts, Income and Expenditure, 1926-1956*, p. 37). New capital investment: Howland, *Some Regional Aspects of Canada's Economic Development*, pp. 95-7.
[a]New capital investment is on a gross basis.

Table V shows index numbers for the growth, in real terms, of per capita personal income, gross product, and new capital investment. Nova Scotia shows practically no growth with respect to any of the three series over the period shown, while the growth for Canada is considerable for all three of them. The dip and subsequent climb in personal income and gross product per capita for Nova Scotia reflect a postwar slump in the region and a gradual recovery from it.

Table VI shows that in 1956 Nova Scotia was below the country as a whole with respect to all of the components of personal income and considerably below for all but government transfer payments. The very low per capita figure for Nova Scotia for net income of farm operators from farm production is in part simply a reflection of the fact that agriculture is relatively less important than for the country as a whole, but is mainly a result of the low farm incomes in Nova Scotia. The subtotal of the first three items, sometimes referred to, although not quite aptly, as "earned income," illustrates further the relatively low

TABLE VI

PERSONAL INCOME PER CAPITA AND SOME OF ITS COMPONENTS:
A COMPARISON OF NOVA SCOTIA AND CANADA,
ON THE AVERAGE FOR 1958–60

	N.S.	Canada	N.S. as % Canada
Wages, salaries, and supplementary labour income[a]	$709	$1,009	70%
Net income of farm operators from farm production[a]	19	67	28
Net income of non-farm unincorporated businesses[a]	115	123	93
TOTAL	843	1,219	69
Interest, dividends, and net rental income of persons[b]	83	144	58
Government transfer payments excluding interest	161	163	99
Personal disposable income	1,069	1,381	77
Personal income	1,129	1,499	75

SOURCE: D.B.S., *National Accounts, Income and Expenditure, 1960* (Ottawa: Queen's Printer, 1961), pp. 40–3, 60.

[a]The comparison between Nova Scotia and Canada must be interpreted with caution in the case of the first three items, especially in the case of the second, as each item is obtained by dividing by total population and not by the part of the population receiving the income.

[b]Includes interest on the public debt paid to persons.

average productivity of the Nova Scotian economy. Net income per capita of non-farm unincorporated business appears to be the strongest component of personal income in Nova Scotia, apart from government transfer payments. Yet even it is significantly below the Canadian level. The relatively low per capita value for Nova Scotia of interest, dividends, and net rental income of persons shows that investment income as well as labour income lags behind the amount for Canada. Per capita personal disposable income is a larger proportion of per capita personal income for Nova Scotia than for Canada, as would be expected since per capita income is smaller for Nova Scotia.

A useful indicator of level of living is per capita retail sales. Although their value for Nova Scotia was almost as large as that for Canada in 1941, the relatively large increase for Canada over the next decade resulted in per capita retail sales for Nova Scotia being only 81 per cent of the amount for Canada by 1951.[21]

Table VII compares the size of population and a number of other aggregates for Nova Scotia with those for Canada. These comparisons

[21]D.B.S., *Ninth Census of Canada, 1951* (Ottawa: Queen's Printer, 1956), X, Part I, p. 519.

TABLE VII

Population[a]	4.3%	Net value of production[e]	2.2%
Number of families (1951)[b]	4.4%	New capital investment[f]	2.2%
Labour force (1951)[b]	4.2%	Retail sales (1951)[b]	3.7%
Personal income[c]	3.3%	Individual income tax	
Gross product[d]	2.9%	collections (federal)[g]	1.7%
		Corporation income tax	
		collections (federal)[g]	1.4%

SOURCES: [a]D.B.S., *National Accounts, Income and Expenditure, 1926–1956*, p. 101. In 1951 the population of Nova Scotia was 4.6 per cent of that of Canada; [b]D.B.S., *Ninth Census of Canada, 1951*, X, Part I, p. 248; [c]D.B.S., *National Accounts, Income and Expenditure, 1955–1957*, Table 29; [d]Gross national product, as in note ([c]), pp. 6, 44 and gross provincial product, as for Table IV; [e]D.B.S., *Survey of Production, 1951–1955* (Ottawa: Queen's Printer, 1958), p. 9; [f]Howland, *Some Regional Aspects of Canada's Economic Development*, p. 94; [g]Department of National Revenue, *Taxation Statistics, 1957* (Ottawa: Queen's Printer), p. 18.

further illustrate the relatively low average productivity of the Nova Scotian economy; they require no special comment.

Norman H. Morse made the estimates in Table VIII showing the percentage contributions of some important economic sectors to the gross provincial product of Nova Scotia and to the gross national product in 1951. He has grouped those manufacturing industries that are a direct outgrowth of the primary industries with these industries, for example, fish processing with fisheries. This classification, which distinguishes between primary and secondary manufacturing, gives a clearer picture of the relative importance of the different sectors than does the one used by the Dominion Bureau of Statistics.[22] The most striking thing revealed by the table is the much larger part of the total included in the service industry grouping for Nova Scotia than for Canada. This grouping includes such categories as transportation, communications, trade, finance, government, education, and the professions. While data are not available to explain satisfactorily the high percentage for service industries in Nova Scotia, it is likely at least partly due to relatively greater expenditures for defence, and to particularly high costs of transportation and distribution arising from having to supply many scattered small pockets of settlement. The table also shows that agriculture and manufacturing are much less important and forestry slightly less important than for Canada, while mining

[22]This distinction between primary and secondary manufacturing is also made in D. H. Fullerton and H. A. Hampson, *Canadian Secondary Manufacturing Industry* (A study for the Royal Commission on Canada's Economic Prospects; Ottawa: Queen's Printer, 1957), Appendix A.

TABLE VIII

PERCENTAGE CONTRIBUTION OF INDUSTRIAL SECTORS TO GROSS
PROVINCIAL PRODUCT AND GROSS NATIONAL PRODUCT FOR
NOVA SCOTIA AND CANADA, 1951, USING MORSE'S
CLASSIFICATION

	Nova Scotia	Canada
Agriculture	5.4%	13.9%
Forestry	7.3	8.7
Fisheries	5.6	.8
Mining	7.7	3.6
Manufacturing	12.8	24.3
Electric power	1.9	1.7
Construction	8.4	8.2
"Service" industries	51.0	38.8
TOTAL GROSS PRODUCT	100.0	100.0

SOURCE: N. H. Morse, "Preliminary Results of Research on
the Economy of Nova Scotia" (A report for the Nova Scotia
Research Foundation; Wolfville, 1954). Morse used his own
estimates of gross provincial product and D.B.S. estimates of
gross national product and net value of production.

and fisheries are much more important for Nova Scotia, and electric
power and construction are of about equal importance to them both.

Using the Bureau's classifications, Morse got the percentage distribution shown in Table IX. The changes are all in the first three and
the fifth sectors. The relative picture is substantially the same as in
Table VIII except that forestry is shown to be more important for
Nova Scotia than for Canada, and manufacturing for Nova Scotia
is of greater importance relative to Canada than in Table VIII,
although it remains a much smaller part of gross product than in the

TABLE IX

PERCENTAGE CONTRIBUTION OF INDUSTRIAL SECTORS TO GROSS
PROVINCIAL PRODUCT AND GROSS NATIONAL PRODUCT FOR
NOVA SCOTIA AND CANADA, 1951, USING D.B.S. CLASSIFICATION

	Nova Scotia	Canada
Agriculture	4.7%	12.5%
Forestry	3.2	2.3
Fisheries	3.5	.5
Mining	7.7	3.6
Manufacturing	19.6	32.4
Electric power	1.9	1.7
Construction	8.4	8.2
"Service" industries	51.0	38.8
TOTAL GROSS PRODUCT	100.0	100.0

SOURCE: As for Table VIII.

case of Canada. This change with respect to manufacturing illustrates that primary manufacturing is a larger part of total manufacturing for Nova Scotia than for Canada, and secondary manufacturing a smaller part.

Finally, Table X compares the percentage deviation of the net value of production per capita for all provinces except Newfoundland from the national average. It shows a strikingly large negative deviation of of 48.4 per cent for Nova Scotia.[23]

TABLE X

PER CAPITA NET VALUE OF PRODUCTION BY PROVINCES IN 1958,
AND PERCENTAGE VARIATIONS FROM THE NATIONAL AVERAGE

	Per capita net value	Variations
Canada	$1,077[a]	
Prince Edward Island	415	−61.5%
NOVA SCOTIA	556	−48.4
New Brunswick	530	−50.8
Quebec	957	−11.1
Ontario	1,320	+22.6
Manitoba	826	−23.3
Saskatchewan	962	−10.7
Alberta	1,242	+15.3
British Columbia[b]	1,111	+ 3.2

SOURCE: D.B.S., *Survey of Production, 1954-58*, (Ottawa: Queen's Printer, 1958), p. 18.
[a]Excludes Newfoundland. This is a weighted average. The unweighted average is $880 and Nova Scotia's deviation from it −36.8 per cent.
[b]Includes Yukon and the Northwest Territories.

The tables in this section show that the Nova Scotian economy is far less productive than that of the nation as a whole and that it gives no indication of catching up. If anything it is getting further behind. They also show that the primary and service industries (except for agriculture) are relatively more important and the manufacturing industries relatively less important than for the nation as a whole.

[23]This deviation would be somewhat smaller if defence expenditures for purposes which are manufacturing by nature, as in the case of H.M.C. Dockyard in Halifax, were included in net value of production, providing that there are disproportionate expenditures for such purposes as well as for over-all defence expenditures.

$\sim\!\!\sim$ III $\sim\!\!\sim$

Federal-Provincial Fiscal Relations

THE HISTORY OF THE FINANCIAL ARRANGEMENTS

THE CANADIAN FINANCIAL STRUCTURE was originally designed to make the Dominion and the provinces sovereign within their respective spheres and so to determine the extent of their functions. Sections 91 and 92 of the British North America Act distribute the powers of jurisdiction between the Dominion and the provinces. Section 91 gives the Dominion power to legislate for the "Peace, Order, and good Government of Canada," except for those exclusive powers given the provinces in Section 92, and lists a series of powers for illustrative purposes. It would appear, then, that residual power rests with the Dominion; but the courts have generally given precedence to the power of the provinces to make laws in relation to property and civil rights, one of the enumerated powers (Clause 13) in Section 92; since practically all matters touch upon property and civil rights in the provinces, this clause has been the operative one. Except in times of dire national emergency, the powers of the Dominion have been confined virtually to its enumerated powers.[1] Concurrent powers over agriculture and immigration are given in Section 95, federal legislation being superior in cases of conflict.

The Dominion executive has the power, by Section 56, to disallow any act of a provincial legislature, and the Dominion appoints the lieutenant-governors of the provinces and can instruct a lieutenant-

---

[1]In recent years there is some evidence of a tendency of the courts to interpret the Dominion's "Peace, Order, and good Government" power more generously. See R. MacG. Dawson, *The Government of Canada* (3rd edition, revised; Toronto: University of Toronto Press, 1957), chap. v, *passim*. See pp. 601, 608–13, for the sections of the British North America Act referred to in this chapter.

governor to withhold his assent from bills and to reserve them for consideration by the Dominion executive, which may refuse assent. These powers of disallowance and veto, which are unitary rather than federal in character, have not been used extensively; federal principles have generally been adhered to in practice.

The division of functions was designed in general to give the Dominion control over matters of national interest and the provinces control over matters of local interest; but in the course of time many matters, such as education, unemployment, public health, and social welfare, have come more and more to be of national as well as local interest.

With regard to raising revenue, two of the enumerated powers of the Dominion in Section 91 entitle it to "The raising of Money by any Mode or System of Taxation" (Clause 3) and "The borrowing of Money on the Public Credit" (Clause 4). Three of the powers given the provinces in Section 92 entitle each province to "Direct Taxation within the Province in order to the Raising of a Revenue for Provincial Purposes" (Clause 2), "The borrowing of Money on the sole Credit of the Province" (Clause 3), and to issue "Shop, Saloon, Tavern, Auctioneer, and other Licenses in order to the raising of a Revenue for Provincial, Local, or Municipal Purposes" (Clause 9). The most important feature of this division of sources of revenue is that the provinces were limited to direct taxation while the Dominion was not.

It was recognized that the independent revenues of the provinces would be inadequate. For even with reduced functions, the loss of their main source of revenue at that time, the customs, to the Dominion left the provinces with insufficient revenues. Consequently, provision was made in the British North America Act for statutory subsidies to be paid by the Dominion to the provinces.[2] These subsidies were intended to be unalterable: "in full Settlement of all future Demands on Canada."[3] This curious phrasing reflects, in retrospect, the wistful nature of this provision. It was consistent, however, with the expectation that provincial functions would remain static and that the

[2]These subsidies were of two types: fixed annual grants in support of the provincial legislatures, totalling $260,000, and annual allowances of 80 cents per capita, based upon the populations of 1861 in Ontario and Quebec, and to grow with the populations in New Brunswick and Nova Scotia until they reached 400,000. In addition, New Brunswick was given an allowance of $63,000 for ten years because of her particularly heavy financial commitments (British North America Act, ss. 118, 119).

[3]British North America Act, s. 118. This phrase was used again as early as 1869, when the Dominion acceded to Nova Scotia's demands for better financial terms, described in the next paragraph.

provinces would play a minor rôle in the federation. It was not expected that the provinces would use their right to levy the then very unpopular direct taxes to any considerable extent, nor *a fortiori* that they would or could levy what were generally regarded as indirect taxes. Nor was it expected that the Dominion would not only enter, but come to dominate, the direct tax fields.

In fact, numerous revisions have been made to the subsidies practically from the outset, beginning with Nova Scotia's successful agitation for "better terms" in 1869.[4] Revisions were inevitable in view of the assumption of new responsibilities by the provinces, of their disparate rates of growth, of the uneven impact of federal policies, and, most immediately, in view of the miscalculation of provincial financial burdens which followed Confederation. If all the provinces had been about equally prosperous and all had expanded their services at about the same rate, they would still have needed larger revenues, although there would have been no basis for claiming differential treatment. But differences in economic development between regions are inevitable in any country, and they are likely to be especially marked in a federation. In fact they are usually largely responsible for its becoming a federation rather than a unitary country. Certainly in Canada the geographical and economic differences of the political regions are very great.

Revisions of federal subsidies and grants to poorer provinces to alleviate their fiscal difficulties have been criticized,[5] with justification, because they did not attack the causes of these provinces' lower taxable capacity, namely their inferior productiveness. Criticisms have, however, generally ignored the possibly favourable effects of these transfers on allocation of resources. Even with perfect allocation of resources, productivity per head of population, and therefore income per head, will be higher in some provinces than in others because variation in endowment of natural resources will result in differing provincial distributions of high- and low-income activities. Differing provincial per capita incomes will mean differing provincial fiscal capacities. Without federal transfers, fiscal pressure would then be heavier on factors in a low-income province than on otherwise similarly situated

[4]These gave Nova Scotia an extra $140,000 per year, $83,000 of it for ten years only. (*Report of the Royal Commission on Dominion-Provincial Relations* [Ottawa: King's Printer, 1940], III, 60.)

[5]See, for example, Government of Nova Scotia, *A Submission on Dominion-Provincial Relations and the Fiscal Disabilities of Nova Scotia within the Canadian Confederation* (A brief submitted by N. McL. Rogers to the Royal Commission: Provincial Economic Inquiry; [Halifax: King's Printer], 1934), p. 30.

factors in a high-income province, because of heavier taxes or inferior services or a combination of both, inducing some factors to move out of the low-income province and inhibiting others from moving into it, with resulting distortion in allocation of resources.

The public demand for elaborate highways, for an ever more extensive system of public education, for greatly expanded services in the fields of public health and welfare, and for public participation in economic development put severe pressure on the provincial revenues. The widening of provincial powers through the judicial interpretation of the British North America Act contributed still further to the need for enlarged provincial revenues.

The Maritime Provinces have been especially vociferous in their demands for better terms from the Dominion. These demands were based mainly on arguments that the area has been adversely affected by Dominion tariff and transportation policies, and that it has not shared fully in the general prosperity and development of the country. Moreover, the financial difficulties that Nova Scotia and New Brunswick faced from the time of their entry into Confederation were probably as strong a reason as any for their agitating for help.

With the growth of their functions, the provinces had to find new sources of revenue. They found it necessary to levy the traditionally unpopular direct taxes on personal and corporate income and duties on estates and successions. Some of them also, like the American and Australian states, at one time levied some property taxes, although somewhat warily since these were the traditional mainstay of local government.[6] The constitutional prohibition on provincial indirect taxes was overcome by levying taxes which, though widely regarded as being indirect, technically fitted John Stuart Mill's definition of a direct tax adopted by the courts: "A direct tax is one which is demanded from the very persons who, it is intended or desired, should pay it." It is this interpretation which has, for example, enabled all ten of the provinces to levy their highly lucrative taxes on gasoline sales and eight of them their general taxes on retail sales.[7] The end result has been accomplished in practice by making the retailer the

[6]Only in 1957, by *Statutes of Nova Scotia* (*S.N.S.*), 1957, c. 41 did Nova Scotia abolish the Municipalities' Highway Tax, levied on its rural municipalities at three-fifths per cent of the value of all ratable property. It continued to make small levies directly on certain categories of property in the rural areas. See "property tax" in Table XI, pp. 46–7, and note *d* to the same table.

[7]British Columbia, Saskatchewan, Ontario, Quebec, New Brunswick, Newfoundland, Nova Scotia, and Prince Edward Island. Nova Scotia has a 5 per cent general retail sales tax to finance its part of the cost of its Hospital Insurance Plan.

agent of the Crown for collecting the tax from the purchaser on whom it is levied.

Other important sources of provincial revenue are motor vehicle licences and the profits from liquor sales monopolies. Income from the public domain is relatively less important in the Atlantic Provinces than elsewhere because of the paucity of natural resources there, but it is of growing importance in Newfoundland and New Brunswick where new developments of natural resources are taking place.

Since the provinces are in fact able to levy even what are commonly regarded as indirect taxes, they are free to levy almost any tax, except one on imports, one which interferes directly with interprovincial commerce, or a sales tax at any stage before retail. They are limited not so much by a paucity of tax bases as by a general paucity of resources in the poor provinces, and by the Dominion's domination of the now important fields of income, succession, and sales taxation.[8] The most important questions in this field, then, centre around the degree to which and the means by which these major tax fields should be shared and the degree to which and the means by which the poorer provinces should be assisted by the Dominion to enable them to attain some minimum standard of services, especially in those services such as education and public health which, though constitutionally the responsibility of the provinces, are of general concern to the whole country. And there is the further important question of whether the poorer provinces in discharging their responsibilities should not at least be able to provide levels of services equal to the national average with the same fiscal pressure on their factors of production as is imposed on similar factors in the richer provinces, to encourage optimum allocation of resources.

The years since Confederation have seen significant developments in both the fields of unconditional and conditional subsidies. Up to the Second World War, the expansion of unconditional subsidies consisted essentially of *ad hoc* adjustments by the Dominion in response to sectional pressures by the Maritimes and the western provinces, with a general revision of the arrangements being made in 1907, but with further adjustments being made after this—in particular, the larger subsidies for the Maritime Provinces recommended by the Duncan Commission in 1926 and the White Commission in 1935.[9] The Royal

[8]The Dominion levies a general sales tax of 11 per cent at the manufacturers' level, with exemptions for some commodities.

[9]The revision in 1907 brought the total annual statutory payments to Nova Scotia up to $611,000, compared with $456,000 at Confederation. Implementation of a recommendation of the Duncan Commission (Royal Commission on Maritime

Commission on Dominion-Provincial Relations, reporting in 1940, recommended some adjustment in the distribution of responsibilities, and the assumption of provincial debt by the Dominion, the transfer of personal and corporate income taxes and succession duties to the Dominion, and payments on the basis of fiscal need to the provinces sufficient to enable them to provide services at a minimum national standard. It eschewed the idea of payments based upon the principle of compensation for adverse effects of Dominion policy. The Dominion was unable, in 1941, to get agreement from the provinces to implement the *Report*, but wartime exigencies led to a development which did set federal-provincial fiscal relations on a new path.

In order to prosecute the war, the Dominion deemed it necessary to gain full control of personal and corporate income taxes for the duration of the war and one full year thereafter. In compensation for vacating these tax fields, it agreed to make payments to the provinces (according to either of two options) which exceeded the loss of revenue for some of them and equalled the loss for the rest and took some rough account of the fiscal need of the provinces.[10]

After the war, an unsuccessful attempt was made by the Dominion to get agreement on a comprehensive set of proposals which would have required the provinces to give up their right to levy personal and corporate income taxes and to co-ordinate their economic policies with those of the federal government (to facilitate the use of anti-cyclical fiscal policy). The proposals also included extensive provisions for social security measures, in particular health insurance and old age pensions, to some of which the provinces were asked to contribute.[11]

As a much less comprehensive alternative the Dominion was able to negotiate separate agreements for the fiscal years 1947–8 to 1951–2

Claims) raised Nova Scotia's annual payment by $875,000. A further increase of $425,000 by implementation of a recommendation of the White Commission (Royal Commission on Financial Arrangements between the Dominion and the Maritime Provinces) brought to $1,300,000 the total increase since 1907 in the amount of the annual payment. This grant was suspended in 1941 while the Wartime Tax Agreements were in force, but was restored in 1947. (J. Harvey Perry, *Taxes, Tariffs, and Subsidies* [Toronto: University of Toronto Press, 1955], II, 517–24.)

[10]For descriptions of the formulae of the Wartime Tax Agreements and of the 1947 and 1952 agreements, see A. Milton Moore and J. Harvey Perry, *Financing Canadian Federation* (Tax Papers, No. 6; Toronto: Canadian Tax Foundation, 1953), pp. 91–2.

[11]See *Dominion-Provincial Conference, 1945* (Dominion and provincial submissions and plenary conference discussions; Ottawa: King's Printer, 1946), *passim*. There is a good summary of these proposals in Perry, *Taxes, Tariffs, and Subsidies*, II, 541–6.

with all provinces except Quebec and Ontario, in which the agreeing provinces gave up the three direct taxes in return for rental payments. These payments could be based upon any of three options, with guarantees of minimum amounts. The rental payments, though not based directly upon any criteria of fiscal need, favoured the poorer provinces. If they levied the three taxes themselves, they would have had to levy them at higher rates than would the richer provinces to obtain the per capita revenues provided by the agreements. Reaction of other provinces to especially favourable treatment initially given British Columbia moved the Dominion to offer the same treatment to the other provinces and to insert guarantees of equal treatment in the agreements:

(1) . . . the Dominion shall not offer better terms or make any extra payment to a province if any two other provinces which have signed agreements object.

(2) . . . if any of the clauses of the agreement, other than the one which fixes the rate of payment, are revised for one province any or all of the other provinces may insist on their agreements being amended in a similar fashion.[12]

While these clauses reduced the possibilities of discrimination and of interprovincial bickering, they did not eliminate the discrimination which arises from the most favourable alternative for one province putting it in a better relative position than the most favourable alternative for another province.

When new agreements were negotiated in 1950 for a further five-year period (fiscal years 1952–3 to 1956–7) the terms were similar to those of the previous agreements, with provision for larger payments and with the addition of another option, favourable to Ontario.[13] (Ontario did come into the agreements in 1952, but even then not with regard to succession duties.) For non-agreeing provinces (the only one was Quebec), tax credits of up to 7 per cent of corporate *profits*, 5 per cent of personal income *tax*, and 50 per cent of succession duties were allowed to provincial taxpayers. In 1955, the Dominion raised the credit for the personal income tax to 10 per cent.

When the time again came in 1955 for considering renewal of the agreements, important changes were made. The Dominion was apparently concerned about the isolation of Quebec from the tax agreements and wished to avoid penalizing a province for not entering into the scheme and thereby giving up some of its taxing powers. The plan

12Canada, House of Commons, *Debates, 1947* (Ottawa: King's Printer), p. 48.
13Perry, *Taxes, Tariffs, and Subsidies*, II, 558–9.

eventually adopted, and implemented April 1, 1957, for five years, accomplished this while preserving most of the advantages of uniformity which would be gained by having the direct taxes solely in the hands of the Dominion.

This plan allowed tax credits on the federal taxes to taxpayers in any provinces which chose to levy any or all of the three direct taxes, on the basis of three "standard" rates of tax: 9 per cent of taxable corporate *income* earned in the province, 10 per cent of federal personal income *tax* payable in the province (raised to 13 per cent, beginning with fiscal year 1958–9), and 50 per cent of the federal succession duties payable in the province. Each province was free (1) to levy and administer any or all of these three kinds of taxes itself at rates of its own choosing; (2) to levy any or all of them at the standard rates and have them collected by the Dominion for a fee; or (3) to rent any or all of them to the Dominion, in which case the Dominion paid to the province a tax rental payment equal to the yield in the province of the standard taxes (for the taxes which were rented) and the province agreed to stay out of the rented tax fields. The second and third alternatives were similar, but the second was expected to have more appeal to Quebec, for it was largely an administrative convenience that would require less surrender of provincial autonomy than the third. At the same time it would require conformity to the standard taxes and so prevent interprovincial variations in the rates of the three taxes. In fact, Quebec chose the first alternative to which it was already constitutionally entitled.

In any case, the Dominion paid to each province an unconditional equalization grant sufficient to make up the difference between what the province's per capita yield was or would be from the standard taxes, and the average of the per capita yields of the two provinces with the highest per capita yields with respect to the standard taxes. Thus the richest province, Ontario, received no equalization grant.

The Dominion also agreed to make stabilization payments if the total payments under the tax-sharing arrangements failed in any year to reach a certain minimum level.[14] And it agreed not to consider a tax on insurance premiums a corporation tax under the fiscal arrangements and to repeal its own tax on insurance premiums of domestic companies.[15] All of the provinces except Quebec and Ontario rented all

[14]For a description of the rather complicated method of determining stabilization payments, see *The National Finances, 1958–59* (Toronto: Canadian Tax Foundation), p. 115.

[15]Nova Scotia's new tax on insurance premiums imposed as a result of this change yielded an estimated $810,000 in the fiscal year 1960–1. Legislature of Nova Scotia, 1961 Session, *Estimates* (Halifax: Queen's Printer, 1961), p. 5.

three of the taxes. Quebec rented none and levied all three on its own; Ontario rented only the personal income tax and levied the other two on its own. In 1957–8, the first year of the new scheme, Nova Scotia received $26.407 million in tax-sharing payments, compared with $22.333 million in the previous year under the 1952 tax agreement.[16]

By making it possible for them to levy direct taxes up to the standard rates without double taxation, this plan left the provinces, especially the wealthier ones, a large measure of autonomy. At the same time, it put the poorer provinces on about the same footing as the wealthier ones with regard to these sources of revenue by giving all the provinces about the same per capita revenues from the three direct taxes; the only departures occurred with respect to those provinces which chose to levy their own taxes at other than the standard rates. The only such departures, in Quebec and Ontario, were not very great.

The tax-sharing arrangements did not compensate the poorer provinces for the fact that other provincial and municipal sources of revenue were less productive for them than for the richer provinces. The special Atlantic Provinces Adjustment Grants inaugurated for a four-year period in the fiscal year 1958–9 did compensate the Atlantic Provinces, although only in part, for their lower fiscal capacity in these other fields.[17] Nova Scotia, like New Brunswick and Newfoundland, received $7.5 million annually; Prince Edward Island received $2.5 million annually.

The new federal-provincial fiscal arrangements for the period 1962–7 are the outcome of a unilateral decision of the federal government rather than of mutual agreement between the federal government and the provinces. They alter the equalization and stabilization elements of the previous arrangements and they constitute an abrupt change with respect to the centralization of control and uniformity of rates of the three direct taxes. They introduced a marked departure from the trend towards greater rationalization of the Canadian fiscal system that had hitherto characterized the war and postwar agreements. The new policy is obviously intended to shift back to the provinces the responsibility for levying their own personal and corporate income taxes at a time of acute need of the provinces for larger revenues and of large

[16]D.B.S., special compilation (Ottawa: October 10, 1958). In the fiscal year 1960–1, it is estimated that Nova Scotia's tax rental payment will be $11.981 million and its equalization payment $20.302 million, making its total payment under the tax-sharing arrangements $32.283 million. *The National Finances, 1960–61*, p. 114.

[17]For a discussion of these grants and a criticism of the formulae upon which they are based, see John F. Graham, "The Special Atlantic Provinces Adjustment Grants: A Critique," *Canadian Tax Journal*, VIII (January-February, 1960), pp. 39–43.

federal deficits. The main provisions of the new arrangements are as follows:

(1) The provinces now levy their own personal and corporate income taxes, at rates of their own choosing, which the federal government collects at no charge to the provinces, providing taxable income is defined in the same way as for the federal levies.

(2) The federal government reduced its own corporate income tax by 9 percentage points and reduced its personal income tax collections by 16 per cent for the first year of the agreement, with provision in this latter case for further reductions of one per cent for each of the following four years, compared with a standard rate of 13 per cent in the old formula.

(3) The federal government continues to pay each province not imposing a succession duty 50 per cent of the yield of the federal tax in that province.

(4) Although equalization payments continue to be paid, the new formula differs significantly from the previous one in that it is based upon the average per capita yield for all provinces, rather than for the two richest ones, from the three direct taxes at the standard rates, and upon 50 per cent of the per capita three-year average of revenues from natural resources collected by all provinces.

(5) The Atlantic Provinces Adjustment Grants are increased from $25 million to $35 million, annually, and the special payment of $8 million annually to Newfoundland is being continued.

(6) There are two guarantees of provincial revenues in the new arrangements: no province entitled to equalization payments under the new formula will be in a worse position than it would have been with the continuation of the previous formula, with respect to the total of tax rental payments, equalization payments, and the Atlantic Provinces Adjustment Grants; and no province will receive revenue less in total than it received on the average in the last two years of the previous (1957–62) agreement.

(7) The federal government agreed to continue the equal sharing with the provincial governments of the income tax collected from power utilities for the full period of the new agreement rather than on a year-to-year basis as previously.

Differences among the provinces in the rates of personal and corporate income taxes are more likely to occur under the new policy of the federal government, although the withdrawal of the federal government from these fields by fixed percentage amounts will, for a time at least, likely produce a tendency towards uniformity. The change in the nature of the new agreements is indicated by the shift from the use of the terms "tax rental" and "tax-sharing" in the agreement of 1957–62 to the use of "tax collection arrangements" with respect to the new agreements.[18]

CONDITIONAL FEDERAL GRANTS: A RÉSUMÉ

In addition to its unconditional grants, the federal government has since 1912 made conditional grants on various terms and for various purposes. These began with grants for agricultural instruction, 1912–24, totalling about $11 million; and included grants for technical education, 1919–39 (about $10 million), for highway construction, 1919–28 (about $20 million), employment offices, 1918–41 (about $150,000 per year), venereal disease, 1919–32 (about $1,700,000), old age pensions, 1926–51 (over $100 million per year in the last years), relief grants-in-aid during the depression, 1930–40 (about $317 million), various forms of health grants, 1948–present, and grants for vocational, apprenticeship, and youth training, for land protection, reclamation and development, for irrigation, water storage, and flood control, for the Trans-Canada Highway, and for improvement and protection of forests.[19]

Some other federal measures which relieved financial pressure on the provinces are unemployment insurance, inaugurated in 1941 by a constitutional amendment; the family allowance scheme, inaugurated in 1945; universal old age pensions for all those 70 years of age and over, inaugurated in 1952 (along with old age assistance, which consists of shared-cost contributions for indigent aged in the 65–69 age group); and agricultural assistance, such as that under the Prairie Farm Assistance Act of 1939 and the Prairie Farm Rehabilitation Act of 1935. The most recent measures are the National Health Plan, under which the federal government shares certain of the costs of provincial free hospitalization plans (Nova Scotia's plan went into effect January 1,

---

[18]For descriptions of these arrangements, see *Canadian Tax Journal*, IX (March–April, 1961), pp. 79–81; and the letter from Prime Minister Diefenbaker to the provincial premiers, of June 16, 1961, in House of Commons, *Debates* (June 19, 1961), Appendix, pp. 6596–8.

[19]Perry, *Taxes, Tariffs, and Subsidies*, II, chaps. 31–3; and J. A. Maxwell, *Federal Subsidies to the Provincial Governments in Canada* (Cambridge: Harvard University Press, 1937), chaps. xv–xvii. Some of the grants which were contingent upon provincial expenditures were those for technical education, highway construction (including those for the Trans-Canada Highway), old age pensions, some of the relief grants, and hospital construction grants (included under "health grants").

1959), and the removal of the so-called "threshold" of .45 per cent from the Unemployment Assistance Act of 1956. Under this act the federal government had agreed to pay 50 per cent of the cost of all relief, for the number of persons on the relief rolls in the province in excess of .45 per cent of its population, to any province which signed an agreement. Removal of the threshold committed the federal government to sharing the cost of all relief.

Perry notes that from 1868 to 1954, the Dominion paid a total of nearly three billion dollars to the provinces, including grants-in-aid and shared-cost contributions, compared with about $200 million it would have paid had there been no alteration to the arrangements made at Confederation[20] which, as already noted, were to be "in full Settlement of all future demands on Canada." In the brief subsequent period, 1954–61, these federal payments amounted to about four and one-half billion dollars.[21]

In 1868, the first year of Confederation, these payments, which then consisted solely of the statutory subsidies, were about 54 per cent of provincial revenues and about 20 per cent of Dominion revenues; in 1929, the total Dominion payments to the provinces were 9 per cent of provincial revenues and 4 per cent of Dominion revenues, while in the fiscal year 1960–1 they were about 36 per cent of provincial net general revenue and 14 per cent of Dominion revenue. However, in Nova Scotia in that year they were about 68 per cent of net general revenue.[22]

THE PRINCIPLE OF FISCAL EQUITY WITH RESPECT TO NOVA SCOTIA

The conditions under which fiscal equity would be achieved in Nova Scotia in relation to the other provinces will now be stated in a general way and some indication will be given of the extent to which these conditions are being met.

If federal grants to a province were sufficient to provide revenues which, along with its own provincial and municipal revenues, would enable it to provide about the same level of services as in other provinces, and if provincial and municipal taxes in the different provinces were similar in nature and levied at about the same rates,

[20]Perry, *Taxes, Tariffs, and Subsidies*, II, 566.
[21]Compilation from Department of Finance, Ottawa.
[22]Moore and Perry, *Financing Canadian Federation*, pp. 78–9. Percentages for fiscal year 1960–1 from D.B.S., *Comparative Statistics of Public Finance, 1956 to 1960* (Ottawa: Queen's Printer, 1960), Part I, Tables 1 and 13; and from a special compilation provided by D.B.S.

fiscal equity could be said to be approximated in that a resident of any province would receive about the same fiscal treatment as a similarly situated resident in any other province.

On the revenue side, the federal tax-sharing arrangements for 1957–62 provided equalization in the provinces with regard to personal and corporate income taxes and succession duties up to the per capita yields at the (quite generous) standard rates on the average for the two richest provinces (Ontario and British Columbia). The special Atlantic Provinces Adjustment Grant provided for partial equalization with respect to other provincial (and municipal) revenues. The magnitude of the equalization with respect to Nova Scotia is indicated by the fact that in the fiscal year 1960–1, about 45 per cent of Nova Scotia's net general revenue came from these two sources and from the statutory subsidies, compared with 21 per cent for all provinces.[23]

The implied principle of the tax-sharing arrangements of 1957–62 was that equalization payments should be based upon the taxable capacity of the two richest provinces. The extension of this procedure to all provincial and municipal sources of revenue would have been consistent with the principle of fiscal equity, assuming that the over-all provincial and municipal costs per capita of providing services are roughly similar between provinces. The new policy for the period 1962–7 of relating equalization payments to average per capita revenues for all provinces is much less in accord with the principle of fiscal equity for, even if this policy were extended to include all provincial and municipal sources of revenue, the fiscal pressure would be heavier in the poorer provinces, because inferior services or heavier tax burdens, or a combination of both, would then be inevitable there.

Nevertheless, Nova Scotia is receiving about $2 million more in fiscal year 1962–3 under the new formula than it would have under the old one; for its lower equalization grant with respect to the three direct taxes is more than offset by the increase in the Atlantic Provinces Adjustment Grant and by the addition of the natural resource element, its per capita revenue from its taxes on natural resources being substantially below the average for all provinces, as is shown in Table XII.

Even with its relatively large federal transfers, Nova Scotia had a combined provincial and municipal net general revenue per capita of only about 79 per cent of that of all provinces, for the fiscal year 1960–1. Moreover, it was only 69 per cent of the average for Ontario and British Columbia, the two richest provinces. It would require

[23]D.B.S., *Comparative Statistics of Public Finance, 1956 to 1960*, calculated from Part I, Tables 1 and 13, and from a special compilation by D.B.S.

about $44 million of additional revenue to bring the amount for Nova Scotia up to the national average, and about $53 million to bring it up to the average for Ontario and British Columbia. Although Nova Scotia's combined provincial and municipal net general expenditure is slightly closer to the national average, it is so only by virtue of a considerable deficit on current and capital account combined—a chronic element in Nova Scotia's provincial budget. A much larger part of its provincial expenditures is taken up by debt servicing (8.9 per cent) than for all provinces taken together (2.5 per cent). On a per capita basis, net debt charges exclusive of debt retirement were about $13 for Nova Scotia and about $4 for all provinces taken together.[24]

What about the burdens of taxation in Nova Scotia compared with those in other provinces?[25] With a gasoline tax of 19 cents per gallon, Nova Scotia shares with Newfoundland the highest rate in all of the provinces. The rates of the other provinces range from 12 cents in Alberta to 18 cents in New Brunswick. The rate for Ontario, the richest province, is 13 cents.[26] The revenues per motor vehicle in Nova Scotia in the fiscal year 1959–60 were $25.46 for all vehicles and $18.50 for passenger automobiles, both slightly lower than those for all of Canada, which were $26.48 and $18.68 respectively.[27]

The large per capita revenue from Nova Scotian liquor profits of $16.20 in fiscal year 1960–1, compared with $10.55 for all provinces taken together, combined with the fact that the ratio of net income from liquor profits to gross sales was .36 for Nova Scotia and .30 for all provinces[28] (for the fiscal year 1958–9), indicates a heavier burden

[24]See pp. 48–9. A comparison of Nova Scotia with each of the other provinces would give a fuller picture, but this comparison with all provinces taken together and with the average for Ontario and British Columbia will suffice for the purpose at hand.

[25]In examining the burdens of taxation, the question arises whether a tax levied at a given rate in a low-income province is more burdensome to the taxpayers than a tax levied at the same rate in a high-income province, assuming similar living costs. The answer is "no" if it is otherwise similarly situated taxpayers who are being considered; for example, a 15 cent per gallon gasoline tax would affect a given taxpayer in the same way regardless of whether he lived in a high- or low-income province. There is really no reason why the *rate* of a given type of tax should be lower in a low-income than in a high-income province. Both have their low-income groups: their unemployed, penniless widows, and indigent aged; and both have their wealthy, and the others in between.

[26]*Canadian Tax Journal*, IX (March-April, 1961), p. 83.

[27]D.B.S., *The Motor Vehicle, 1959* (Ottawa: Queen's Printer, 1960), Tables 3 and 6.

[28]D.B.S., *Comparative Statistics of Public Finance, 1956 to 1960*, per capita values calculated from Tables 1 and 13; and D.B.S., *Financial Statistics of Provincial Governments, 1958* (Ottawa: Queen's Printer, 1958), revenue and expenditure, actual, ratios calculated from Table 9. Only British Columbia had a

in Nova Scotia than in other provinces. This burden is further increased by the 5 per cent general retail sales tax which is applied to alcoholic beverages.

The burden of the general retail sales tax in Nova Scotia (raised from 3 per cent to 5 per cent April 1, 1961) is heavier than in most of the other provinces. Newfoundland and British Columbia have the same rate. The rate is 3 per cent in New Brunswick, Saskatchewan, and Ontario, and 4 per cent in Prince Edward Island and Quebec. Alberta and Manitoba levy no tax.[29]

Because of the diversity among the provinces in the kinds of natural resources, in the types of ownership of them, and in the methods of taxing them, no satisfactory way has yet been found of comparing the relative burdens of taxation on them.[30] Although satisfactory over-all interprovincial comparisons cannot be made of property taxes, the main source of municipal tax revenue, because of variations in assessments and in assessment practices, the Commission to Investigate the Taxation System in the City of Halifax, reporting in 1957, did attempt to make comparisons of property tax burdens between Halifax and twenty-two cities in other provinces. While it found the residential tax burden in Halifax to be in line with such burdens in other cities, the Commission found the tax burden on commercial property in Halifax to be over twice the average in these cities.[31]

---

higher per capita revenue ($16.69); the values for the other provinces ranged from $4.81 (Newfoundland) to $14.53 (Alberta), Ontario's being $9.55. Nova Scotia had the highest ratio of net income to gross sales, the others ranging as low as .21 (Manitoba). The ratio for Ontario was .31 (*ibid.*). Provincial consumption of alcoholic beverages per capita should also be taken into account in assessing the burden of provincial government liquor revenues. Per capita sales in the fiscal year 1960–1 for the part of the population twenty years of age and over in Nova Scotia, using the 1956 census, with amounts for all provinces except Prince Edward Island shown in parentheses, were, in gallons: spirits 1.16 (1.34), wine .68 (.71), beer 10.76 (19.83), all alcoholic beverages 12.59 (21.88). This evidence indicates that per capita consumption is less in Nova Scotia than in the rest of the country. The burden of provincial government liquor revenues is all the greater on that account in this province. (D.B.S., *The Control and Sale of Alcoholic Beverages in Canada*, fiscal year ended March 31, 1959 (Ottawa: Queen's Printer, 1960), p. 6; and D.B.S., *Census of Canada, 1956* (Ottawa: Queen's Printer, 1958), bulletin 3–3, Table 1.

[29]The rates of sales and other provincial taxes given here are those at the time of writing. They may well be quite different by the time this study is published, as provincial tax rates have recently been changing rapidly.

[30]The Canadian Tax Foundation has studied this problem, but has not so far found a satisfactory way of making the comparison (letter from Marion H. Bryden, the Foundation statistician, July 2, 1959).

[31]City of Halifax, *Report of the Commission to Investigate the Taxation System in the City of Halifax* (Halifax, 1957), pp. 21–33.

TABLE XI

ESTIMATES OF NET GENERAL REVENUE[a] FOR NOVA SCOTIA AND ALL PROVINCES
FOR THE FISCAL YEAR ENDED NEAREST TO DECEMBER 31, 1960
($'000)

	Nova Scotia	Nova Scotia % distribution	All provinces % distribution
Taxes			
On corporations, including corporate income	810[b]	.9	10.8
On personal income	nil	nil	2.4
Succession duties	1[c]	—[e]	2.0
Property	105[d]	.1	.3
Sales			
Motor fuel and fuel oil	16,295	17.7	15.7
General	9,785	10.6	8.3
Other commodities and services	707	.8	2.2
Other	97	—[e]	6.7
TOTAL TAXES	27,800	30.2	48.4
Privileges, licences, and permits			
Liquor control and regulation	272	.3	..[f]
Motor vehicles	6,430	7.0	..[f]
Natural resources	1,373	1.5	..[f]
Other	575	.6	..[f]
TOTAL PRIVILEGES, ETC.	8,650	9.4	20.8
Liquor profits	11,700	12.7	7.4
Other revenue	1,739	1.9	2.4
SUBTOTAL, EXCLUDING FEDERAL TRANSFERS	49,889	54.1	79.0
From Government of Canada			
Tax rental	11,981	13.0	11.6
Tax equalization	20,273	22.0	7.0
Revenue stabilization	nil	nil	nil
Atlantic Provinces Adjustment Grants	7,500	8.1	1.0
Share of increase in tax on public utilities	450	.5	.3
Statutory subsidies	2,057	2.2	1.1
TOTAL GOVERNMENT OF CANADA	42,261	45.9	21.0
TOTAL NET GENERAL REVENUE	92,150	100.0	100.0

Net general revenue per capita for Nova Scotia	$127
Net general revenue per capita for all provinces	$144
Ratio of net general revenue per capita for Nova Scotia to net general revenue per capita for all provinces	.89

SOURCE: D.B.S., *Comparative Statistics of Public Finance, 1956 to 1960* (Ottawa, Queen's Printer, 1960), Part I, Federal, Provincial, and Municipal Governments: Tables 1 and 13; and special compilation, Department of Finance. The statistics for the fiscal year 1960–1 are forecast estimates. They were the latest data at the time of writing. Although they are bound to differ from the actual revenues and expenditures, it was thought that they would likely give a more accurate picture than the actual data for an earlier year, especially in view of the newness of Nova Scotia's general retail sales tax.

ᵃ"Net general revenue" excludes revenues which can be specifically related to services rendered. Treated in conjunction with "net general expenditure," which is based upon the same principle, it gives a measure of the "net" cost to the government of its services. Accordingly, it is arrived at by deducting the following from "gross general revenue": (a) all revenue of provincial government institutions, (b) revenue in the form of interest, premium, discount, and exchange, (c) grants-in-aid and shared-cost contributions, and (d) all capital revenue. The surplus position is the same for both gross and net receipts.

ᵇTax on premium income of insurance companies.

ᶜCollection of arrears.

ᵈAbout one-quarter provincial Fire Tax (for fire protection), levied at seventy-five cents per one hundred acres on each owner, occupant, or lessee of timberlands or uncultivated land of 200 acres or more; and about three-quarters Land Tax levied on occupants of more than 1,000 acres of land at one per cent of its value.

ᵉThe symbol "—" means too small to be expressed.

ᶠThe symbol ". ." means not available.

For three of the provincial revenues examined (the gasoline tax, revenue from the sale of alcoholic beverages, and the general sales tax) and for the local property tax, for Halifax at least, it can be said that the burdens of taxation are significantly heavier than in at least some of the other provinces.[32] The only exception is the burden of the motor vehicle revenues, which appears to be slightly less than the average for all provinces. Since the substantially lower levels of provincial and municipal expenditures in Nova Scotia probably reflect a lower level of services there than in the provinces of central and western Canada, it appears that the principle of fiscal equity cannot at present be fully applied in Nova Scotia in relation to these provinces. It is still pertinent, nevertheless, to determine how the principle can be applied by the Government of Nova Scotia within the province with respect to the Nova Scotian municipalities.

CURRENT PUBLIC FINANCE IN NOVA SCOTIA

The accompanying tables largely speak for themselves, but it might be helpful to point out a few things of particular interest in them and to add some information about combined provincial and municipal revenue, expenditure, and debt.

Tables XI and XII illustrate Nova Scotia's heavy dependence, relative to other provinces, upon profits from the government liquor sales monopoly, and payments from the Government of Canada, especially the tax-sharing arrangements; and its relatively small revenue from

[32]Those who do not use alcohol, drive cars, or ride regularly on motor buses would not be treated very differently with regard to tax burdens than their counterparts in other provinces, except in provinces that have no sales tax.

TABLE XII

	Nova Scotia	All provinces
Taxes on corporations, corporate and personal income taxes, and succession duties	$ 1.12	$ 21.91
Tax on motor fuel and fuel oil	22.54	22.50
General sales tax	13.53	11.96
Motor vehicle licences	8.89	7.85[a]
Liquor profits	16.18	10.55
Natural resources	1.90	15.63[a]
TOTAL MAJOR REVENUES FROM PROVINCIAL SOURCES	64.16	90.40
From Government of Canada	58.45	30.13
TOTAL MAJOR REVENUES	122.61	120.53
Other revenues	4.83	22.97
TOTAL NET GENERAL REVENUE	$127.44	$143.50
Grants-in-aid and shared-cost contributions from the Government of Canada	28.47[b]	21.88
TOTAL NET GENERAL REVENUE AND GRANTS-IN-AID, ETC.	$155.91	$165.38
Major general revenues per capita as percentage of total net general revenue per capita	96.2	84.0

SOURCE: Calculated from D.B.S., *Comparative Statistics of Public Finance, 1956–1960*, Part I, Tables 1 and 13.
[a]Not shown separately in source. Estimated by using same prorating of items under "privileges, licences, and permits" as for fiscal year ended March 31, 1958.
[b]These total $20,583,000, distributed as follows (thousands omitted): agriculture 132, health 2,327, hospital insurance 8,901, welfare 3,286, vocational training, etc. 634, highways and transportation 3,313, resource development 1,110, civil defence 110, and other 770.

natural resources, a serious weakness in Nova Scotia's fiscal structure compared to other provinces, which reflects the relative paucity of these resources. This disadvantage is now partially overcome by the inclusion of the natural resource element in the new equalization formula.

Table XIII shows a distribution of expenditures for Nova Scotia quite similar to that for all provinces. Debt charges are a striking exception. On a per capita basis they were $13.14 for Nova Scotia compared with only $3.92 for all provinces. As would be expected, Nova Scotia has a relatively large debt. Its net direct funded debt per capita was $304, compared with $151 for all provinces, as at the end of the fiscal

TABLE XIII

ESTIMATES OF NET GENERAL EXPENDITURES[a] AND GRANTS-IN-AID AND
SHARED-COST CONTRIBUTIONS[b] FOR NOVA SCOTIA AND ALL PROVINCES
FOR FISCAL YEAR ENDED NEAREST TO DECEMBER 31, 1960
(in thousands of dollars, except per capita figures)

	Nova Scotia	Nova Scotia % distribution	All provinces distribution
General government	4,530	4.2	4.2
Protection to persons and property	4,185	3.9	5.2
Transportation and communications	29,460	27.6	25.7
Health	19,630	18.4	18.0
Social welfare	6,520	6.1	8.0
Education	24,720	23.2	24.2
Natural resources and primary industries	4,400	4.1	6.7
Debt charges, net, exclusive of debt retirement	9,500	8.9	2.5
Contributions to municipal governments	1,050	1.0	2.6
All other expenditures and adjustments	2,655	2.5	2.9
		100.0	100.0

	Nova Scotia	All provinces
Total net general expenditure exclusive of debt retirement	106,650	2,757,270
Grants-in-aid and shared-cost contributions from Government of Canada	20,583	388,980
TOTAL	127,233	3,146,250
Net general expenditure per capita excluding debt retirement	$147.51	$155.09
Grants-in-aid, etc. per capita	28.47	21.88
TOTAL PER CAPITA	175.98	176.97

SOURCE: D.B.S., *Comparative Statistics of Public Finance, 1956–1960*, Part I,
Tables 2 and 14.

[a]For the meaning of "net general expenditure" see Table XI, note ([a]). The term
"general" means that capital expenditures are included.

[b]Shown to give a truer picture of the extent of services rendered by the provinces.

year ended nearest to December 31, 1960. The relatively larger expenditures by Nova Scotia on transportation and communications are probably in part accounted for by the fact that the Government of Nova Scotia is responsible for all public roads in the province apart from those in towns and cities, while in some provinces local governments are responsible for many of the roads in rural areas; but they are likely in part due to a relatively higher priority being assigned to highway building by the provincial government.

Per capita revenue, expenditure, and debt for provincial and municipal governments combined are of interest because the distribution of functions and of revenues varies from province to province. For the fiscal year ended nearest December 31, 1960, the combined provincial and municipal net general revenue per capita for Nova Scotia was about $182—about 79 per cent of that for all provinces, $229. Its combined net general expenditure per capita was about $214—about 81 per cent of that for all provinces, $264. At the fiscal year ended nearest to December 31, 1958, the combined net funded direct debt per capita for Nova Scotia was $410—about 117 per cent of that for all provinces, $350.

Municipal Organization and Finance in Nova Scotia

NOVA SCOTIA BECAME COMPLETELY ORGANIZED for purposes of local government by the County Incorporation Act of 1879, which established twenty-four rural municipalities. These still exist, with the same boundaries as in 1879. The boundaries of twelve of them coincide with those of counties. The other six counties were divided into two rural municipalities each.[2] Prior to this act, the City of Halifax, and five towns had been incorporated,[3] all by special acts of the legislature, in response to local agitation. The County Incorporation Act, then, organized the rest of the province into units of local government. Three additional towns[4] were incorporated by special legislation before the legislature passed the Towns' Incorporation Act of 1888, which provided for incorporation of towns if a majority of ratepayers voting

[1]Much of the material in this section has been obtained from the introduction in Government of Nova Scotia, *Annual Report of Municipal Statistics, 1959* (Halifax: Queen's Printer); Donald C. Rowat, *The Reorganization of Provincial-Municipal Relations in Nova Scotia* (A report prepared for the Government of Nova Scotia by the Nova Scotia Municipal Bureau, Institute of Public Affairs, Dalhousie University; Halifax, 1949); J. Murray Beck, *The Government of Nova Scotia* (Toronto: University of Toronto Press, 1957); and from interviews.

[2]The 18 counties developed as electoral districts, as the province was gradually opened up, rather than as units of local government. The whole province was divided into counties by 1851. Today the counties serve as geographical and census as well as electoral divisions. The term "county" is also frequently used for a rural municipality which comprises a whole county. See Beck, *Government of Nova Scotia*, pp. 54–6, 112–13.

[3]Halifax (1841), Dartmouth (1873), Pictou (1874), Truro (1875), New Glasgow (1875), and Windsor (1878).

[4]Sydney (1885), North Sydney (1885), and Kentville (1886).

at a poll favoured it, and if the area of the locality in question was at least 500 acres and its population at least 700.[5]

Local government was slow to develop in Nova Scotia in its pre-Confederation days, partly because it was discouraged by the Legislative Council in accordance with the policy of the Crown to maintain centralized administration, and partly, especially in the case of the rural areas, because of a reluctance of the people to accept the responsibilities and burdens involved. When rural municipal organization did come it was imposed on the rural communities to force them to levy much-despised property taxes for the maintenance of roads and bridges and so to relieve the province of the responsibility for this service at a time of financial stringency, rather than being granted in response to popular demand.[6] In view of this, it is ironical that the province later took over responsibility for public roads and bridges in the rural municipalities (partly in 1917 and completely by the late nineteen-twenties). A number of other functions which had been added meanwhile, however, including ones relating to education, health, and welfare (the performance of most of which was also required by the province), as well as the regulative and service functions commonly performed by localities, justified the continued existence of rural municipal government.

Today, Nova Scotia is completely organized for purposes of local government into 66 municipal units, consisting of three cities (Halifax, Dartmouth, and Sydney), 24 rural municipalities, and 39 towns.[7] The boundaries of the rural municipalities and the locations of the cities and towns, along with their populations, are shown on the accompanying map (Figure 1). The populations of the towns in the 1961 census ranged from 800 (Annapolis Royal) to 24,180 (Glace Bay) with a mean of 4,425, and of the rural municipalities from 3,123 (St. Mary's) to 86,246 (Halifax) with a mean of 16,306. The areas of the rural municipalities range from about 220 square miles (Barrington) to about 2,190 square miles (Halifax), with a mean of about 860 square miles.[8]

[5]Since amended (by Geo. VI, c. 3) to 640 acres and 1500 inhabitants. The new requirements were not made retroactive.

[6]Beck, *Government of Nova Scotia*, pp. 302–3.

[7]Sydney became a city in 1904, and Dartmouth, after absorbing some of its fringe areas, in 1961. Three towns (Port Hood in 1946, Wedgeport in 1947, and Joggins in 1949) surrendered their incorporated status and became part of the rural municipalities which geographically contain them because, according to Beck (*ibid.*, p. 304), they found the burden of town organization too great. The last towns to incorporate were Berwick and Mulgrave, both in 1923. (*Annual Report of Municipal Statistics, 1956*, p. 3.)

[8]*Annual Report of Municipal Statistics, 1959*, p. 12. The area given for the

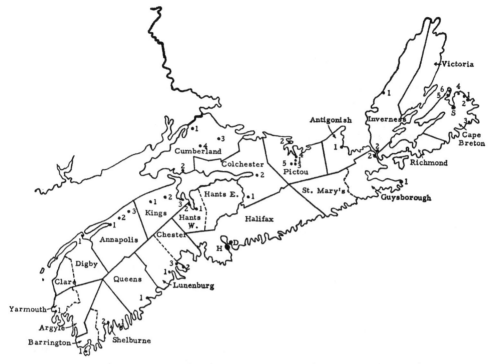

FIGURE 1. LOCATION AND 1961 POPULATION OF NOVA SCOTIA'S 24 RURAL MUNICIPALITIES, 39 TOWNS, AND 3 CITIES

Broken lines are used to show the boundaries of rural municipalities where counties are split into two municipalities. The towns (designated by numerals) and cities (designated by letters) are listed under their respective rural municipalities in the population figures. The population figures for the rural municipalities do not include the towns or cities within their geographical boundaries.

ANNAPOLIS	18,885	CUMBERLAND	17,838	3. Wolfville	2,413
1. Annapolis Royal	800	1. Amherst	10,788		
2. Bridgetown	1,043	2. Parrsboro	1,834	LUNENBURG	18,416
3. Middleton	1,921	3. Oxford	1,471	1. Bridgewater	4,497
		4. Springhill	5,836	2. Lunenburg	3,056
ANTIGONISH	10,016			3. Mahone Bay	1,103
1. Antigonish	4,344	DIGBY	9,369		
		1. Digby	2,308	PICTOU	16,966
ARGYLE	7,810			1. New Glasgow	9,782
		GUYSBOROUGH	7,855	2. Pictou	4,534
BARRINGTON	5,596	1. Canso	1,151	3. Stellarton	5,327
1. Clark's Harbour	945	2. Mulgrave	1,145	4. Trenton	3,140
				5. Westville	4,159
CAPE BRETON	40,917	HALIFAX	86,246		
1. Dominion	2,999	D Dartmouth	46,966	QUEENS	9,443
2. Glace Bay	24,186	H Halifax	92,511	1. Liverpool	3,712
3. Louisburg	1,417				
4. New Waterford	10,592	HANTS, EAST	10,866	RICHMOND	11,374
5. North Sydney	8,657				
6. Sydney Mines	9,122	HANTS, WEST	10,374	SHELBURNE	4,668
S Sydney	33,617	1. Windsor	3,823	1. Lockeport	1,231
		2. Hantsport	1,381	2. Shelburne	2,408
CHESTER	7,926				
		INVERNESS	15,263	ST. MARY'S	3,123
CLARE	8,539	1. Inverness	2,109		
		2. Port Hawkesbury	1,346	VICTORIA	8,266
COLCHESTER	20,844	KINGS	33,440	YARMOUTH	6,940
1. Stewiacke	1,042	1. Berwick	1,282	1. Yarmouth	8,636
2. Truro	12,421	2. Kentville	4,612		

As is the case throughout Canada the municipal units are the creatures of the provincial government. The British North America Act divided power between the federal government and the provinces, giving the provinces jurisdiction over what at the time were regarded as matters primarily of local concern. Each province was free to organize local governments and to delegate or assign to them any of its functions and revenue sources it wished.

The powers of the three cities, Halifax, Dartmouth, and Sydney, are contained in their charters, which are separate pieces of provincial legislation and are amended from time to time by the legislature, usually at the request of the cities. The powers of the towns are derived from the present version of the Towns' Incorporation Act, and of the rural municipalities, from the Municipal Act, the present version of the original County Incorporation Act. The Municipal Affairs Act, which regulates municipal borrowing powers, relates to all of the municipal units. Certain important functions required of the municipalities are contained in special acts, such as the Education Act and the Public Health Act. In addition, the Village Service Act permits a community of more than 100 people to incorporate village commissions, usually consisting of three elected commissioners, to provide certain specific services of a local improvement nature, such as street lighting and fire protection, additional to those provided by a rural municipality. These villages, of which there are 15, remain part of the rural municipality which contains them. They obtain the revenue necessary for the services they provide by extra levies on the property of their residents, using the assessment rolls of the rural municipalities of which they are a part. They may collect these taxes themselves or, what is the commoner practice, have the rural municipalities collect the taxes for them. About 20 other commissions similar to the village commissions have been created by special acts of the legislature.

The rural municipalities are divided into districts for electoral and other administrative purposes. These districts are based upon the old townships, which had never served effectively as units of local government and which were established mainly for provincial electoral purposes. Any semblance they had of being independent units of local government disappeared when the rural municipalities were formed. The rural municipalities are also divided into many small school sections, about 70 on the average; they at one time had considerable

Municipality of Halifax County does not take account of the absorption in 1961 by the new City of Dartmouth of some of its fringe areas which were formerly part of the county.

independence with regard to building and financing schools, but are now essentially administrative divisions under the school boards of the rural municipalities.

The Municipal Act and the Towns' Incorporation Act contain lists of regulatory functions which relate mainly to the maintenance of law and order and to the protection of the welfare of the inhabitants. These acts also give the general power to preserve peace, health, and good order. The city charters of the three cities grant similar but more extensive powers. Other functions, such as the provision of roads and educational facilities and the support of the poor and unemployed, were at one time principally local functions, but have come more and more to be of provincial and even national interest as well. Roads were once entirely a local responsibility in Nova Scotia. The province is now responsible for all those in the rural areas and even bears some of the cost of those in towns and cities.

The municipalities, then, are concerned in varying degrees with providing services relating to roads, education, welfare, public health, public utilities, regulation, redevelopment, and recreation. Some of these services have seen larger and larger participation by the provincial and federal governments as time progressed, but since the range and amounts of services which concern the municipalities have also grown, so have the responsibilities and financial burdens of the municipalities.

All of the municipal units are governed by elected councils. The chairman of each rural municipal council, the warden, is elected by the council from their own number, while that of each town and city council, the mayor, is elected at large by the voters. Each rural municipality is divided into districts for electoral purposes. Some of the towns are divided into wards for electoral purposes and some are not, at each town's discretion. All three cities, Halifax, Dartmouth, and Sydney, are so divided. In all three kinds of municipal unit there is provision for staggering the terms of council members so that not all of them come up for election in any one year.

School boards are chosen partly by the councils and partly by the province; the town boards having three members out of five chosen by the councils; the municipal boards, four out of seven; Halifax City, six out of twelve; and Sydney, four out of seven. It is likely that the Dartmouth city charter, when ratified by the legislature, will provide for a larger school board than the five members it still had at the time of writing, probably for nine members, five chosen by the council.

The separation of the rural municipalities from the towns and cities is a distinctive feature of local government in Nova Scotia, in contrast to the organization in most of the other provinces, and in practically all of the American states. A consequence of this separation was that it left some of the units too weak financially and too small in population to provide some kinds of services economically (especially institutions such as court houses, jails, poor houses, and mental hospitals, and functions such as law enforcement). Provision was therefore made for a system of joint expenditure so that services and their costs could be shared by a rural municipality with one or more towns or a city or another rural municipality. Costs are apportioned according to the assessed value of property in the municipal units concerned. The objects of joint expenditure and the allocation of the costs are determined by arbitration committees of three members elected from the council of each participating municipal unit. If assessments were made on a uniform basis in each such unit, this method of sharing costs would probably be satisfactory. It would mean that a unit with a larger per capita assessment would pay more in proportion to population than a unit with a smaller per capita assessment, relative population being taken as a measure of the degree of benefit of each unit from the service. This result would generally hold for towns and cities in relation to the rural municipalities.

In fact, assessments have not been made on a uniform basis, although some progress has been made towards uniformity. The sharing arrangement has therefore not been satisfactory, for it has had the unfortunate effect of encouraging competitive under-assessment in all three kinds of municipal unit to minimize the share of the costs of the joint expenditures, at the expense of the other municipal units participating. The recently abolished Municipalities' Highway Tax,[9] a provincial tax on the rural municipalities based on real property, was initially imposed in 1917 when the province began to assume responsibility for rural public roads. It had the similar effect of inducing rural municipalities to keep their assessments low to minimize the burden of the tax.

MAJOR RESPONSIBILITIES OF THE MUNICIPALITIES

AND PROVINCIAL PARTICIPATION

The services of the municipalities can be divided roughly according to whether they are of a local or of a general nature; that is, according to whether the benefits from them accrue only to the inhabitants

---

[9]Abolished in 1957, effective after 1956 (*S.N.S.*, 1957, c. 41). In the calendar year 1956 this tax, which was levied at 60 cents per $100 of assessment of real property, yielded $245,924. (*Annual Report of Municipal Statistics, 1956*, p. 30.)

of the municipalities or whether they are spread throughout the province or the nation. All of the services presently provided by the municipalities were at one time considered, by the province at least, to be most appropriately performed locally. But it would be stretching a point to say that all of them were at the time they were undertaken considered to be only, or primarily, of local interest. This may be said perhaps of those functions directly related to serving local residents, such as fire and police protection, the construction and maintenance of streets, sanitation and waste removal, suppression of public nuisances, and even of the provision of welfare services. But practically from the beginning, public education in Nova Scotia, which today accounts for by far the largest single part of local expenditures (see Table XVII) was considered to confer a general benefit.[10] The municipalities assumed responsibility for it not because they wanted to but because the province said they must, in the belief that education, although it conferred a general benefit, could be most effectively administered and in large part financed, without undue hardship, at the local level. This view no doubt stemmed in part from a feeling that education was only one step from the family unit and so assumed such a degree of intimacy that it should be largely under local control. Many of the same views as the foregoing about education were held with regard to services relating to health.

In the field of social welfare, the benefit is confined more narrowly to the individual upon whom the service is directly conferred than in the case of education and public health, and so in this sense can be considered a local one. Provision for the needy was long regarded as being primarily of local concern. If the indigent aged and other destitute could not be provided for by their families it was a matter of local pride for the community to see that they were cared for. The provincial government in Nova Scotia was acting in accordance with the social attitude of the day in assigning the responsibility for such care to the municipalities. But the general attitude of society has changed to the point where not only services which confer a general benefit, like education and health, are considered to be of general interest and

[10]As evidenced, for example, in the following statement by Joseph Howe, one of Nova Scotia's most famous statesmen: "Start with the principle that every child shall have the rudiments of education, that from Cape North to Cape Sable there shall not be a family beyond the reach of common schools—not a child who is not acquainted with reading, writing and arithmetic. Give them the means for the highest progress if you will, but make sure of the broad basis for all." Cited in Government of Nova Scotia, *Report of the Royal Commission on Public School Finance* (Halifax: Queen's Printer, 1954), p. 84.

therefore appropriate objects of expenditure for the larger units of government. The assurance of a minimum measure of economic security has come to be considered as being in the interest of all and as a right to which all are entitled. Welfare can therefore now be grouped with the other general services. This change is in part attributable to the development of democracy in that those in the low- and middle-income groups have exerted pressures to have the government provide them with a minimum of security. It is also attributable to the fact that most of the members of a highly specialized and urbanized industrial society are less independent and therefore more vulnerable economically than in a lower income, predominantly agricultural society. People in the rural areas also get the benefit of welfare measures; otherwise there would appear to be discrimination against them, a condition no government can likely ignore for long.[11]

The distinction between local and general services is of interest because it permits a division into those functions which are more or less clearly the preserve of the local government and those in which the province might appropriately assume an interest. The province can, of course, aid the municipalities financially with respect to local as well as to general services; but if adjustments are to be made in the kinds of services provided by local government, it is in the area of the general services that they will likely have to be made.

One of the outcomes of the increasing amounts and quality of the general services demanded from the municipalities has been that many municipal units are too weak financially and too small from the administrative point of view to provide them at adequate levels.[12] The financial disparity of the municipal units was not so serious when much less was expected of government generally and when the austere view that each locality should provide only what it could afford to provide was commonly held.[13]

[11]Unemployment insurance benefits were not, however, initially extended to the mainly rural industries, fishing, agriculture, and forestry, largely because of their seasonal nature. The trend is now towards extending benefits even to these industries.

[12]See Rowat, *Reorganization of Provincial-Municipal Relations*, Part 1, *passim*. It is to remedying these shortcomings that much of Rowat's study is directed.

[13]This attitude is not dead in Nova Scotia. A warden of a rural municipality in Nova Scotia, a well-educated and thoughtful man, said in an interview that in his opinion the guiding principle of municipal finance should be "What we can't afford, we can't have." He said, for example, he thought it was ridiculous to say that every child should have the same educational opportunity regardless of where he lived in the province. He believes that the level of services provided by a municipality should be only what it can provide with its own resources and that benefits should not be the same everywhere. He added, however, that a municipality

TABLE XIV
REVENUES OF NOVA SCOTIAN MUNICIPALITIES IN 1959 (CALENDAR YEAR)

	Cities ($'000)	Cities (%)	Towns ($'000)	Towns (%)	Rural muns. ($'000)	Rural muns. (%)	All muns. ($'000)	All muns. (%)
Taxation revenue^a								
General								
Real property	9,069	58.8	6,666	53.6	8,094	65.3	23,829	59.2
Personal property	2,225^b	14.4	2,812	22.6	1,663	13.4	6,700	16.6
Poll	271	1.8	329	2.6	475	3.8	1,075	2.7
Special assessments and charges	92	.6	128	1.0	82	.7	302	.8
TOTAL TAXATION REVENUE	11,657	75.6	9,935	79.8	10,314	83.2	31,906	79.3
Licences and permits; rents, concessions, and franchises; fines and fees	651	4.2	347	2.8	52	.4	1,050	2.6
Interest, tax penalties, etc.	200	1.3	108	.9	96	.8	404	1.0
Contributions, grants, subsidies								
Governments								
Dominion^c	1,545	10.0	379	3.0	208	1.7	2,132	5.3
Province of Nova Scotia^d	683	4.4	1,155	9.3	1,693	13.6	3,531	8.8
Municipal	—	—	8	.1	—	—	8	.0
Government enterprises	298	1.9	193	1.6	9	.1	500	1.2
Other	332	2.2	284	2.3	—	—	616	1.5
TOTAL CONTRIBUTIONS, GRANTS, SUBSIDIES	2,858	18.5	2,019	16.3	1,910	15.4	6,787	16.8
Miscellaneous (including recreation and community services)	49	.3	26	.2	23	.2	98	.2
TOTAL CURRENT REVENUE^e	15,415	100.0	12,435	100.0	12,395	100.0	40,245	100.0
TOTAL CURRENT REVENUE PER CAPITA	$123		$65		$33		$58	

SOURCE: Government of Nova Scotia, *Annual Report of Municipal Statistics, 1959*, (Halifax: Queen's Printer), pp. 3, 12, 14, 24, 31.
^aIncludes all taxes levied for municipal and school purposes.
^bThe part for Halifax consists of household tax, business tax, and payment by Maritime Telephone & Telegraph Co. of 3 per cent of gross subscriber revenue.
^cPayments in lieu of municipal taxes on federal property.
^dSee Table XV.
^eDoes not include adjustments for deficit or surplus from previous years or for deficit or surplus of current year and so differs slightly from the totals in *Annual Report of Municipal Statistics, 1959*.

TABLE XV

ANALYSIS OF CONTRIBUTIONS, GRANTS, AND SUBSIDIES FROM THE
PROVINCE OF NOVA SCOTIA TO THE MUNICIPALITIES IN 1959[a]

	Cities ($'000)	Towns ($'000)	Rural muns. ($'000)	All muns. ($'000)
General purposes grant	421	449	116	986
Debt charges on school capital term debt	7	203	841	1,052
Capital expenditures out of revenue—school purposes	—	261	173	434
Discount on debentures issued for school purposes	1	4	57	62
Province's share of maintenance of street approaches	—	29	—	29
Assistance under Social Assistance Act—municipal relief	143	143	395	681
Assistance under Local Asylums Act—mentally ill	64	12	82	158
Dues under Lands and Forests Act	—	—	5	5
Winter works programme	17	36	21	74
Other[b]	29	17	2	48
TOTAL	683	1,155	1,693	3,531

SOURCE: Obtained directly from the Department of Municipal Affairs.
[a]There are slight rounding errors in some of the totals.
[b]Mainly civil defence.

Tables XIV to XVIII, showing the expenditures and revenues of
municipalities in Nova Scotia, give a general idea of the relative
importance at present of different types of expenditures and revenues
of the three kinds of municipal unit. They show how the variety and
amount of services decline from the cities to the towns to the rural
municipalities, and how very important property taxes are as a source
of revenue. Grants from the provincial government appear to be relatively unimportant as a revenue source, but the large grants for education are not shown. In 1959 these totalled $13,673,000,[14] an amount
equal to about 33 per cent of all municipal expenditures in the calendar year 1959.[15]

Many changes have taken place in provincial-municipal fiscal relations in Nova Scotia in the last half century, both by adjustments in the

can usually afford to pay more than it thinks it can. When pressed slightly, even
he conceded that there is some merit in equalization grants for a service like education which bestows general benefits beyond the boundaries of the municipality.

[14]See Table XX. Government of Nova Scotia, *Annual Report of the Department
of Education*, for the year ended July 31, 1960 (Halifax: Queen's Printer, 1961),
p. xxi.

[15]*Annual Report of Municipal Statistics, 1959*, calculated from pp. 27 and 34.

TABLE XVI

PER CAPITA REVENUES OF NOVA SCOTIAN MUNICIPALITIES^a

IN 1959 (CALENDAR YEAR)

	Cities $	Towns $	Rural muns. $	All muns. $
Taxation revenue:				
General				
Real property	72.28	34.76	21.44	34.30
Personal property	17.73	14.66	4.40	9.64
Poll	2.16	1.72	1.26	1.55
Special assessments and charges	.73	.67	.22	.43
TOTAL TAXATION REVENUE	92.90	51.81	27.32	45.92
Licences and permits; rents, concessions, and franchises; fines and fees	5.19	1.81	.14	1.51
Interest, tax penalties, etc.	1.59	.44	.25	.58
Contributions, grants, subsidies				
Governments				
Dominion	12.31	1.98	.55	3.07
Province of Nova Scotia	5.44	6.02	4.48	5.08
Municipal	—	.04	—	.01
Government enterprises	2.38	1.01	.02	.72
Other	2.65	1.48	—	.89
TOTAL CONTRIBUTIONS, GRANTS, SUBSIDIES	22.78	10.53	5.05	9.77
Miscellaneous	.39	.14	.06	.14
TOTAL CURRENT REVENUE PER CAPITA	122.85	64.73	32.82	57.92

SOURCE: As for Table XIV.
^aBased on 1956 population data.

division of responsibilities between the province and the localities, and by the payment of grants to the localities.[16] There has been practically no adjustment by altering the revenue bases available to the municipalities, apart from the loss of the income tax by the municipalities as a result of the province's tax rental agreements with the Dominion for which they were compensated by an annual unconditional grant from the province. The remainder of this chapter will chronicle these changes in provincial-municipal fiscal relations and describe the functions of the municipalities in sufficient detail and with sufficient historical perspective to give an understanding of provincial-municipal fiscal relations at the present time.

As general government is mainly concerned with administration,

[16]See Rowat, *Reorganization of Provincial-Municipal Relations*, pp. 12–22, on "The Increased Participation by Senior Governments."

TABLE XVII

EXPENDITURES OF NOVA SCOTIAN MUNICIPALITIES IN 1959 (CALENDAR YEAR)

	Cities		Towns		Rural muns.		All muns.	
	($'000)	(%)	($'000)	(%)	($'000)	(%)	($'000)	(%)
General government	1,107	7.1	769	6.1	932	7.3	2,807	6.8
Protection to persons and property[a]	2,866	18.4	1,648	13.0	108	.8	4,622	11.3
Public works	1,088	7.0	1,137	9.0	28	.2	2,253	5.5
Sanitation and waste removal	577	3.7	276	2.2	—	—	853	2.1
Health[b]	744	4.8	265	2.1	711	5.6	1,720	4.2
Social welfare[c]	467	3.0	406	3.2	852	6.7	1,725	4.2
Education	4,505	28.8	3,681	29.1	5,953	46.9	14,139	34.5
Recreation and community services	529	3.4	192	1.5	47	.4	768	1.9
Debt charges[d]	3,055	19.6	2,212	17.5	2,040	16.1	7,307	17.8
Utilities and other municipal enterprises[e]	13	.1	70	.6	—	—	83	.2
Provision for reserves	128	.8	295	2.3	260	2.0	683	1.7
Capital expenditure provided out of revenue	45	.3	974	7.7	423	3.3	1,442	3.5
Joint or special expenditure	385	2.5	527	4.2	1,260	9.9	2,172	5.3
Miscellaneous expenditure	103	.6	188	1.5	83	.6	374	.9
TOTAL EXPENDITURE[f]	15,612	100.0	12,640	100.0	12,697	100.0	40,947	100.0
Population (1956 Census)	125,463		191,753		377,501		694,717	
TOTAL EXPENDITURE PER CAPITA	$124		$66		$34		$59	

SOURCE: *Annual Report of Municipal Statistics, 1959*, pp. 3, 12, 25–7, 32–4.
[a]Includes fire and police protection, law enforcement and corrections, street lighting, etc.
[b]Mainly for general and mental hospitals and, in Halifax, public health.
[c]Mainly for municipal homes, outdoor relief, and child welfare.
[d]Including schools.
[e]Deficits of and levies for utilities.
[f]Does not include adjustment for deficit of previous years or surplus for current year and so differs from the totals in the source.

TABLE XVIII

PER CAPITA EXPENDITURES OF NOVA SCOTIAN MUNICIPALITIES[a]
IN 1959 (CALENDAR YEAR)

	Cities $	Towns $	Rural muns. $	All muns. $
General government	8.82	4.01	2.47	4.04
Protection to persons and property	22.84	8.59	.29	6.65
Public works	8.67	5.93	.07	3.24
Sanitation and waste removal	4.60	1.44	—	1.23
Health	5.93	1.38	1.88	2.48
Social welfare	3.72	2.12	2.26	2.48
Education	35.91	19.20	15.77	20.35
Recreation and community services	4.22	1.00	.12	1.10
Debt charges	24.35	11.54	5.40	10.52
Utilities and other municipal enterprises	.10	.36	—	.12
Provision for reserves	1.02	1.54	.69	.98
Capital expenditure provided out of revenue	.36	5.08	1.12	2.08
Joint or special expenditure	3.07	2.74	3.34	3.13
Miscellaneous expenditures	.82	.98	.22	.54
TOTAL EXPENDITURES PER CAPITA	124.43	65.91	33.63	58.94

SOURCE: As for Table XV.
[a]Based on 1956 population data.

its cost will vary with the other responsibilities assumed by the localities, and so it is not really an independent item and is not of much interest to this study. Protection to persons and property, and public works will be discussed briefly, but most attention will be given to problems of the localities and for most of the difficulties in provincial-education, health, and welfare, for they are responsible for most of the municipal relations. The last few years have seen fundamental changes with regard to provincial participation in all three of these fields.

Protection to Persons and Property

This category includes such services as fire protection, police protection, law enforcement, and street lighting. There is not much here that concerns this study. These are mostly traditional local functions which have remained local in character.

Police protection, to the extent it is provided by localities, is provided mainly by the towns and cities; the rural municipalities are policed by the Royal Canadian Mounted Police, who by a contract with the provincial government, act as provincial as well as federal police in Nova Scotia. They also police Inverness, Pictou, and Windsor, by special contract with these towns.

Some change might be made in the responsibility for providing jails and lock-up houses. At present the localities must provide these for prisoners awaiting trial or sentence and for those serving sentences of less than two years. Prisoners serving longer sentences are sent to the federal penitentiary at Dorchester, New Brunswick. The system of numerous small local jails is unsatisfactory as it provides insufficient segregation of prisoners of different categories and as it is not conducive to the best reformatory practices.[17] The federal government has recently proposed that it take over responsibility for prisoners sentenced to more than one year and is expected to introduce legislation to eliminate sentences for federal crimes of over six months up to one year.[18] The new federal prison at Springhill was established to provide some of the expansion of federal penal facilities necessitated by these changes. The Nova Scotian government has proposed to the federal government that the province be permitted to board its prisoners serving terms of three months or more in the federal prison. Such an arrangement would mean that the federal prison would take the responsibility for most of the training and rehabilitation of prisoners and that the municipal jails would be used only for those prisoners serving sentences of less than three months and for those awaiting trial or sentence. This group nevertheless comprises on the average about three-quarters of those serving sentences or being held in local jails, about one-third of the total being held for drunkenness.

Public Works

Sewers, sidewalks, and drainage are local responsibilities, as are most of the streets in towns and cities. As already mentioned, the province, through its Department of Highways, assumes responsibility for all public roads in the rural municipalities. This practice has relieved the rural municipalities of a big burden, but one consequence has been that the province is in fact providing streets in built-up areas, which are technically classed along with other roads. To compensate the

[17]For a good description of conditions in local jails in Nova Scotia and of the need for reform, see Government of Nova Scotia, *Fifty-fifth* and *Fifty-sixth Annual Reports on Penal Institutions* (Halifax: Queen's Printer, 1956 and 1957), *passim*. A good deal of progress has been made towards improving conditions since these reports.

[18]The changes in the federal government's policy are based on recommendations in the *Report of the Committee to Inquire into the Principles and Procedures Followed in the Remission Service of the Department of Justice of Canada* (Called the Fauteux Committee, after the chairman, Mr. Gerald Fauteux; Ottawa: Queen's Printer, 1956).

towns and cities for the less favourable treatment accorded them with respect to roads and streets, the province, in the fiscal year 1960–1, began to make them an annual grant of $200 per mile of street. These grants are administered by the Department of Municipal Affairs, the amounts budgeted being $190,000 for 1960–1 and $200,000 for 1961–2.[19] The province also shares the capital and maintenance costs of sections of highways passing through towns and cities, up to a maximum of 50 per cent.[20] In the fiscal year 1959–60, the province's share of aid to towns for maintenance and capital expenditures was about $128,000 compared with total maintenance and capital expenditures on highways from provincial funds of about $27,686,000,[21] and compared with a total expenditure of towns and cities for public works in 1959 (calendar year) of about $2,225,000.[22]

It is in keeping with the division between local and general services that those city and town streets which form parts of highways should at least in part be regarded as general services, since it is of value to all who use them to have them well looked after, and since the towns and cities should not have to bear the full cost of building and maintaining streets which are largely used by outsiders passing through.

In an effort to introduce more care in laying out new suburban developments in rural municipalities, the province made provision in 1956 for the Minister of Highways to enter into agreements with rural municipalities for the province to bear 40 per cent of the cost of putting in pavement and curbs and gutters in such areas, the rural municipalities to pay 20 per cent, and the owners of the abutting property, 40 per cent. In 1957, the provincial share was increased to 45 per cent and the municipal share reduced to 15 per cent. The outlay of the province for this purpose in the year ending March 31, 1960, was $200,000, the whole sum being for Halifax County, the only rural municipality with which the province had an agreement in that year. The Minister also may, with the approval of the Governor-in-Council, share with the rural municipalities the costs of building sidewalks along public highways to the extent of 50 per cent. The province's

[19]Legislature of Nova Scotia, 1961 Session, *Estimates* (Halifax: Queen's Printer, 1961), p. 42.

[20]R.S.N.S., 1954, c. 235, Public Highways Act, s. 25. This means in fact, that the province pays the maximum of 50 per cent. An amendment to the act, s. 25A, permits the Minister to pay up to 100 per cent for major trunk highways passing through towns and for costly bridges.

[21]Government of Nova Scotia, *Annual Report of the Department of Highways*, for the fiscal year ended March 31, 1960 (Halifax: Queen's Printer, 1960), table beginning on p. 110.

[22]*Annual Report of Municipal Statistics, 1959*, p. 25.

expenditure for this purpose in the fiscal year 1959–60, was $63,423.92.[23]

Education[24]

As early as 1808 there was authority in Nova Scotia for the establishment by the inhabitants of school sections of free schools, supported by local property taxes,[25] with provision for some financial aid by the government of Nova Scotia. But it was not until the series of Education Acts of 1864, 1865, and 1866, that the principle of free public education for all children in the province, supported mainly by compulsory levies on real and personal property in local school sections, was put into effect. At the time, there was strenuous opposition to the legislation, especially by many of those who had no children and by those who wished to educate their children privately. These acts provided for provincial grants of a fixed sum for the construction and support of County Academies[26] and Superior Schools, for provincial salary grants to teachers according to licence, for the establishment of a Municipal School Fund in each county supported by levies in that county[27] and distributed to the school sections in proportion to the number of teachers in each, and for the local school sections to raise any money required in addition to the provincial and municipal grants, by levies on real and personal property.[28] The allocation of costs for selected years is shown in Table XIX.

This system of finance prevailed until 1942. One significant feature of it was the designation of poor sections, usually in sparsely populated areas. They received special assistance both from the Municipal School Fund and from the provincial government. The financial weakness of these sections was a continual problem and one which became espe-

[23]Obtained directly from the Department of Highways.

[24]Most of the material in this section is from the *Report of the Royal Commission on Public School Finance*. This excellent report will hereinafter be referred to as the *Pottier Report*, after the Commissioner, The Honourable Vincent J. Pottier, Q.C. Also useful is H. P. Moffatt, *Educational Finance in Canada* (The 1957 Quance Lectures in Canadian Education; Toronto: W. J. Gage Limited, 1957).

[25]Other sources of support used at various times after the first Education Act in 1766 included religious denominations, private subscriptions, excise taxes, allocation of lands, and government grants.

[26]These were high schools, some of which came to have a very high standard of instruction.

[27]At first equalling two-thirds of the provincial grant to the county and later being at a rate of so much per inhabitant, beginning at 30 cents in 1866 and rising to $1.00 in 1921.

[28]They were at first required to do this only for obtaining or erecting school houses.

TABLE XIX

ALLOCATION OF COSTS OF EDUCATION IN NOVA SCOTIA FOR SELECTED YEARS,
1870–1940

Year	School Sect. levy	% of total	Munic. fund	% of total	Prov'l grant	% of total	Total	% of total
1870	$ 266,160	50.0	$ 91,762	17.2	$ 174,602	32.8	$ 532,524	100.0
1900	519,620	58.5	119,923	13.5	248,309	27.9	887,852	100.0
1920	1,978,242	73.2	224,025	8.3	500,405	18.5	2,702,672	100.0
1930	2,529,293	63.7	523,876	13.2	916,856	23.1	3,970,025	100.0
1940	2,900,290	61.4	516,616	10.9	1,304,521	27.6	4,721,427	100.0

SOURCE: Based on the table, p. 5, of Government of Nova Scotia, *Report of the Royal Commission on Public School Finance* (Halifax: Queen's Printer, 1954), hereinafter *Pottier Report*.

cially acute in the depression of the 1930's, when at one point the rural and village school sections were almost half a million dollars in arrears.[29]

The school section system of financing had never worked well in the rural areas, because of the very small size of the sections.[30] What was clearly called for was a larger unit of school finance. In 1938, the Commission on the Larger Unit declared itself in favour of the larger unit for educational finance in the rural areas becoming the province itself. The provincial government was to determine a minimum programme, in terms of teachers' salaries and maintenance of schools, and levy a uniform property tax throughout the province. The commission further suggested that any deficit resulting from the failure of this tax to cover the minimum programme be made up by an equalization fund drawn from other provincial revenues.[31] These radical proposals, which would have ended the practice of making localities assume considerable financial responsibility for education, were not put into effect. Instead, an alternative suggestion of the commission was translated into enabling legislation in 1942. This legislation, which provided for the establishment of a municipal school unit, was adopted by all rural municipalities by 1946.

The new legislation was designed to equalize the tax burden within each rural municipality and to establish a minimum programme throughout the province for teachers' salaries and, in village and rural

[29]*Pottier Report*, p. 7.

[30]Rowat, writing in 1949, noted that their average population was only 185, and that their breadth, averaging only 4 miles, was mainly determined by the distance a child could walk to school. (*Reorganization of Provincial-Municipal Relations*, p. 3.)

[31]Government of Nova Scotia, "Report of the Commission on the Larger Unit," *Journals of the House of Assembly*, 1940, Appendix 8.

sections, for maintenance expenditures on schools. The provincial
government committed itself to make up the difference between the
cost of the minimum programme and the revenue raised in each
municipality by a uniform levy. The uniform tax rate in each rural
municipality was determined by taking the median of the rates for
the sections in the municipality for the school year 1941–2 and reducing
it by 10 per cent. Capital costs were still borne by the school sections.
One defect of this scheme was that the tax rate in relation to market
values of property varied from one municipality to another. Another
defect was that the scheme was based upon municipal assessments
which varied greatly from one municipality to another, with the result
that a more wealthy rural municipality with low assessments in relation
to market values of property could receive more aid than a less wealthy
rural municipality with higher assessments in relation to market value.
The plan did work in the general direction of equalization, however,
even though there was nothing in the "formula" itself to bring it about
in any systematic way; for most of the wealthier municipalities were
closer to the minimum programme to begin with and so received less
money from the province than the poorer ones. In spite of its shortcomings, the reform was a step in the right direction in bringing about
the formation of a larger unit for financing school operations; and it
did cope with an emergency situation.

The minimum programme was adjusted upwards a number of times
over the next ten years, the salary increases being paid by the province.[32] Since the municipal school tax rates were fixed at the 1942
levels and since assessments changed very little, practically the whole
of the other increases was also paid by the province. When the rapid
increase in enrolment after 1948, as a result of the high wartime birth
rate, further increased the demand for classrooms, most of the burden
of the operation of the additional classrooms fell on the province.

In 1948, the province informed the rural municipalities that it would
not further increase the school maintenance grants of the minimum
programme. In 1951, it amended the Education Act to protect itself
further from increased financial commitments. The amendment froze
the equalization fund used to pay the provincial share of the minimum
programme in the rural municipalities at $1,211,040, the amount paid
in 1950–1. The freezing did not apply to salary grants. The province

[32]". . . the amount paid by the Province for teachers' salaries and pension
benefits increased from approximately $975,000 in 1942 to over $5,000,000 in
1953, exclusive of the Equalization Fund and grants for Rural and Regional
High Schools." (*Pottier Report*, p. 9.)

continued to pay other provincial aid and salary grants and full grants for conveyances in operation in 1952, but agreed to pay only half the cost for new conveyances after that year. The province's new policy meant that the rural municipalities were required to pay basic salaries for new classrooms, the full cost of maintenance of additional classrooms, any additional maintenance costs for existing classrooms, and one-half of added conveyance costs.

In 1946, the province began an ambitious plan of developing rural and regional high schools for grades 7 to 12, called Rural High Schools if built in the rural municipalities, and Regional High Schools if built in towns and serving surrounding rural areas as well. It paid all of the capital costs for the Rural High Schools. And it paid the capital costs for the Regional High Schools to the extent they were incurred to serve village and rural pupils, and part of the balance of the costs, the amount depending on the agreement arrived at with the particular town. It also paid 75 per cent of the operating costs for the rural pupils in the Regional High Schools and 30 to 50 per cent of the cost for town pupils in these schools, depending on the proportion it had paid of the costs of operating the old high schools in the towns before the Regional High Schools were built. The part of the province's educational programme relating to Rural and Regional High Schools, like the other parts, took no systematic account of the ability to pay of the rural municipalities and towns.

The province later established a School Loan Fund ($2,000,000 in 1954) to assist the school sections with capital expansion and repairs, and in addition guaranteed their debentures to enhance the sections' borrowing power. The Pottier Commission argued: "*In many instances . . . the obligation of repaying the principal and interest placed an excessive tax burden on the local school sections,* particularly when this was in addition to the general Municipal tax rate, the Municipal tax rate for schools, and special taxes for other services, such as regional libraries and local improvements."[33] It added that these burdens bore little relation to the taxpaying ability of the sections.

A greater measure of aid was given to the rural municipalities than to the towns and cities, where grants for teachers' salaries were the only important source of help towards operating expenses. As these salary grants, established in 1948, bore an inverse relation to the salaries paid by the towns in 1945–6, there was no necessary connection between the level of salaries in that year and a town's ability to pay.

[33]*Ibid.*, p. 13, italics as in the report.

The provincial share of the costs of education varied a good deal in the twelve years preceding the Pottier Commission. In 1941–2 it was 36.52 per cent; in 1950–1, 61.45 per cent; and in 1953 (calendar year), 49.93 per cent.[34]

Such were the conditions of educational finance in Nova Scotia at the time of the appointment of Justice V. J. Pottier as a one-man Royal Commission on Public School Finance, on March 2, 1953, to make a thorough investigation of educational finance in the province, and to make appropriate recommendations. Justice Pottier aimed at a solution similar in many respects to the one of the Commission on the Larger Unit but, as Beck puts it, ". . . broadened it to include all the sixty-six municipalities and clothed its skeletal outlines with the details needed to give it practical effect."[35]

The principal propositions on which his recommendations were based are:

(1) That all children in the province should "have at least an opportunity to obtain an adequate foundation education."[36] The plan to provide this opportunity was defined in terms of what Pottier termed a "Foundation Program."[37]

(2) That all publicly provided educational services should be included in the Foundation Program, that is instruction, maintenance of schools, transportation of pupils, and even capital cost, the last to include new construction, interest on present and future debt, and debt repayment.

(3) That the tradition of local responsibility for schools should be continued, while at the same time the province should equalize the financial burdens on the different localities in the provision of the Foundation Program.

(4) That since by far the most important source of revenue of the localities was the property tax, the contribution made by each municipality should be according to its ability to pay,[38] as measured by a uniform rate of tax on the market value of real and personal property.

---

[34]*Ibid.*, p. 10.

[35]Beck, *Government of Nova Scotia*, p. 323.   [36]*Pottier Report*, p. 15.

[37]The commission's reason for using the term "foundation" rather than "minimum" is given as follows: "The Commission is strongly opposed to referring to such programs as a 'minimum' or a 'minimum foundation program.' The word 'minimum' leaves the impression that the plans are to produce the lowest type of program. The proper approach is not the lowest type of program of education which could be adopted but on the contrary the highest type of program which all resources available can finance and in which every child can participate." (*Ibid.*, p. 16.)

[38]"Ability to pay" was used by the commission to mean the revenue-raising capacity of the municipal unit itself, not the ability to pay of the individual taxpayer, which is the more common meaning.

The commission defined the Foundation Program in terms of a minimum salary scale for teachers, cost of maintenance of schools, cost of transportation of pupils, and capital costs; that is, in terms of the four services in (2) above, and accordingly recommended that auditoriums, gymnasiums, and cafeterias not be included in the Program, although there was to be nothing to prevent a municipality from adding these entirely at its own expense. It also made certain recommendations about vocational schools and schools for the blind and the deaf.

In order to obtain a good basis for ability to pay, the commission undertook the heroic task of equalizing assessments. Since it was impractical to do this by reassessing each individual property in the province, the commission made estimates at the level of the municipal unit. In the case of real property, it appraised 6,000 properties on a sampling basis, examined records of sales, and solicited the opinions of assessors and others who were well-informed about property values. By these means, a ratio of market to assessed value was obtained for each of the 66 municipal units and applied to the total assessed value to get an estimate of total market value.

In the case of personal property, the commission found the assessment practices generally so chaotic that it could not use this ratio method and instead worked out estimates of values based upon the assessments of some of the localities which did have good practices and upon what other relevant information it could obtain.

Having obtained uniform assessments by municipal unit, the commission next tackled the job of determining the rate of levy to use to determine the localities' contributions to the Foundation Program. It arrived at a solution by initially examining the median effort being made by the municipal units on an equalized assessment basis and the total amount of funds required from all of the municipal units. The median rate was about 62 cents per $100 of assessment in 1953 and was estimated to be about 65 cents in 1954. The commission was of the opinion that the sharing of the costs of the Foundation Program by the municipal units and the province should be on a fifty-fifty basis. Since to bring the municipal units' share up to approximately half would require a rate of 80 cents, this was the rate decided upon.[39] The

[39]The amount required from the municipal units to make up 50 per cent was about $9 million. It is interesting to observe, as an indication of the range of effort which the municipal units had been making, that if the least effort made by a municipal unit were used as the over-all rate it would have yielded municipal contributions of about $3 million, and if the greatest effort were used, $22 million. (Honourable Mr. Justice Pottier, "Background of School Finance in Nova Scotia," *Proceedings of the Golden Anniversary Convention of the Nova Scotia Union of Municipalities* [1955], p. 50.)

application of the 80-cent rate to the uniform assessments was simply the method by which each municipal unit's contribution to the costs of instruction, maintenance, and transportation in the Foundation Program was determined. How it was actually to raise its share was its own affair, but in effect it meant applying the rate on its own property assessments necessary to raise the required amount.

The ratio of each municipal unit's share to the total allowed costs of instruction, maintenance, and transportation, in the Foundation Program was denoted as the "partnership ratio" for that municipal unit. (The provincial relative share of these costs for each unit has come to be called the "provincial proportion" and the municipal share, the "municipal proportion.") This ratio was to be used to determine the municipal and provincial shares for payment of present and future capital costs (including both interest and debt repayment) incurred by the municipal unit. The partnership ratio was to be used for this purpose to avoid penalizing municipal units which had already built and paid for schools and to avoid committing the province to un- limited outlays for payment of capital costs above the fixed local contribution. Otherwise the cost of the Foundation Program would be greater, and a heavier burden would have to be imposed on all municipalities.

The commission was very critical of the province's programme for Rural and Regional High Schools. It saw no reason why the full cost of the Rural High Schools should be borne by the province, since it meant preferred treatment of rural areas and loss of local interest. And it charged that the share of costs by a town, in the case of a Regional High School, was "a wrangled figure . . . usually arrived at by compromise,"[40] with no particular connection with the town's ability to pay. To remove this anomaly, the commission proposed that the capital costs for both types of school be assumed as an obligation of the municipal units served by them, repayment of the costs to be borne by the municipal units and the province according to the partnership ratio. To do otherwise, it was felt, would be unjust to those municipal units which would have to build such schools in the future and share in their cost.[41]

Up to this point the commission was consistent in applying the principles it had developed for provincial and municipal sharing of

[40]*Pottier Report*, p. 51.
[41]One member of a municipal council who was interviewed argued, on the other hand, that it was unjust for the province to build a school with the assurance that it would be no charge on a municipality and then, at a later date, charge back part of the cost of it to that municipality.

costs. If it had gone no further, however, it would have meant that a few municipal units would have received no provincial aid at all, since the 80-cent levy would cover all of their costs in providing the Foundation Program. To encourage general acceptance of its other recommendations, the commission added a further one: "that no Municipal unit is to receive less than 25% of said Foundation Program total cost . . . regardless of its ability, it being understood that this modification shall not apply in any way to determining partnership ratio for the purpose of repayment of existing and future capital costs."[42] By way of explanation, it continued:

> The Commission recommends the minimum contribution by the Province of 25% as above because experience elsewhere has shown that unless a minimum is granted, the finance program will not be accepted by the units which have the greatest ability and would not otherwise benefit. There seems always to be the contention that they have a right to a share in Provincial contributions regardless of their ability and to end by making any other plan practically unworkable. The Commission believes that Nova Scotia would have the same experience under the same circumstances.[43]

This provision is an example of a carefully considered, if imperfect, formula being compromised for the sake of political expediency. All of those whom the writer asked about the provision have agreed that the compromise was necessary, despite the fact that the principle of allocation is not vague and arbitrary, but, not withstanding the criticisms of it to be taken up later, is far clearer and more just than that in the previous system of grants. Nevertheless, the implementation of the report was an act of considerable political courage, even with the compromise.[44]

To ease the initial impact of the programme on those municipalities for which the increase in the tax rate would be considerable, the commission proposed that the rate on the equalized assessment should be increased by 10 cents each year until it reached 80 cents.[45]

One effect of the commission's recommendations was to transfer still more responsibility from the rural and village school sections to the municipal school boards, especially the responsibility for capital costs. It left the sections with only the responsibilities of seeing that the school property is well cared for and that the schools are being operated according to the regulations.

The report was submitted in 1954 and was largely implemented in

[42]*Pottier Report*, p. 76.
[43]*Ibid.*
[44]Compare Beck, *Government of Nova Scotia*, p. 325.
[45]*Pottier Report*, p. 79.

a new Education Act which went into effect January 1, 1956. There were some changes from the commission's recommendations. One was the inclusion of cafeterias or lunchrooms (where enrolment is in excess of 500 pupils) and auditorium-gymnasiums in the capital costs part of the Foundation Program.[46] Another was the provision for any school section to add to the programme of the rural municipality, the cost to be covered by an additional levy in the section. But the present legislation essentially embodies the recommendations made by the commission. Table XX gives a summary of the expenditures of the localities and the province in 1959 (calendar year).

TABLE XX

MUNICIPAL AND PROVINCIAL OUTLAYS FOR PUBLIC EDUCATION
IN 1959 (CALENDAR YEAR)

		% of Total
Towns and Cities		
Amount provided by town or city council	$7,977,623	67.8
Provincial grants, including grant for debt service charges	3,791,262	32.2
TOTAL	11,768,885	100.0
Rural Municipalities		
Amount provided by municipal councils, including local school area section levies	5,851,327	37.2
Provincial grants, including grant for debt service charges	9,882,219	62.8
TOTAL	15,733,546	100.0
All Municipalities		
Amount provided by municipalities	13,828,950	50.3
Provincial grants	13,673,481	49.7
TOTAL	$27,502,431	100.0

SOURCE: *Annual Report of Municipal Statistics, 1959*, pp. 50, 54.

Since the localities make some expenditures in addition to the Foundation Program, the provincial share of the Foundation Program is slightly more than the 49.7 per cent shown. The province pays about two-thirds of the educational costs of the rural municipalities and less than one-third of those of the towns and cities. This disparity simply reflects the greater ability of the urban areas to support services. The above calculations do not take into account the administrative costs of the Department of Education, or such items as the cost of textbooks provided free by the province to students up to grade eight, or the costs of vocational education. In the fiscal year ending March 31, 1960,

[46]Government of Nova Scotia, *The Education Act and Related Acts* (Education Office Bulletin No. 1, 1956–7; Halifax: 1956), p. 67.

the total expenditures of the department, excluding the Nova Scotia Technical College, the Provincial Library, the Nova Scotia Museum of Science, and grants to universities, were $19,020,230. Without allowing for the difference in years, this brings the total outlay for the localities and the province to $32,849,480, and the provincial share to about 58 per cent. The corresponding share in the first year of the new plan was about 56 per cent.[47]

The government has since, in 1957, agreed to share the cost of teachers' salaries above the Foundation Program scale in accordance with the provincial proportions, the amounts to vary with the qualifications of teachers, the 25 per cent minimum not to apply in this case. In December, 1958, the Minister of Education announced the province's willingness to share, in accordance with the provincial proportions, in further salary increases up to $400 for teachers holding the three highest certificates, who are teaching in grades 7–12 more than 50 per cent of the time, the 25 per cent minimum again not to apply. The purposes of the latest salary grants are to encourage the best-qualified teachers to teach in the higher grades and to make the teaching profession more attractive to people with university training. The Nova Scotia Teachers' Union and some other organizations concerned with education oppose the method of paying these grants. They argue that teachers should be paid according to qualifications regardless of the grades they teach, to encourage the use of each teacher in the grade where he is most effective. Beginning September 1, 1960, the government provided for increased remuneration in the Foundation Program for superintendents, supervisors, and supervising principals, the 25 per cent minimum applying. There have also been increases in the allowable capital costs in the Foundation Program for libraries, science and household science laboratories, rooms for industrial arts, and auditorium-gymnasiums. These increases are effective from January 1, 1961; but they cover all buildings built since January 1, 1956, on the basis of an amortization period of twenty years. Lastly, the government now shares, according to provincial proportions, at foundation standards, the discounts on municipal debentures for financing construction of schools.[48]

[47]*Annual Report of the Department of Education*, for the year ended July 31, 1960, pp. xxi–xxii.

[48]The information in this paragraph about changes in the Foundation Program was obtained directly from the Department of Education. As there has been a tendency for the provincial government's percentage of the cost of the Foundation Program to increase in subsequent years, the uniform rate used to calculate the municipalities' share was increased to 90 cents per $100 of equalized valuation,

The new Pottier programme has been operating since January 1, 1956; and while there are numerous complaints about details of the scheme, as, for example, over the amounts allowed for the maintenance of schools in the Foundation Program, there seems to be general agreement that the new scheme is a vast improvement over the old one. Some municipalities do feel, however, that the operation of the scheme has seriously aggravated the financial pressure on them to the point where they are in serious financial straits. (Some criticisms of the formula by which the provincial grants are calculated are offered in chapter VIII.)

Sections 91 and 92 of the Education Act provide that the Governor-in-Council may from time to time appoint a commission to make reassessments of property in the municipalities and that the provincial and municipal contributions to the Foundation Program shall be revised accordingly. The first such reassessment was made public in December, 1958. The total of the new assessments was about 30 per cent higher than that of the Pottier assessments made in 1954. The increase was unevenly distributed, some municipalities even receiving reductions from the 1954 assessment. The result has been some shifting in education costs among the municipalities and a slight reduction in the over-all provincial share of the Foundation Program (from 53.60 per cent to 52.84 per cent on the basis of the cost of the Program in 1957).[49] Beginning in 1961, provision has been made for annual revisions of the valuation of property, so that the basis for sharing costs may be kept right up to date.

Health

Three general aspects of health with which the provincial and municipal governments are concerned are of interest here: hospital care, mental hospitals, and public health, the last being a catch-all for a wide variety of functions, most of them of a protective and preventive nature.

Hospital care. There are about fifty hospitals serving the public in Nova Scotia, apart from mental hospitals. Four are operated by the province, of which one is the large Victoria General Hospital in Halifax, a referral centre for the whole province; two of the others are tuberculosis hospitals; and the fourth is a general hospital. Most of the others are local general hospitals. Seven of these are operated by

---

beginning with 1962. This change was not announced in time to be taken into account in this study, but it in no way alters the argument. See also p. 92, n. 81.

[49]Obtained directly from the Department of Education.

municipalities, seven by the Roman Catholic Church, and the rest by private non-religious organizations (eleven of these are small Red Cross hospitals). Of the remainder, two are maternity hospitals (one in Halifax and one in Sydney) run by the Salvation Army, one is a tuberculosis hospital run by the City of Halifax, and one a privately-run convalescent hospital in Halifax.[50]

The Hospital Insurance Plan, by which Nova Scotia participates in the National Health Plan, came into effect January 1, 1959. Before this plan is discussed, something will be said about provincial participation in hospital finance before the plan was adopted.

In the year ending March 31, 1957, the province made grants of about $393,000 to forty-three local public hospitals[51] under the provision in the Local Hospitals Act[52] for grants of up to 50 cents per patient-day. In order to receive these grants a hospital had to be established or maintained by a municipal unit (or declared by a municipal council to be a public hospital), receive a grant from the municipality of at least $500, and have a representative of the municipality on its governing board.[53] The municipalities made grants of about $67,000 to hospitals in the same year.[54] The provincial government made additional grants in this period of about $407,000, most of which went to seven local hospitals for free tuberculosis treatment, as it assumes practically full financial responsibility for all hospital treatment of tuberculosis in the province.

In recent years, by the Local Hospitals Act, each municipality was responsible for delinquent bills of any patient who had settlement within its boundaries, regardless of where in the province the patient was being treated.[55] This requirement imposed a heavy and growing burden on the municipalities, costing the towns and cities $440,609 and the rural municipalities $704,766 in 1955, compared with $131,408 and $174,036, respectively, in 1949.[56] The municipalities were far from

[50]D.B.S., *List of Canadian Hospitals, 1959* (Ottawa: Queen's Printer, 1958), pp. 8–10 and Government of Nova Scotia, *Seventy-first Annual Report on Humane Institutions*, 1956–7 (Halifax: Queen's Printer, 1957), Table XIX, p. 37.

[51]Government of Nova Scotia, *Public Accounts*, for the fiscal year ended March 31, 1957 (Halifax: Queen's Printer, 1958), pp. 201–2.

[52]*R.S.N.S.*, 1954, c. 161, as amended by *S.N.S.* 1955, c. 31, s. 3. This act has been superseded by the Public Hospitals Act (*S.N.S.*, 1958, c. 11) which brings the legislation into conformity with the Hospital Insurance Plan, which began January 1, 1959.

[53]Local Hospitals Act, s. 5.

[54]*Seventy-first Annual Report on Humane Institutions*, 1956–7, Table XX, p. 38.

[55]Local Hospitals Act, ss. 9–16.

[56]*Annual Report of Municipal Statistics, 1949* and *1955*, pp. 16 and 21, and 17 and 22, respectively.

satisfied with this arrangement. They maintained that the legislation gave protection to the hospitals without sufficient safeguards for the interests of the municipalities, that the incentive of hospital administrators to collect bills from patients was weakened, and that the scheme was badly abused by irresponsible patients who could pay their own bills. In the view of local officials, the province in requiring these payments from the municipalities was protecting the hospitals at the expense of the municipalities.

The whole picture regarding hospitalization was very much changed when the province's participation in the National Health Plan began January 1, 1959. The province now provides free public ward care and diagnostic services to all residents of Nova Scotia, under the Hospital Insurance Act. This plan excludes tuberculosis and mental hospitals, nursing homes, and homes for the aged (which provide some care for chronic invalids). The province has entered into an agreement with the federal government, whereby the latter will pay Nova Scotia 25 per cent of national per capita cost of the services covered by the plan plus 25 per cent of provincial per capita cost of these services. The cost of administering the plan is not shared by the federal government. Because, initially at least, per capita expenditures have been higher for Canada as a whole than for Nova Scotia, the federal government paid about 54 per cent of the cost of the shared part of the plan in 1960.[57] Although the plan is an extra burden on the provincial government because most hospital costs assumed publicly were previously borne by individuals, it has reduced the direct burden for hospital costs on the residents of the province because of the federal contribution.[58]

The federal and provincial governments also contribute to hospital construction costs, the federal government paying $2,000 per bed, and the provincial government paying the required matching $2,000 plus an additional $1,000 per bed. These payments at costs in 1961 together represented about 35–40 per cent of estimated construction costs.

In his budget speech on April 9, 1958, the Premier, as Provincial Treasurer, estimated that the province would need over $6 million in

[57]Obtained directly from the Hospital Insurance Commission.
[58]"If we did not have the hospital plan, Nova Scotians would have to pay an estimated fourteen million dollars in 1959 for general hospitalization. Under the plan, Nova Scotians will have to provide only about half that amount." (Premier Robert L. Stanfield, *Speech on Second Reading: Hospital Tax Act* [Halifax: 1958].) The federal contribution is not a net gain, since it is in part paid for by Nova Scotians in higher taxes or alternative services foregone.

1959 for its share of the programme, and in his speech on the second reading of the Hospital Tax Act he implied that another million dollars would be required for construction grants, making a total of over $7 million needed in 1959. The amounts in later years were expected to be even larger. Without the scheme, the province would have paid about $1,800,000 for similar purposes, so the extra cost was expected to be over $5,200,000. (In fact, the province's share of operating costs in fiscal year 1959–60 was about $7,640,000.) In considering how to raise the extra money, the Premier dismissed a uniform premium plan as being inequitable and after examining taxes on minerals and special sales taxes on liquor, tobacco, luxuries, power bills, telephones, and fuel oil, he settled on a general retail sales tax, with higher than the general rate on tobacco and liquor, and with exemptions designed to make the tax more equitable. "Heavy taxation of a few items would be discriminatory," he argued, "and it would not produce the necessary money."[59] The Hospital Tax Act was duly passed, effective January 1, 1959, providing for a tax of one-tenth of a cent per cigarette purchased, of 5 per cent on tobacco in other forms and on spirituous liquors, and 3 per cent on other retail purchases except those specifically exempted. The tax was raised to 5 per cent on April 1, 1961, to pay for the rising costs of the plan; the rates on cigarettes, other tobacco, and spirituous liquors were not changed. In fact, in the fiscal year 1959–60, its first full year, the new tax yielded $9,906,583; in 1960–1 it yielded an estimated $9,500,000; and in 1961–2, at the higher rate, it is estimated that it will yield about $15,700,000.[60]

The plan relieved the municipalities of their considerable hospital costs which arose from their responsibility for delinquent bills and from other general hospital operating costs.[61] However, the Premier made it clear that, while the province has relieved the municipalities from most of their hospital operating costs, the building and operating of general hospitals continue to be a local and regional responsibility,

[59]*Ibid.* In considering the distribution of the burden of the tax, the Premier said: "This tax should not bear heavily on the ordinary man. Much of what he buys will be tax exempt. It may be said the tax makes no allowance for ability to pay. But it does make a very considerable allowance. The man who spends $6000 a year will pay over twice the tax of the man who spends $3000—because a substantial proportion of the $3000 will be on tax exempt commodities." (*Ibid.*)

[60]Legislature of Nova Scotia, 1961 Session, *Estimates* (Halifax: Queen's Printer, 1961), p. 6.

[61]To provide some immediate relief, the province paid the municipalities in 1958 50 per cent of their hospital costs incurred in 1957. This payment was about one million dollars.

except of course for the grants-in-aid of construction mentioned above.[62] In 1959 the provincial government passed an amendment to the Public Hospitals Act establishing a Hospital Capital Fund financed by an annual levy on each municipality. The levy is fifty cents per capita for the first one thousand of population and one dollar per capita for the remainder. It produces about $660,000 on the basis of the 1956 census. The revenue received from each municipality is divided among the public hospitals according to the number of patient-days of treatment each hospital provides to patients from that municipality. The grants to which the provincially owned hospitals would be entitled are distributed among the other public hospitals in proportion to the number of patient-days of treatment they provide. The grants have to be used towards capital costs of public hospitals incurred by hospital boards and municipalities. One virtue claimed for this measure is that it compels municipalities that have inadequate hospital facilities, requiring that some of their residents be treated elsewhere in the province, to help pay for the capital costs of the hospitals where they are treated. The chief objection to the levy is that it takes no account of ability to pay, even at the level of the municipal unit. The executive of the Union of Nova Scotia Municipalities has opposed the levy on the ground that the Union passed a resolution at two consecutive annual meetings approving in principle the adoption of the health scheme provided it imposed no burden on the municipalities. Arguments given in support of this stand were that the municipalities needed the money released by the health scheme for other urgent purposes, and that the levy would be larger than the hospital costs currently being incurred by some towns, even though the total outlay of all municipalities would be reduced.

Mental hospitals. Responsibility for hospitals for the mentally ill is divided between the province and the municipalities. The province cares for the curable and violent insane at the Nova Scotia Hospital at Dartmouth. The harmless, incurable insane are the responsibility of the municipalities. They are cared for in institutions operated by the municipalities, some of them under systems of joint expenditure described earlier. Until recently there were seventeen municipal mental hospitals. Only four were exclusively mental hospitals, the other thirteen being used to house welfare cases (indigent sane) as well. In most of the combined institutions there was inadequate provision for segregation of the mentally ill and the chronically ill and other poor.

---

[62]Address at Provincial-Municipal Conference, December 17, 1957 (mimeographed).

There were also five municipal homes exclusively for the poor.[63] Mentally defective children capable of being trained in any degree are looked after at the Nova Scotia Training School at Truro run by the province. Only seriously mentally retarded or defective children are kept in the municipal mental hospitals. Nova Scotia is now the only province which does not assume full responsibility for the care of the mentally ill; but on the other hand, Nova Scotia bears a larger part of the cost of the public health programme than do other provinces.[64]

At a provincial-municipal conference on December 19, 1957, the province agreed to pay one-third of the net cost of operating municipal mental hospitals, provided that certain standards are met.[65] The provincial government clearly desires to raise the standards of these institutions and it has refused to associate itself with the running of substandard institutions. The provincial contribution was raised to one half beginning January 1, 1960. The grants for operating costs totalled $315,680 in the fiscal year 1959–60 and rose to $577,600 in 1960–1.[66]

The introduction of the new programme of grants was almost immediately followed by a vast improvement in the operation of the municipal mental hospitals. By the end of 1958, the first year, nearly all mental and welfare cases were being cared for in separate institutions. There were eight exclusively mental hospitals and only one combined mental hospital and poor home, in Lunenburg,[67] and the mental hospitals

[63]*Seventieth Annual Report on Humane Institutions*, 1955–6 (Halifax: Queen's Printer, 1956), Tables V and VI. But the criterion as to whether the inmates of these municipal institutions were mentally ill or not was the technical one of whether they had actually been committed. Many not technically classed as mentally ill could have been legally committed. (See *Seventy-first Annual Report on Humane Institutions*, 1956–7, pp. 34–5.)

[64]*Seventieth Annual Report on Humane Institutions*, 1955–6, pp. 35–6.

[65]Speech of Premier Robert L. Stanfield at the conference (mimeographed). The proposed standards have to do with administration; staff; buildings, furnishings, and grounds; medical facilities and services; occupational and recreational facilities; food services; religious instruction; and general care of patients. Until the adoption of these standards for qualifying for these grants and of the standards for qualifying for the grants for poor houses (discussed in the section on social welfare), the province's influence on the standards of these institutions was mainly through its Inspector of Humane Institutions, who inspected both municipal mental hospitals and poor homes. His powers were confined to the making of recommendations. That these recommendations were frequently ineffective as means of control is documented vividly in the *Seventieth Annual Report on Humane Institutions*, 1955–6, *passim*.

[66]Obtained directly from the Department of Public Health.

[67]Mental hospitals in the counties of Annapolis, Cape Breton, Kings, and Pictou were already separate. Of the formerly combined homes and mental hospitals, Inverness's is now closed and Cumberland's no longer cares for welfare patients. Halifax County and Halifax City acquired separate buildings for their welfare patients.

of Cape Breton and Halifax counties and the City of Halifax had already qualified for grants. The separation was brought about partly as a result of the new grants for the mental hospitals and those for municipal poor homes, and partly as a result of a determined effort to achieve segregation on the parts of the Departments of Public Health and Public Welfare. Moreover, the federal government refused to share the cost of welfare cases in combined institutions, under the Unemployment Assistance Act. By mid-1961 the mental hospital of Kings County had also qualified for grants and it was likely that the one in Cumberland County would soon qualify and that the small mental hospital in Annapolis County would encorporate before long with one of the others; the mental hospital in Pictou County and the one in Lunenburg, still a combined institution, gave no indication of attempting to qualify. The four that had qualified accounted for about 70 per cent of all of the patients in municipal mental hospitals.[68]

One effect of the separation is that localities without mental hospitals or poor homes have to board their own people in hospitals or homes of localities that have them (or in local private nursing homes). There has always been some such boarding, but the specialization of functions has made the practice commoner. The specialization might make it possible to obtain some economies of administration that make it easier for the mental hospitals to qualify for grants. But it also means that a municipality which previously provided for its mental patients in its own combined institution at a low cost may, now that it no longer has this way of caring for its mental patients, have to pay a higher cost to board its patients in mental hospitals of other municipalities, if these are meeting the provincial standards to qualify for the grants. Still, a municipality may, now that the province will pay half of the operating costs, increase the net costs of its mental hospital by as much as 100 per cent in order to qualify for the provincial grant, at the expense of the province. For example, if the weekly net cost per patient was $14 before standards were met, the municipality operating the hospital could increase it to $28 at no expense either to itself or to other municipalities boarding patients in its hospital, as the province would then pay one-half of $28, or $14. Moreover, grants from the federal and provincial governments for construction of mental hospitals are available to the municipalities on the same terms as for general hospitals.

[68]The information in this paragraph was obtained directly from the Department of Public Health.

Public health. Responsibility in the field of public health is a dual one. The duties of the province and of the localities are set out in the Public Health Act. Every locality is required to have a board of health. In Halifax and Sydney, it is a separate city health board. This may now also become the practice in Dartmouth. In the towns it is a committee of the council (it may be the whole council), with the mayor as chairman. The medical health officer is also a member. In the rural municipalities, a committee is appointed for each polling district with a councillor from the district as chairman, the council being empowered to unite more than one district under one board. There is also provision for the establishment of county boards of health which have jurisdiction over the local boards, and of joint boards of health in those rural municipalities and the towns and cities contained by them, where there are joint expenditure boards or committees. The county and joint boards have supervision over the local boards and share their functions. Each town and rural municipal council is required to appoint a medical health officer, and a sanitary inspector, the latter functioning under the authority of the former. These officials are responsible for seeing that sanitary and other conditions conducive to good health in the community are maintained.

Because of the inactivity of the local boards of health, however, the province, ever since it established a separate Department of Public Health in 1938, has been increasingly active in the field of public health. The department derives its powers from the same Public Health Act as the municipalities do. Many of its powers overlap those of the local boards. The result has been that the department itself performs many of the functions over which the municipalities also have jurisdiction. The province has been divided into eight divisions, each with a medical health officer in charge, and each having its own public health nurses, nutritionists, and sanitary inspectors. The over-all programme is directed from Halifax, where various provincial laboratories which serve the whole province are also located.

Halifax City is an exception. It carries the full responsibility for public health and conducts an extensive programme. On the other hand, it is relieved of the responsibility of operating a general hospital because of the operation by the province in Halifax of the Victoria General Hospital.

The expenditure of the province on preventive public health activities in the fiscal year 1959–60 was about $2,235,000, of which about $1,120,000 was paid by the federal government for various purposes under its National Health Grants Program.[69] The expenditures of all municipalities on public health, in the calendar year 1959, were $280,395, of which $213,348 was accounted for by the City of Halifax, $8,196 by Sydney, $40,010 by the towns, and $18,841 by the rural municipalities.[70]

Social Welfare

Until 1958, the Poor Relief Act of Nova Scotia, which stemmed directly from the English Elizabethan poor law of 1601, stipulated that the municipalities were to take complete responsibility for poor relief for their residents. Under this act the rural municipalities were required to organize themselves into poor districts (a rural municipality could constitute itself as one poor district) and to appoint three rate-payers as overseers of the poor in each district and who were to furnish relief to persons in need in their district. The council in a town, and the council or a committee of the council in a city, were also deemed to be overseers and were charged with the same responsibilities. Some of the poor receiving relief under this legislation were cared for in the municipal homes already referred to in the discussion of municipal mental hospitals. Some of these homes were operated under the system of joint expenditures. As already mentioned, until the reforms effected in 1958, only five out of eighteen of these homes were exclusively for the poor, the rest housing mentally ill persons as well. With the reforms, there were, in mid-1961, fifteen municipal homes caring for needy persons, all of them completely separate institutions. Lunenburg, which, as already mentioned, continues to operate a mixed institution, does not attempt to qualify for provincial aid by meeting provincial standards.

The municipalities must also provide relief to those in need not cared for in municipal homes. The term "outdoor relief" is sometimes used to denote this kind of relief, although recently the term "municipal assistance" has come to be used in Nova Scotia. The advent of many provincial and federal welfare measures, such as unemployment insurance, old age pensions, family allowances, and mothers' allowances, has made the burden of relief in the municipalities much lighter than it would otherwise have been.

In February, 1958, the province signed an agreement with the Dominion bringing Nova Scotia under the federal Unemployment

[69]Government of Nova Scotia, *Public Accounts*, for the fiscal year ended March 31, 1960 (Halifax: Queen's Printer, 1960), pp. 221, 230.
[70]*Annual Report of Municipal Statistics, 1959*, pp. 25, 32.

Assistance Act described in the previous chapter. Under this act the Dominion pays 50 per cent of the costs of relief in the province. Signing the agreement was an important step for Nova Scotia, for it brought the province indirectly into the field of municipal assistance. It could have decided simply to pass the federal money on to the municipalities with no strings attached and so continue its old policy regarding these services. In fact, it decided upon a fundamental departure from its old policy. First of all, it decided to add a grant equal to 16⅔ per cent of the costs of local relief to the Dominion's 50 per cent, bringing the total grant to 66⅔ per cent. (The province increased the total to 83⅓ per cent for February, March, and April of 1959, as an emergency measure to cope with particularly great unemployment in some localities.) Secondly, it set up standards which the municipalities must meet in order to qualify for both the federal and provincial grants. The province is in effect saying to the municipalities that it will not pass the municipalities' claims along to the federal government or share in the costs itself unless these standards, applying to both outdoor relief and homes, are met. At the outset it seemed likely that nearly all of the municipalities would benefit at least to some extent from this offer, in that their own expenditures for relief would be reduced; for even though they had to meet higher standards, they could treble their expenditures at no cost to themselves. In fact their own costs have not diminished significantly, because of the combination of higher standards and larger number of people served.

In the calendar year 1959, the total expenditure for all of the municipalities for municipal assistance (indoor and outdoor relief), including provincial grants, was $1,142,000. Social assistance grants of $681,000 from the province reduced the cost to the municipalities to $461,000, compared with a total expenditure of $464,000 for these purposes in 1956, when the municipalities bore the whole cost.[71]

To stimulate improved municipal administration of welfare services, so that the municipalities will be able to handle the new municipal assistance adequately, the province in fiscal year 1958–9 began to pay 50 per cent of the administrative expenses of municipal welfare offices, or of the municipal payments to social agencies, such as the Children's Aid Society, administering services on a municipality's behalf, providing certain requirements designed to centralize and improve local

[71]*Annual Report of Municipal Statistics, 1956*, pp. 22, 29; and *ibid., 1959*, pp. 26, 33. The estimates of provincial grants for 1959 were obtained directly from the Department of Municipal Affairs. The estimates are rounded to the nearest $1,000.

welfare administration are met. The new conditional grants for administration are proving effective in achieving their purpose. Nine municipalities had already qualified for them by mid-July, 1961. The grants totalled $28,000 in 1959–60, and $55,000 was budgeted for them for 1960–1.[72]

Legislation regarding the care of neglected, mentally retarded, and delinquent children is embodied in the Child Welfare Act. The policy of the province is to encourage local private and public interest and support in caring for neglected children, with over-all supervision by the provincial Division of Child Welfare through its five regional offices, and with some financial support from the province. There are twelve Children's Aid Societies scattered throughout the province, covering all areas except Antigonish, the City of Dartmouth, Guysborough, Digby, and the Municipality of Halifax County. Where there are Children's Aid Societies, they do the actual case work, the provincial department doing it elsewhere. There are also a number of privately sponsored child-caring institutions. Placing children in these homes and in foster homes is mainly done by the Children's Aid Societies and the Director of Child Welfare. The maintenance costs of children being so cared for are paid partly by the province and partly by the municipalities, the municipal share being set down in the act.[73] Where no place of settlement can be established, these costs are paid by the province. The child-caring institutions are supported by voluntary subscription, and receive a maintenance allowance of $14 per

[72]Legislature of Nova Scotia, 1961 Session, *Estimates*, p. 57. The information on the number of municipalities qualifying for grants was obtained directly from the Department of Public Welfare.

[73]S. 37, ss. 2. There is a complicated system of provincial grants for child welfare in Nova Scotia, with no general principle to explain them. There are shared grants for the maintenance of indigent children. As in mid-July, 1961, if a child was in a boarding home, the payment was $8.96 per week, with the province and municipality sharing 50–50; if in an institution, the amount of the payment was $14 per week, $6 being paid by the municipality and the balance by the province. In the Nova Scotia Training School for retarded children at Truro, the municipalities paid $350 per year, the province the balance of about $2,000 per year, for each child. In the case of delinquent children boarded in private institutions, the municipalities paid $350 per year per child, the province, $850. For delinquent children placed in the provincial training school at Shelburne, the municipality paid $350 per child, the province the balance of about $2,000. Except for the training schools at Truro and Shelburne, the sharing was initially on a 50–50 basis, the departures coming about when the total payments per child had to be raised because of rising costs. The municipalities, feeling they were unduly squeezed by the pressure put on them by the Education Act to increase their expenditures for education, have persuaded the province to absorb disproportionate shares of the increases. (Information obtained from the Department of Public Welfare.)

week for the wards of the Children's Aid Societies, and for the wards
of the Director of Child Welfare, $8 of which is paid by the province
and $6 by the municipality of settlement.

The Children's Aid Societies obtain funds for their operation from
voluntary subscriptions, from municipal grants, and from provincial
grants. In the fiscal year 1960–1, apart from voluntary private subscriptions, the societies received $41,441 in municipal grants and $129,134
in provincial grants. The provincial grants are of three kinds: (1)
matching grants ($58,660) equal to 50 per cent of the voluntary sub-
scriptions of the previous year; (2) matching grants ($20,721) equal
to 50 per cent of the municipal grants of the previous year; and (3)
population grants ($58,250) of $1,000 for each 10,000 of population
and for fractional amounts in excess of 5,000.[74] The total cost to
the localities for child welfare in 1959 (calendar year) was $518,893,
of which $124,568 was for the cities, $139,927 for the towns, and
$254,398 for the rural municipalities.[75]

OTHER PROVINCIAL FINANCIAL RELIEF TO THE MUNICIPALITIES
IN RECENT YEARS[76]

A quite recent development is the payment of unconditional grants
by the province to the municipalities. Prior to 1942, some of the municipalities levied personal income taxes on individuals, and some levied
"personal" property taxes on branches of banks based upon the net
income from business done in the locality, the minimum annual levy
being $150 per branch. The wartime tax rental agreement between the
provincial and the federal governments in depriving the provincial
government thereby deprived the municipal governments of the right
to levy personal and corporate income taxes. (The provincial govern-

[74]Obtained directly from the Department of Public Welfare. When the basis
for calculating population grants was introduced in 1959–60, the province made
provision that no society would receive less than it had received in the previous
year. In previous years the province paid a population grant of 10 cents for each
person if the population of the area covered by the society was less than 15,000,
and 4 cents per person if the population was 15,000 or more; and it paid a
grading grant which depended on the standards met by the society. There were
A, B, C, and D grades and grants of $2,000, $1,500, $1,000, and $500 respectively.
The weakness of the grading grants was that the lower grants went to poorer
societies. Their strength was that they stimulated support for societies in areas
which could afford to give it. The method of calculating the matching grants
has not been changed.
[75]*Annual Report of Municipal Statistics, 1959,* pp. 26, 33.
[76]Most of the data in this section were obtained directly from the Department
of Municipal Affairs.

ment had never itself levied a personal income tax.) To compensate the municipalities for the loss of their personal income and bank taxes, the province in 1942 paid them $119,231, the amount they had received from these taxes in 1940. The province also continued distributing a grant of $30,330 paid to the localities in lieu of taxes on the property of the Canadian National Railways, making the total grant $149,564. The grants were continued at practically the same amounts up to and including 1947, when a new Dominion-provincial tax rental agreement was negotiated. A new principle was then adopted for the payment of unconditional grants to municipalities. The grants were now designed not as the previous ones had been, simply to compensate the localities which had levied income taxes and bank taxes for their loss of revenue, but rather to compensate all of the localities for the loss of these potential tax bases. The formula decided upon by the province was to take the per capita income tax that had been highest in each of the three types of municipality in the last year they had levied this tax, increase it by about 50 per cent, and pay each municipality in each category the resulting amounts per head of population. The resulting grants per head were $1.53 for cities, $1.00 for towns, and $.10 for rural municipalities. At the same time, it was decided to make a flat rate payment of $225.00 for each bank branch in each locality. The payment in lieu of taxes for the Canadian National Railways was continued. The total grant in 1948 was $408,235.

In 1949, the per capita grants were increased by 50 per cent to $2.295, $1.50, and $.15 for cities, towns, and rural municipalities, respectively. The grant for each bank branch was also increased by 50 per cent to $337.50. The Canadian National Railways payment remained unchanged. The basis for the grants remained the same through 1951, the total amount in that year being $597,038. No adjustments were made for changes in the number of bank branches.

For 1952, there was an "across the board" increase in grants of 40 per cent for all localities and the three items were not separated, making the grants in that year $835,853.

In 1953, there was a reversion to the three types of grant. The per capita grants were raised 40 per cent above the 1951 level to $3.213 for cities, $2.10 for towns, and $.21 for rural municipalities; and were based on the 1951 census. The grant for bank branches was reduced back to $337.50 and based upon the number of branches currently in operation. The Canadian National Railways grant was again paid on the old basis. No municipality was to receive less than it had received in 1952. Total grants in 1953 were $920,807.

TABLE XXI

UNCONDITIONAL PROVINCIAL GRANTS TO NOVA SCOTIAN MUNICIPALITIES
AS RATIOS OF TAX RENTAL AND TAX-SHARING PAYMENTS FROM THE
DOMINION AND, FOR SELECTED YEARS, OF MUNICIPAL TAX REVENUES

Calendar year	Unconditional grants to municipalities[a] ($'000)	Fiscal year ending March 31	N.S. income from tax rental and tax-sharing agreements[b] ($'000)	Provincial grants as ratio of tax rentals, etc.	Grants as ratio of municipal tax revenue[c]
1942	150	1943	3,348	.045	
1943	153	1944	2,911	.053	
1944	151	1945	2,911	.052	
1945	151	1946	2,911	.052	
1946	151	1947	4,085[d]	.037	
1947	151	1948	7,525	.020	
1948	408	1949	10,673	.038	
1949	599	1950	9,836[e]	.061	
1950	597	1951	13,203[e]	.045	
1951	597	1952	14,336[e]	.042	.037
1952	836	1953	20,484	.041	.044
1953	921	1954	19,788	.047	.046
1954	921	1955	20,775	.044	.043
1955	922	1956	20,212	.046	.041
1956	922	1957	22,571	.041	.040
1957	982	1958	26,808	.037	.036
1958	987	1959	35,359	.028	.034
1959	987	1960	39,678	.025	.031

SOURCE: [a]obtained directly from the Department of Municipal Affairs; [b]obtained directly from the Public Finance Section, Dominion Bureau of Statistics. From 1950 on, includes provincial share of public utilities tax. From 1959 on, includes Atlantic Provinces Adjustment Grant; [c]Tax revenues (for calendar years) obtained from *Annual Report of Municipal Statistics*, issues for 1951–9.

[d]Includes $1.611 million earned by the province under the 1951 agreement, but withheld until the termination of the agreement.

[e]Includes 5 per cent tax on provincial corporate income, collected by the Dominion and paid to the provinces.

The province in 1953 also began paying about $55,000 to assist the towns and municipalities which had a money loss as a result of the abolition of the Municipal School Fund.[77]

The same basis of making these grants has been continued, except that the 1957 grants were based upon the 1956 census, raising them to $982,201. In 1958 and 1959, they were $986,589, and in 1960, $988,614, the increases being due to additional bank branches.

Table XXI shows that the growth of these unconditional grants has

[77]The operation of the Municipal School Fund had resulted in the cities and some of the towns contributing more to the Fund than they received back from it. Hence, when the Fund was abolished, some rural municipalities and towns lost this revenue, for which they were partly compensated by special grants by the province. These were discontinued in 1956 when the new education programme was introduced.

been roughly commensurate both with the growth of tax rental and tax-sharing payments and the growth of municipal tax revenues, until the last three years shown, when they have declined in relation to these two series. At the same time, one should bear in mind the considerable expansion of conditional grants to the municipalities, already described.

The distribution of the part of these grants in lieu of the income tax among the cities, towns, and municipalities is still tied to the highest per capita yields of each tax in each kind of municipality back in 1940. This was not a very good basis for distributing the grants in the first year it was adopted in 1948; it is even less appropriate today. There is some logic in giving the urban localities larger per capita grants than the rural areas, since they provide more services, but the present system follows even this tenuous principle in only a very crude way, as Table XXII shows.

TABLE XXII

A COMPARISON OF UNCONDITIONAL GRANTS PER CAPITA AND
EXPENDITURE PER CAPITA FOR THE THREE TYPES OF MUNICIPALITY[a]

	Total expenditure per capita in 1959	Unconditional grants per capita in 1959	Grants per capita as ratio of total expenditure per capita
Cities	$122.85	$3.36	.027
Towns	64.73	2.34	.036
Rural municipalities	32.82	.31	.009

[a]Calculated from data in *Annual Report of Municipal Statistics, 1959,* and from data obtained from the Department of Municipal Affairs. Grants for bank branches and the grant from the Canadian National Railways are included in the calculation of unconditional grants per capita.

It appears that the rural municipalities are being discriminated against, especially in view of their more limited taxable capacity, and that the cities are less favourably treated than the towns. It is of interest to see what happens when other provincial contributions are eliminated by relating the grants to local taxation per capita, as has been done in Table XXIII. This table reveals practically the same pattern as Table XXII.

The municipal sharing of particular provincial revenues does not play an important part in Nova Scotian public finance. The only instance is that of licences to cut timber. Section 43 of the Lands and Forests Act provides that the Minister may pay to the municipalities in which the lands are situated 5 per cent of the licence dues payable to

TABLE XXIII

A COMPARISON OF UNCONDITIONAL PER CAPITA GRANTS WITH TOTAL
TAX REVENUE PER CAPITA FOR THE THREE TYPES OF MUNICIPALITY[a]

	Total tax revenue per capita in 1959	Unconditional grant per capita in 1959	Grants per capita as ratios of tax revenue per capita
Cities	$92.90	$3.36	.036
Towns	51.81	2.34	.045
Rural municipalities	27.32	.31	.011

[a]Calculated from data in *Annual Report of Municipal Statistics, 1959,* and from data obtained from the Department of Municipal Affairs.

the Crown. The total amount paid in the fiscal year ending March 31, 1960, was only $6,496.[78]

In recent years the province has given relief to the municipalities in other ways as well as in the ones already mentioned. In 1947 the province assumed the full cost of hospital care for tuberculosis patients, a service which cost the municipalities over $95,000 in 1946. In 1948 the province relieved the municipalities of charges for patients at the Nova Scotia (mental) Hospital. In 1947 these charges cost the municipalities $131,632. In 1948 the cities and towns were relieved of the highway tax, which had cost them $128,066 in 1947. In 1949 the province relieved the rural municipalities of the highway poll tax which had cost them over $75,000 annually.[79] More recently, in 1957, it relieved them of the Municipalities' Highway Tax, which in 1956 cost them about $246,000.[80]

THE POSTWAR REVOLUTION IN PROVINCIAL PARTICIPATION
IN LOCAL FUNCTIONS

There has been no integrated reorganization in provincial-municipal fiscal relations in Nova Scotia in the postwar period; but there have been four major departures from long-established policies significant enough taken together to constitute a revolution. In the field of education, the province has taken much of the power of determining standards out of municipal hands, has compelled the municipalities to make a specified effort to pay for educational services, and has com-

[78]Government of Nova Scotia, *Annual Report of the Department of Lands and Forests,* for the fiscal year ending March 31, 1960 (Halifax: Queen's Printer, 1960), p. 24.
[79]Obtained from the Department of Municipal Affairs.
[80]*Annual Report of Municipal Statistics, 1956,* p. 30.

mitted itself to underwriting the balance of the allowable costs of the Foundation Program.[81] In the field of health, it has introduced a comprehensive hospital plan which has relieved the municipalities of most of the operating costs of hospitals and of some of their capital costs. In the field of care for the mentally ill, the province has departed from its long-established practice of insisting that support of the incurable, harmless insane was purely a local responsibility, by making grants to the municipalities contingent on meeting the provincial standards. Similarly, it has for the first time departed from the principle of the Elizabethan poor law that direct relief is a purely local responsibility, by making grants under its programme of social assistance to the municipalities for both indoor and outdoor relief, again subject to provincial standards. In the cases of education and hospitalization it has become much more deeply involved than previously in both financing and controlling these services. In the cases of care for the mentally ill and relief for the indigent, it now has committed itself both to exerting control over the level of services and to contributing to their cost, whereas previously it did neither. Provincial activity in the fields of public health and child welfare and in the sharing of the costs of the parts of highways running through towns and cities has resulted in further reductions in municipal responsibility for services of a general nature. Moreover, the recent practice of the provincial government of contributing, on a mileage basis, to the cost of maintaining urban streets is a significant step by the province towards helping the municipalities to provide local services.

Whatever the best arrangements may be for the carrying on of those general services for which the municipalities currently have some responsibility, or for financing local services, the question of whether or not there will be provincial financial participation is no longer an issue. At the practical level, the new provincial participation greatly broadens the scope for fiscal adjustment in provincial-municipal relations.

[81]In December, 1962, the government announced its intention to increase the scale of costs according to which it will pay grants with respect to teachers' salaries and maintenance of classrooms, and to add an allowance of $100 per classroom for teaching equipment and supplies. As these supplements for teachers' salaries are payable at the option of the municipalities, they represent a departure from the basic principle of the Foundation Program of a uniform minimum standard throughout the province, although, in fact, many municipalities are already paying amounts at least as high as the new ones allowable and the others will likely soon follow suit.

$$\sim\!\!\sim\!\!\sim V \sim\!\!\sim\!\!\sim$$

Why Nova Scotia is a Low-Income Province

NOVA SCOTIA MIGHT BE A LOW-INCOME PROVINCE either because its resources do not permit as high productivity per head as in other provinces or because they are not being used to their best advantage relative to other provinces, or because of a combination of both factors. Chapter II gave a general picture of the growth, size, and productivity of the Nova Scotian economy compared to that of Canada. It answered affirmatively with empirical data the question: "Is Nova Scotia a low-income province?" There follows an examination of the province's resources compared with those of the nation as a whole, and an investigation of the effectiveness with which the province's resources are being used, with some suggestions for improvement in their use.

THE NATURE OF ITS RESOURCES

Natural Resources: Their Kind, Quality, and Quantity

Certainly Nova Scotia is not generously endowed with natural resources in which it has strong natural advantages. If one examines the natural resources of the province in themselves, *in situ*, in comparison with those in other parts of the country, most of them do not give the impression of being either high in quality, or abundant in quantity in terms of offering opportunities for the use of mass production techniques of exploitation. If one examines them in relation to Canadian and foreign markets, they appear even less attractive, because of the added costs of getting the products to distant markets and because of the competitive advantage of better-placed producers—better-placed with respect to the large central Canadian markets because of the superior location of central Canadian producers and better-placed with respect to foreign markets because of both superior location of foreign producers and the existence of tariffs and other import restrictions. There are exceptions, as in the cases, to some extent, of fishing and forestry resources. And, of course, one must not ignore the element of comparative costs in assessing Nova Scotia's competitive strength.

It is true that while freight costs act as a barrier to selling goods outside of the region, in central Canada, they also act to some extent as a protective barrier for the development of regional industry. The protective barrier argument is valid for goods which are local in character, such as beverages and food, and for industries which rely on regional sources of raw material and which have an optimum size commensurate with the small size of the regional market. The regional market, however, is largely confined to the three Maritime Provinces, since shipping costs to Newfoundland are usually lower from Montreal than from the Maritimes. The size of this market is only about 1,400,000 persons and the degree of protection in it diminishes as one moves westward through it towards central Canada. Furthermore, the lack of any really large marketing centre in the region is a hindrance to Maritime industrial development. Where the optimum size of a firm is greater than that necessary to supply the region the protective barrier argument breaks down. It also breaks down badly for an industry which must bring in its raw materials from outside the region.[1]

In the field of agriculture, the soil is not generally of high quality to begin with. The legacy of subsistence farms (from an age to which they were more suited), too small in size,[2] often unsuited topographically to the use of machinery, and often poorly located in relation to markets, still dominates much of the agricultural picture of Nova Scotia. The fact that in 1956 the ratio of improved farmland to total occupied farmland was 23 per cent for Nova Scotia compared with 58 for Canada is an indication of the province's poor agricultural resources.[3] The average net farm income per farm over the period

[1]Most of the material in this paragraph is based upon argument in a letter received from a confidential source.

[2]The average size of farms in Nova Scotia in 1956 was 131.7 acres compared with 302.5 acres for Canada. (D.B.S., *Census of Canada, 1956* (Ottawa: Queen's Printer, 1958), Bulletin 2–3, Table 1; Bulletin 2–11, Table 1.)

[3]D.B.S., *Census of Canada, 1956*, Bulletin 2–11, Table 15. In 1951, 92.2 per cent of farms had not more than 69 acres of improved land. (Government of Nova Scotia, *Report of the Royal Commission on Rural Credit* [Halifax, 1957], p. 17.) Improved land consists of cultivated crop and pasture land, barnyards, home gardens, lanes, and roads.

1951–5 was only $963 for Nova Scotia compared to $2,772 for Canada.[4] Even more striking is the fact that in 1951, 72 per cent of Nova Scotian farms sold products valued at less than $1,200, compared with 38 per cent for Canada.[5] It is clear that Nova Scotia's agriculture is heavily weighted with unproductive farms, even allowing for the larger percentage of part-time farms in Nova Scotia (23 per cent) compared with Canada (10 per cent).[6]

In the field of forestry it is difficult to be as specific; but there seems to be no doubt that the province's forestry resources are less attractive than for the nation as a whole. Certainly the opportunities for large-scale exploitation are lacking, especially compared with those in Quebec, Ontario, and British Columbia. Their limited extent is also a problem where scale in manufacturing is a consideration. One recent study of the Canadian forestry industry observes: "The Maritime Provinces have a long history of logging, fire, and insect attack. The stands of timber have been left generally in an understocked condition."[7] Although the forest area comprises 70.3 per cent of the total area of the province (compared with about 22 per cent for Canada),[8] the volume of wood per acre of forest land is only 680 cubic feet compared with 1,010 for Canada.[9]

In connection with logging operations, Howland writes:

The evidence suggests that a relatively high proportion of the cut in the Maritimes . . . is carried out by small-scale operators. However, the biggest factors contributing to the relatively low net value per worker appear to be related to the greater seasonal amplitude of logging in the region and to differences in the value of particular species of wood where the product is marketed as lumber. The white pines and hardwoods of Ontario yield, as lumber, about twice the price received for the spruce and balsam of the

[4]W. M. Drummond, W. Mackenzie, *et al.*, *Progress and Prospects of Canadian Agriculture* (A study for the Royal Commission on Canada's Economic Prospects; Ottawa: Queen's Printer, 1957), p. 334. If only full-scale farms are included (28.0 per cent of the total number in Nova Scotia and 62.1 per cent in Canada), net farm income was $2,688 for Nova Scotia and $4,165 for Canada. (*Ibid.*)

[5]Drummond, Mackenzie, *et al.*, *Progress and Prospects*, p. 332.

[6]*Ibid.*, the percentages are for 1951.

[7]John Davis, *et al.*, *The Outlook for the Canadian Forest Industries* (A Study for the Royal Commission on Canada's Economic Prospects; Ottawa: Queen's Printer, 1957), p. 172. This proposition is emphatically corroborated in Government of Nova Scotia, Department of Lands and Forests, *The Forest Resources of Nova Scotia* (1958), *passim*. The report emphasizes (p. 64): "Forest practices have resulted in a rapid and too great an accumulation of forest lands in young age classes. The objective should be to develop balance of age classes and acreage which will provide the allowable annual cuts without removing immature stands, and without accumulating overmature stands."

[8]Davis, *et al.*, *Outlook for Canadian Forest Industries*, p. 165.

[9]*Ibid.*, p. 167.

Atlantic Region; while veneer birch logs in Ontario bring up to three times as much.[10]

The seasonal amplitude of logging in Nova Scotia is determined partly by climate and partly by the part-time nature of operations by farmers and fishermen. Not only is a large proportion of forest land privately owned in Nova Scotia (about 70 per cent compared to about 10 per cent for Canada),[11] but it is owned to a considerable extent in small woodlots, some of it by absentee landowners. These kinds of ownership combined with a considerable amount of part-time operations are probably in part responsible for the small-scale operations, and also for the difficulties encountered in putting production on a sustained yield basis.[12] However, these difficulties are by no means insuperable and the prospects for the industry, especially with regard to pulpwood production, are quite favourable.

Fisheries are one resource with which Nova Scotia is well endowed. But the fishing industry in the Atlantic Provinces is not a high-income activity.[13] To the extent this is attributable to the resources themselves, it is due mainly to the fact that landings are more heavily weighted by varieties low in value per pound than is the case in British Columbia, as well as being lower in value for a given amount of fishing effort. In the latter province in recent years, two-thirds of the

[10]R. D. Howland, *Some Regional Aspects of Canada's Economic Development* (A study for the Royal Commission on Canada's Economic Prospects; Ottawa: Queen's Printer, 1958), p. 179. One person interviewed, who is familiar with the forestry industry in Nova Scotia, was sceptical about the importance of either of the factors Howland emphasizes.

[11]Davis, et al., *Outlook for Canadian Forest Industries*, p. 166.

[12]See Howland, *Some Regional Aspects of Canada's Economic Development*, p. 181.

[13]See H. Scott Gordon, "The Economic Theory of a Common Property Resource: The Fishery," *Journal of Political Economy*, LXII (April, 1954), for an explanation of why fishing tends to be a low-income activity. In brief, he argues that since the sea fisheries are a common property resource, no one is in a position to appropriate economic rent. As a result, all fishermen aim at getting the maximum average product per unit of "fishing effort" and in so doing tend to drive the average revenue per unit of output down to average cost. (He assumes marginal and average cost per unit of fishing effort to be constant and therefore equal.) Since opportunity incomes of fishermen are included in average and marginal costs, and since revenues tend to just cover costs, fishermen tend to earn only their opportunity incomes and so do not become wealthy. (Although Gordon does not mention it, some fishermen may, of course, earn quasi-economic rents by virtue of unusual skill in their calling.) He contends that in fact fishermen tend to earn even less than their opportunity income because of their "great immobility" (due to their relative isolation and their romantic attachment to the sea) and because they are characteristically gamblers hoping for a lucky catch and optimistic about getting it. As a result, they earn less than those in other occupations of comparable risk and skill.

value of fish landings have been accounted for by salmon, a high-value fish which is sufficiently uniform with respect to size and shape to be processed by highly mechanized techniques. In the Atlantic fisheries, lobsters and several other high-value species such as salmon, scallops, oysters, swordfish, and tuna together account for only slightly over 40 per cent of the value of landings; the lower-value cod, haddock, herring, and mackerel account for most of the balance. In recent years the Atlantic fisheries have generally accounted for about two-thirds of the national catch in weight but only about one-half of the landed value of fish.[14]

In 1951 the median earnings of male workers in primary fishing, hunting, and trapping were $701 for Nova Scotia, $831 for Canada, and $2,268 for British Columbia.[15] The most significant comparison is with British Columbia, since the Canadian figure is heavily weighted by the other three Atlantic Provinces which have fisheries resources similar to Nova Scotia's. The big difference in earnings is not by any means only due to the difference in resources. The much greater use of capital and the greater rationalization of the industry in British Columbia are important factors.[16] But certainly the difference in the nature of resources is a factor in that both the kinds and the high value of the west coast resources make it possible and profitable to employ greater amounts of capital than on the Atlantic coast.

It has already been noted that mining in the province is dominated by a high-cost coal industry heavily supported by freight subventions. In 1960 coal accounted for about $46 million of the province's total mineral production of about $65 million.[17] There are no known large deposits of precious or base metals, and no large sources of very cheap power which could be used as a basis for smelting imported minerals.[18]

[14]*Report of the Royal Commission on Canada's Economic Prospects* (Ottawa: Queen's Printer, 1958), pp. 182, 184; and D.B.S., *Fisheries Statistics of Canada, 1955 and 1958* (Ottawa: Queen's Printer, 1958 and 1960), pp. A-10, A-11.

[15]D.B.S., *Ninth Census of Canada, 1951* (Ottawa: Queen's Printer, 1956), X, Table 73. Trapping is of very small relative importance.

[16]Department of Fisheries of Canada and the Fisheries Research Board, *The Commercial Fisheries of Canada* (A study for the Royal Commission on Canada's Economic Prospects; Ottawa: Queen's Printer, 1958), pp. 111–17.

[17]D.B.S., *Preliminary Report on Mineral Production, 1960* (Ottawa: Queen's Printer, 1961), pp. 6, 40.

[18]Except possibly tidal power in the Bay of Fundy. This source of power has been talked about for many years, but harnessing it has not yet been shown conclusively to be feasible from the engineering or economic point of view. If transmission costs could be drastically reduced, Grand Falls on the Hamilton River in Labrador could conceivably become a major source of power for Nova Scotia. Both projects are very much in the speculative future.

There are large deposits of gypsum and barytes which are being exploited; operations can be expanded as markets develop. The gypsum deposits could, when regional markets become sufficient some time in the future, become the basis of secondary manufacturing of building products and chemicals. But the mining industry, even with all the fundamental weakness of the coal-mining sector, is not responsible for Nova Scotia's being a low-income province. In 1959, the average of weekly wages and salaries in the Nova Scotian mining industry was $68.61. While this was considerably less than the $90.76 for mining for Canada as a whole, it was not very far below the "industrial composite" for Canada ($73.47), and it was considerably above the "industrial composite" for Nova Scotia ($60.17).[19]

In 1957, per capita generation of electrical energy in Nova Scotia was 2,201 k.w.h. compared with 5,717 k.w.h. for Canada. Forty-one per cent of the energy in Nova Scotia was generated by water power compared with 93 per cent for Canada, the balance being generated by thermal power.[20] Practically all of Nova Scotia's hydro-electric capacity is now harnessed although some additions to installations are still being made. In 1955 installed turbine capacity was 114 per cent of the available power at ordinary six months' flow. The percentage for Canada was 45 and for Ontario, the province with the next highest percentage, 74.[21]

In 1958, the federal government, under the Atlantic Provinces Power Development Act, began paying a subvention on coal used for supplying industrial users of electric power in the Atlantic Provinces. The subvention of about $1.80 per ton of coal represents the difference between the price paid for coal by these users and the price paid by Ontario Hydro for its generating plants in Toronto and Windsor. In the year ending November 30, 1960, the subvention for Nova Scotia was $955,771, distributed among over 630 users.[22]

Although Nova Scotia, unless the harnessing of tidal power is found to be economically feasible, is not favoured with the large amount of cheap hydro-electric power available in Quebec, Ontario, and British Columbia, which might itself stimulate major industrial de-

---

[19]D.B.S., *Review of Employment and Payrolls, 1959* (Ottawa: Queen's Printer, 1960), pp. 38, 47, 56. For coal mining the amounts were $68.90 for Nova Scotia and $69.07 for Canada. (*Ibid.*)

[20]D.B.S., *Canada Year Book, 1960* (Ottawa: Queen's Printer), p. 604.

[21]Howland, *Some Regional Aspects of Canada's Economic Development*, p. 135.

[22]*Statutes of Canada*, 6 Eliz. II, c. 25; and Government of Nova Scotia, *Forty-first Annual Report of the Nova Scotia Power Commission*, for the year ended November 30, 1960 (Halifax: Queen's Printer, 1961), p. ix.

velopment on the basis of imported raw materials, as in the case of the aluminium smelter at Kitimat in northern British Columbia, it would appear that its resources are sufficient to cope with quite substantial demands at fairly low rates.[23] Lack of power resources is not in itself a reason for Nova Scotia's being a low-income province.

The attractiveness of the province scenically and climatically, especially in the summer, is a natural resource that not only provides the basis of a thriving tourist industry, but is also an inducement to industrial location in that people like to live in the province and in that some able people are willing to apply their entrepreneurial talent and capital there for a smaller reward than they might obtain elsewhere.

A factor highly relevant to a discussion of natural resources, and one that is frequently crucial in the industrial development of an area, is location. Closely linked to location is transportation. Something has already been said about both, the conclusion being that given its resources, and given the barriers of transportation with respect to domestic markets and of import restrictions with respect to foreign markets, and with strong competition in both, the province is not favourably located.

Since Nova Scotia is unfavourably located for competing in general Canadian markets, freight rates are an important matter to the province, as they are also to the other Atlantic Provinces. Policies in setting railway rates have long been a bone of contention in this region. Originally rates were adjusted in the region's favour to allow for the all-Canadian uneconomic route of the Intercolonial Railway (now part of the Canadian National Railways), since the route was chosen for defence reasons. A departure from this policy in the period 1912–26 brought the rates up to those in Ontario. The Maritime Freight Rates Act of 1927 restored the more favourable structure by reducing rates on outbound and internal movements by 20 per cent, and compensating the railways for the reduction with federal subventions. A series of horizontal rate increases since 1948, allowed because of rising costs incurred by the railways, and only partly ameliorated by federal

[23]This view was expressed by several of the people interviewed. See *Halifax Chronicle-Herald*, July 18, 1958, for a report of similar views expressed by members of the power committee of the Atlantic Provinces Economic Council. It is frequently contended, as it is by this committee, that the Atlantic Provinces can provide additional thermal power for considerable industrial expansion at rates comparable to those anywhere on the North Atlantic seaboard. It is important, however, to bear in mind that that area is not where Nova Scotia's competition for industry generally lies.

subventions introduced in 1957 and 1959, have, as Howland puts it, appeared "to accentuate once again the pressure of geography and economic facts toward the fragmentation of the Canadian economy."[24] Horizontal increases harm the competitive position of a Maritime producer in the central Canadian market because they add a larger absolute amount to his freight costs than to the freight costs of a central Canadian competitor. Probably even more important in accounting for the widening difference in the freight bills of the Maritime and central Canadian producers is the practice of the railways of reducing their rates to meet the competition of truckers. Since this competition is keener for the shorter hauls in more densely populated central Canada, rates tend to be reduced more there than for the longer hauls between central Canada and the Maritimes.

Howland suggests that the practice of charging lower rates on low-value bulk commodities and higher rates on high-value manufactured commodities discourages the development of manufacturing, since it favours the movement of raw materials out of the province before processing.[25] On the other hand, high rates on imported manufactures favour the development of manufacturing for the regional market (with the important qualifications made at the beginning of this section), especially since the rate reductions financed by subventions apply only on outbound and, to a lesser extent, on internal traffic.

Opinion is very much divided on the importance of the freight rate structure as a deterrent to economic development of the Atlantic Provinces. The transportation of goods gives rise to costs which are bound to work against producers in outlying regions trying to sell in central Canadian markets. Central Canadian producers selling in the outlying regions have the advantage of being able to develop their production on the basis of a large easily accessible local market, which is lacking in the Atlantic region. Location is no doubt an important factor in the lower average productivity of the Nova Scotian economy. Although its unfavourable effects could be mitigated somewhat by removing discriminatory elements from the freight rate structure, the locational disadvantages are a fact of the Nova Scotian economy that could be tempered only by some form of subsidy. The opinion of some well-informed people in the province is that, while there are undoubtedly some aspects of the freight rate structure which

[24]Howland, *Some Regional Aspects of Canada's Economic Development*, p. 185. "Horizontal increases" are uniform percentage increases applied over the whole freight rate structure, or over sections of it, pertaining to the whole country.
[25]*Ibid.*

impose an undue burden on the provincial economy, too much of a bogey has been made out of it. Partly in this connection, one highly placed person stated in a confidential interview: "The force of conventional arguments is still terrific in Nova Scotia."

One of the principal tasks given the Royal Commission on Transportation, appointed May 13, 1959, was to "consider and report upon inequities in the freight rate structure, their incidence upon the various regions of Canada and the legislative and other changes that can and should be made, in furtherance of national economic policy, to remove or alleviate such inequities."[26] Contrary to expectations, the commission did not make proposals to reduce the freight rate differential in central Canadian markets between goods of Maritime producers and those of their central Canadian competitors, on the ground that to do so would have been outside their terms of reference. It did, however, admit the feasibility of using transportation policy to accelerate the economic growth of the Atlantic Provinces and suggested "should it . . . be deemed desirable to give special transportation assistance to the Atlantic Provinces to overcome economic lag, such special assistance might well be designed to assist the movement of the products of secondary industry where it may have the greatest employment generating impact."[27]

In its examination of the Maritime Freight Rates Act of 1927, the commission recommended the elimination of the 20 per cent subvention within the region, except with respect to Newfoundland, on the ground that there was no good justification for it, as the purpose of the act was to make central Canadian markets more accessible to Maritime products, and on the ground that its elimination would be a stimulus to competition among carriers and therefore to greater efficiency. It also recommended the extension to non-rail carriers of the 20 per cent subvention on westbound traffic from the region, on the ground that a policy designed to help a region or industry should not distort the transportation industry itself by favouring rail over non-rail carriers. It was also envisaged by the commission that regional discrimination hitherto ensuing from horizontal rate increases would no longer be an issue if rates were set according to competitive principles as it recommended. It is now clear that if transportation policy is to become a major instrument for the economic development of the Atlantic Provinces, it will have to be devised by the federal government itself.

[26]*Report of the Royal Commission on Transportation* (Ottawa: Queen's Printer, 1961), I, Appendix A.   [27]*Ibid.*, II, 218.

In his study, Howland expresses net values of production per worker for Nova Scotia as percentages of the values for Ontario for 1953 in those sectors for which data are available. The percentages are: agriculture 53.3, forestry 28.3, fishing 82.0; agriculture, forestry, and fishing combined 57.8; mining 68.6; and primary manufacturing 43.1.[28] While these figures are not precise measures of the relative values of resources in the two provinces, they do support the general contention made in this section: that Nova Scotia is relatively poorly endowed with exploitable natural resources compared with the country as a whole. It is clear that to a considerable extent Nova Scotia is a low-income province because of its paucity of natural resources.

One can say, "But look at Switzerland, where highly advanced manufacturing industries, such as watchmaking, were established on the basis of acquired skills and imported raw materials. Why can this sort of thing not be done in Nova Scotia?" Conceivably it could, as it could almost anywhere, although the province lacks the strategic marketing location of Switzerland. Such an industry requires a very adaptable labour force, capable of becoming highly skilled, and the willingness of entrepreneurs interested in some new industry of this type to locate in Nova Scotia. It is questionable that the province has this kind of labour force at present; but labour in general is a very versatile resource and such a labour force might be developed in time. Nova Scotia is faced with the situation, as a compact national unit like Switzerland is not, of the pulls on skilled labour and entrepreneurial ability being stronger elsewhere in the country where such factors are frequently more productive and better paid, with no national barriers to their moving there. Differences in rewards are less easily maintained between provinces within a nation than between nations. Even if ventures of the type envisaged here could be successful, the fact remains that there is no evidence at present that they are likely to be launched, although a concerted programme of regional development accompanied by strong federal and provincial inducements to industry to locate in Nova Scotia might alter the outlook.

Labour[29]

Size of Labour Force. In 1951, Nova Scotia with 4.6 per cent of the Canadian population had 4.2 per cent of the Canadian labour force.

[28]Howland, *Some Regional Aspects of Canada's Economic Development*, p. 171. As the salt water fisheries of Nova Scotia differ considerably in nature from the fresh water fisheries of Ontario, the percentage for fisheries is probably not of much significance.

[29]As the latest detailed data on the labour force at the time of writing are

TABLE XXIV

MEMBERS OF THE LABOUR FORCE WITHOUT JOBS SEEKING WORK AS A
PERCENTAGE OF THE TOTAL LABOUR FORCE, FOR NOVA SCOTIA
AND CANADA,[a] FOR SELECTED YEARS

	Nova Scotia	Canada	Nova Scotia as a ratio of Canada
1947	5.4%	2.0%	2.70
1951[b]	3.3	2.0	1.65
1954	5.7	4.3	1.33
1956	4.6	3.1	1.48
1957	6.2	4.3	1.44
1958	9.1	6.6	1.38
1959	7.0	5.6	1.26
1960	7.9	6.8	1.16

SOURCE: *Ninth Census of Canada, 1951*, V, Tables 1 and 2; D.B.S., *The Labour Force, November 1945–July 1958* (Reference Paper No. 58, 1958 revision; Ottawa: Queen's Printer, 1958), Table 12; list of number of registrations for work with the National Employment Service, for three Maritime Provinces, 1947–57, supplied directly by the Research and Development Division of the Dominion Bureau of Statistics. Data for 1958–60 obtained from *Labour Gazette*, various issues.

[a]The percentages for Canada were calculated using averages of the size of the labour force and the number without jobs seeking work, for each year (from quarterly data for 1947 and 1951, monthly data for 1954 and 1956–9, and data for the first eight months of 1960). Since labour force data are not given separately for Nova Scotia (except for 1951), but for all three Maritime Provinces grouped together, the percentages for Nova Scotia had to be estimated. These estimates were based upon two assumptions: (1) that the ratio of the labour force to total population was the same in each of the three provinces throughout the period as it was at the time of the 1951 census, making allowance for relative changes in their populations; and (2) that those without jobs seeking work were distributed among the three provinces for the years covered in the same proportions as the number of registrations for work with the National Employment Service (which are available for each province). The registration figures used were averages of four quarterly readings for 1947 and 1951, and of twelve monthly readings for the other years. The writer is indebted to Mr. D. H. Jones of the Dominion Bureau of Statistics for his suggestion of a somewhat similar method of obtaining the Nova Scotian estimates and for supplying the data on registrations for work.

[b]The percentages calculated from the 1951 census data (for the week ending June 2, 1951) were 3.2 per cent for Nova Scotia and 1.7 per cent for Canada, which are quite close to the estimates shown here, especially allowing for the fact that these estimates are based on the average of four quarterly readings.

Nova Scotia's labour participation rate[30] in that year was 49.7 per cent, the same as for the Maritime Provinces as a whole, while Canada's was 53.1 per cent.[31] In 1955 the labour participation rate was 48.6 per cent

those of the 1951 census, it will be necessary in some instances to use figures for that year. Where possible, figures for later years will be used.

[30]The "labour participation rate" is the size of the labour force expressed as a percentage of population 14 years of age and over.

[31]Calculated from the *Ninth Census of Canada, 1951*, X, 248.

for the Maritime Provinces and 53.6 per cent for Canada.[32] The median number of weeks employed during the 12 months prior to the 1951 census date, for the wage earners in the labour force, was 50.6 for males and 50.7 for females in Nova Scotia and 50.9 and 50.8, respectively in Canada,[33] the difference between Nova Scotia and Canada being very small in each case.

Not only is the labour force of Nova Scotia smaller relative to total population and relative to the part of population of working age than for Canada, but the rate of unemployment is higher for the postwar period, as Table XXIV shows, even for years of generally high levels of employment. Both factors contribute to the low average income of the province.

Occupational Distribution. Table XXV shows the occupational distribution of male wage and salary earners for Nova Scotia and Canada in 1951. The weighted median for Nova Scotia, using the percentage distribution for Nova Scotia for weighting, was $1,855. Using the median earnings for Nova Scotia but the percentage distribution for Canada, the weighted median would have been $1,961. This suggests that the difference in occupational distribution to some extent accounts for the lower average income in Nova Scotia, although, since the self-employed are excluded, the picture is not complete.[34]

Age Distribution of the Population. The size of the labour force is in part determined by the age distribution of the population. Table XXVI, containing the age distribution for Nova Scotia and Canada for 1951 and 1956, shows that Nova Scotia's population is weighted less heavily than Canada's with the productive age group 15–64, and more heavily with the young and old age groups 0–14 and 65 and over. This weighting in part accounts for the size of Nova Scotia's labour force being smaller relative to the total population than Canada's. The difference in distribution is no doubt largely accounted for by the emigration of members of the population in the productive age group

[32]Howland, *Some Regional Aspects of Canada's Economic Development*, p. 78. Howland observes: "The regional labour force represents . . . the number of people of the region who consider themselves to be part of the working force, and the rate of growth of the labour force may reflect a change in the participation rate, or the percentage of the population who choose to identify themselves with the labour force by working or by seeking work. The participation rate is usually higher where economic activity is at a high level and where the economy is sufficiently well diversified to offer attractive employment opportunities for females." (*Ibid.*)

[33]*Ninth Census of Canada, 1951*, X, 279.

[34]The calculations cannot be made for females since for a number of occupational groupings there are no entries for Nova Scotia.

TABLE XXV

DISTRIBUTION OF MALE WAGE AND SALARY EARNERS BY OCCUPATIONAL
GROUPS, AND MEDIAN EARNINGS FOR EACH GROUP,
FOR NOVA SCOTIA AND CANADA, 1951

Occupational group	Nova Scotia		Canada	
	% dist'n. of wage earners	Median earnings ($)	% dist'n. of wage earners	Median earnings ($)
All occupations	100.0	1,773	100.0	2,121
Primary (except mining)	8.4	703	7.6	904
Agricultural	3.9	690	4.4	772
Fishing, hunting, trapping	1.7	701	.3	831
Logging	2.8	720	2.9	1,172
Mining & quarrying	8.7	2,273	2.2	2,398
Manufacturing & mechanical	15.6	1,924	23.0	2,315
Construction	8.8	1,645	8.3	2,104
Transportation	11.4	1,701	10.3	2,101
Communication	1.6	2,030	1.3	2,390
Commercial	4.5	1,710	6.1	2,203
Managerial	4.3	3,042	5.3	3,596
Professional	3.9	2,531	5.9	2,927
Clerical	5.8	1,947	8.1	2,164
Financial	.4	2,967	.7	3,073
Service	12.4	1,892	8.5	1,822
Personal	3.0	1,379	4.1	1,619
Protective	9.3	1,995	4.1	2,061
Other	.1	1,486	.2	2,030
Labourers	12.2	1,033	10.9	1,552
Not stated	1.9	1,427	1.6	1,546
TOTAL NUMBER OF MALE WAGE EARNERS	136,494		3,011,322	

SOURCE: Calculated from *Ninth Census of Canada, 1951*, X, Part II, Table 73

from Nova Scotia to other parts of the country (particularly the younger members of the group).[35] But it is in part accounted for by the fact that the more prosperous parts of the country receive more immigrants from abroad relative to population than Nova Scotia; and most immigrants are in the productive age groups.[36] A likely explanation for the larger percentage of old people in Nova Scotia is also that it is common for Nova Scotians who spend their working years outside of the province to return when they retire.

Sex Distribution of the Population. In the productive age group 15–64, 50.5 per cent of the population in Nova Scotia was male in

[35]For a good analysis of this and other aspects of the distribution of population in the Atlantic Provinces, see Kari Levitt, *Population Movements in the Atlantic Provinces* (Halifax and Fredericton: Atlantic Provinces Economic Council, 1960), *passim*.

[36]Over the period 1946–55, Nova Scotia, with about 4.5 per cent of the Canadian population received only 1.9 per cent of immigrants to Canada. (Howland, *Some Regional Aspects of Canada's Economic Development*, p. 120.)

TABLE XXVI

POPULATION DISTRIBUTION BY AGE FOR NOVA SCOTIA
AND CANADA, 1951 AND 1956

	Nova Scotia		Canada	
Age group	1951	1956	1951	1956
0–4	12.8	12.4	12.3	12.3
5–9	10.7	11.8	10.0	11.2
10–14	9.1	9.7	8.1	8.9
15–19	8.0	8.1	7.6	7.2
20–24	7.2	7.1	7.8	7.0
25–34	14.5	13.0	15.5	15.0
35–44	12.9	12.9	13.3	13.3
45–54	9.0	9.5	10.0	10.0
55–64	7.2	7.0	7.7	7.2
65–69	3.0	2.9	3.1	2.9
70+	5.5	5.6	4.7	4.8
TOTAL	100.0	100.0	100.0	100.0
0–14	32.6	33.9	30.4	32.4
15–64	58.8	57.6	61.9	59.7
65+	8.5	8.5	7.8	7.7
TOTAL	100.0	100.0	100.0	100.0

SOURCE: D.B.S., *Census of Canada, 1956*, Bulletin 3–3,
Table 2.

1951, and 51.0 in 1956, compared with 50.4 and 50.6 for Canada.[37]
These discrepancies are too small to have much effect on the relative
size of the labour force in Nova Scotia and Canada. Table XXVII
shows that the labour participation rates for both males and females
are lower for Nova Scotia than for Canada, the difference being somewhat greater for females. The lower participation rate for women in
the Atlantic Provinces is a reflection of fewer types of employment
suitable for women there, compared to Ontario, for example, where
light secondary manufacturing industries are commoner.[38] The
especially low female participation rate contributes, though not greatly,
to the explanation of why Nova Scotia is a low-income province.

Productivity of the labour force. There is little doubt that the
Nova Scotian labour force is less productive than that of Canada as
a whole. Table XXV shows that only in the "protective" part of the
category "service" (which includes members of the armed forces) were

[37]Calculated from *Census of Canada, 1956*, Bulletin 3-3, Table 1.
[38]Howland, *Some Regional Aspects of Canada's Economic Development*, pp.
160–1.

TABLE XXVII

PERCENTAGE OF MALE AND FEMALE POPULATION IN THE
LABOUR FORCE IN NOVA SCOTIA AND CANADA IN 1951

	Nova Scotia	Canada
Percentage of population 14 years of age and over in the labour force	49.7%	53.1%
Percentage of male population 14 years of age and over in the labour force	79.5	82.2
Percentage of female population 14 years of age and over in the labour force	19.4	23.6
Females as percentage of males in the labour force	24.0	28.3

SOURCE: *Ninth Census of Canada, 1951*, X, 248.

median earnings of male wage earners higher in Nova Scotia than in
Canada. Table XXVIII, compiled by Howland, shows that net value of
production per worker in 1953 was considerably less in Nova Scotia
than in Ontario for every industry included, except for electric power.
The percentage for all industries shown is only 56.1.

The lower productivity in Nova Scotia is due to inferior resources,
to less application of capital, to the small scale of organization and
prevalence of part-time activity in the primary industries, and perhaps
in some areas to intrinsically inferior labour resources. It is highly
probable that in a region which has experienced almost continual
migration over a long period there has been a severe drain on some
of the province's most vigorous and productive stock. Howland suggests that the greater seasonal amplitude in employment in the

TABLE XXVIII

NET VALUE OF PRODUCTION PER WORKER BY
INDUSTRY IN NOVA SCOTIA AS A PERCENTAGE OF
NET VALUE OF PRODUCTION IN ONTARIO, 1953

Agriculture, forestry, and fishing	57.8%
Agriculture	53.3
Forestry	28.3
Fishing	82.0
Mining	68.6
Manufacturing	61.3
Primary manufacturing	43.1
Secondary manufacturing	71.8
Electric power	123.3
Construction	73.4
TOTAL	56.1

SOURCE: Howland, *Some Regional Aspects of Canada's Economic Development*, p. 171.

Atlantic Provinces is also an important factor contributing to low incomes.[39]

Table XXIX shows that the advanced educational level of the Nova Scotian labour force in 1951 was less for Nova Scotia than for the country as a whole and that Nova Scotia had a larger percentage of its labour force in the 0–4 years category.

TABLE XXIX

EDUCATIONAL LEVEL OF THE LABOUR FORCE
FOR NOVA SCOTIA AND CANADA, 1951

Years of schooling	Nova Scotia	Canada
0– 4	8.1%	7.1%
5– 8	40.6	43.2
9–12	43.8	39.4
13 and over	7.5	10.3

SOURCE: Howland, *Some Regional Aspects of Canada's Economic Development*, p. 79.

On the other hand it also had a larger percentage in the 9–12 category. It is likely that its smaller percentage in the higher education grouping is the result of many of its college-trained graduates taking jobs outside of the province. In 1951, 49.0 per cent of the Nova Scotian population in the age group 15–24 was in school compared to 45.2 per cent for Canada, and 49.2 per cent for Ontario. However, it is those who stay in the province who are of interest here. If higher education is weighted more heavily than secondary education, it appears that on balance the educational level of Nova Scotia's labour force is at least slightly inferior to the average for the nation, although the evidence is not very conclusive.

Reliable empirical evidence about the quality of Nova Scotian labour in terms of its willingness to work hard and efficiently and in terms of its adaptability is lacking. But the consensus seems to be that in the construction industry, at least, Nova Scotian labour is less productive than in central Canada. This seems particularly true of the Halifax area, and appears to be in part owing to poor organization and supervision of the men on construction projects and in part to their poor training and an inadequate apprenticeship programme. One man prominent in the construction industry said that Montreal firms add about 5 per cent to their estimates for projects in the Halifax

[39]The average seasonal amplitude of employment over the period 1947–51 for non-agricultural industries was 16.6 per cent for Nova Scotia compared with 4.4 per cent for Ontario, seasonal amplitude being defined as the difference between the high and low levels of employment when they are expressed as percentages of the average level. (*Ibid.*, pp. 162–5.)

area compared with estimates for similar projects in Ontario and Quebec, in part, at least, to allow for lower labour productivity around Halifax. It is also not uncommon to hear informed people say that labour productivity is in general lower in Nova Scotia than in central and western Canada. Attempts to interest fishermen in learning skills which they could apply during their off-season in some secondary manufacturing industries of a "putting out" sort (such as the making of jewelry and cutlery) have not met with favourable reactions. There has even been some difficulty in getting fishermen to harvest Irish moss, a seaweed used in the food processing industry, although it is ready in their off-season, pulling it in is quite easy, and it is a profitable sideline linked closely to their main occupation. On the other hand, some employers maintain that their working forces are unusually skilful, adaptable, and reliable.

Howland estimated the importance of the different factors accounting for the difference in per capita earned income in the Atlantic Provinces and in Ontario in 1951. His results are shown in Table XXX.

TABLE XXX

ESTIMATED IMPORTANCE OF VARIOUS FACTORS ACCOUNTING FOR
THE DISPARITY IN PER CAPITA EARNED INCOME BETWEEN
ONTARIO AND THE ATLANTIC REGION, 1951

TOTAL DISPARITY	$545	100%
Proportion ascribed to differences in:		
(1) Relative size of the labour force	158	29
A. Due to different age distribution of the population	103	19
B. Due to the lower participation of the working-age population in the Atlantic Provinces	55	10
(2) Weeks worked per annum by paid workers	55	10
(3) Occupational or industrial pattern	65	12
(4) Rates of earnings	267	49

SOURCE: Howland, *Some Regional Aspects of Canada's Economic Development*, p. 158.

It is likely that the percentages would not be very much different for Nova Scotia. The table puts in a more concrete and succinct form much of what has been said above. The large part of the difference (49 per cent) attributed to the difference in the rate of wages is of course in turn attributable to more fundamental factors, especially to differences in the abundance of resources and in the ways they are used. Poor resources are less attractive to capital than good resources, so naturally the productivity of labour working with the resources will be less and so also will its remuneration.

Capital—Adequacy of Supply

There are insufficient data on the stock of capital in Nova Scotia to compare the amounts of capital in use in the different industrial sectors or to make comparisons with the rest of the country. However, if recent levels of investment expenditure are any indication, the use of capital in Nova Scotia is less extensive than in the rest of the country. Table III (p. 24) shows that capital investment expenditure per capita in Nova Scotia over the period 1949–56 was only 58.8 per cent of the amount for the country as a whole. The figure for all of the Atlantic Provinces was 58.3 per cent.[40] These figures are for both business and institutional investment. Business investment per capita for the Atlantic Provinces in 1956 was 47.7 per cent of the national average, and business investment per worker 55.2 per cent of the national average.[41] To some extent these great departures of investment in Nova Scotia and the other Atlantic Provinces from the national average are a reflection of the relatively greater expansion in other parts of the country (especially Ontario, Alberta, and British Columbia) which has required larger amounts of both industrial and social capital. But the differences are also partly due to the inferior nature of Nova Scotia's natural resources compared with those available for exploitation elsewhere. The relatively small size of business firms both in secondary manufacturing and primary industries[42] probably also restricts the profitable application of capital.

No doubt increased application of capital would increase the per capita production of the area but this does not necessarily mean that the increased application would be profitable, or that an increase in average income would result. From the financial point of view, it is practically certain that Nova Scotia is and has long been a net exporter of private capital through the partial transfer of current savings of Nova Scotians by banks, insurance companies, and trust and loan companies for use outside of the province, and through the investment of Nova Scotians in bonds and stocks of companies operating outside of Nova Scotia. To the extent that Nova Scotians' savings are invested more profitably elsewhere, their incomes are higher than if they were invested in Nova Scotia.

Even so, there is no evidence of an over-all shortage of capital

[40]*Ibid.*, p. 113.
[41]*Ibid.*, p. 115.
[42]For example, in 1958, the average number of employees in all manufacturing establishments was 22 for Nova Scotia, 37 for Canada, and 46 for Ontario. (D.B.S., *General Review of the Manufacturing Industries of Canada, 1958* (Ottawa: Queen's Printer, 1961), pp. 118–19.

funds in Nova Scotia[43] for firms which can make good use of them, although there may be important shortages of particular kinds of capital. Large established firms can generally rely upon internally-generated capital funds or upon well-established lines of credit from banks and other financial institutions. They also have the organized security markets available to them.

Banks supply mainly working capital to firms of all sizes but also some medium-term capital. New firms, of course, have greater difficulty getting capital than well-established firms, because of the greater risk; and small and medium-size firms have more difficulty than large firms, because funds from insurance and loan companies and from the organized securities markets are generally not available to them. Some equity capital is available to both small and large firms from private individuals; but the problem of obtaining equity capital is a serious impediment to the development of some of the small firms that characterize much of Nova Scotian industry. Failure to obtain sufficient equity capital may inhibit the establishment or growth of a firm, or force it to rely too heavily upon borrowed funds and so commit itself to crippling fixed interest charges. Professor Cairncross suggests as a partial solution that public lending agencies such as the Industrial Development Bank provide equity capital more freely than they are presently inclined to do.[44]

It appears that the principal gaps for small and medium-size firms are for equity capital, medium-term credit secured by chattel mortgages, and long-term credit for purchase of plant. These gaps are in part filled by the federal government's Industrial Development Bank (an agency of the Bank of Canada) and the provincial government's Industrial Estates Limited and Industrial Loan Board, and the provincial government's power to lend directly to business under the Industrial Development Act. The Industrial Development Bank and the Industrial Loan Board will supply medium- and longer-term credit to enterprises considered too risky by private suppliers of credit. Both institutions supply mainly loan capital (usually secured by mortgages) and require that the applicant have a minimum amount of the capital required for the enterprise (50 per cent in the case of the Industrial Loan Board), although the Industrial Development Bank sometimes takes an equity position as well. Industrial Estates Limited has wide

[43]Much of the material on the availability of capital in this section is based on information obtained from a study made for the Government of Nova Scotia, Department of Trade and Industry.

[44]A. K. Cairncross, *Economic Development and the Atlantic Provinces* (Fredericton: Atlantic Provinces Research Board, 1961), pp. 143–4.

power, but basically it provides complete financing of buildings by designing and constructing them for suitable applicants. It can also lend money on equipment. It offers financial inducements in its rental terms on buildings and can make special tax deals with local authorities, the pattern apparently being a tax of one per cent of the cost of construction of the building, which is considerably below the ordinary rates of all Nova Scotian municipalities. This special tax treatment is limited to a period of ten years.

In the field of agriculture, Nova Scotia's Royal Commission on Rural Credit reported in 1957 that the supply of short-term credit from private sources and of medium-term credit provided by the chartered banks under the Federal Farm Improvement Loans Act was adequate. However, it felt that the supply of long-term credit, which is mainly provided by federal and provincial governmental agencies, should be improved, principally by some consolidation of federal and provincial lending agencies, by the increase of the maximum amounts of loans, and by increasing the maximum age of borrowers by which loans must be repaid, from 61 to 66 years.[45] Since the commission made its report, both the federal government, through its Farm Credit Corporation which replaced the Farm Loan Board in 1959, and the provincial government, through its Farm Loan Settlement Board, have substantially increased the size of loans they will make to farmers. Loans have increased notably in response to the new policies which should enable farmers to expand the size of their enterprises and to make them more profitable.[46]

Special capital aid for the fishing industry in the form of subsidies and loans is available, under a variety of federal and provincial measures, for the acquisition of boats and other fishing equipment and for the construction and modernization of cold storage and processing plants.[47]

Hand in hand with the question of the amount and kinds of capital

[45]Government of Nova Scotia, *Report of the Royal Commission on Rural Credit,* chap. v.
[46]Government of Nova Scotia, Department of Agriculture and Marketing.
[47]A fisherman buying a longliner (a versatile boat about 50–60 feet in length, which can be used for offshore fishing) costing $35,000, can get a federal subsidy of about $9,000 (at $165 per ton), a provincial loan of $19,700, and supply a down payment of only $6,300 for the balance. The federal government has announced a new policy of paying subsidies on large boats of $165 to $250 per gross ton on boats 45 feet and over. This will probably have considerable effect in stimulating the construction of trawlers. (Government of Nova Scotia, Department of Trade and Industry, Fisheries Division.) The longliner is so-called because of the long fishing lines it draws behind it. These lines have baited hooks spaced along them and are drawn in by a powered winch.

available goes the question of the cost of capital. There is no indication known to the writer that the cost of capital is any higher in Nova Scotia than elsewhere in Canada for investments of comparable risk. In Canada's nation-wide branch banking system, policies regarding interest rates are generally uniformly applied throughout the country and are limited by the Bank Act. The other private lending institutions in Canada are sufficiently attuned to rate differentials to eliminate them quickly by competition. Rates on loans made by federal agencies, such as the Industrial Development Bank and under the Canadian Farm Loan Act and the Farm Improvements Loans Act, are applied uniformly throughout the country. Loans by provincial lending agencies are made at lower rates than could be obtained from private lenders.

It appears that although there are some types of loans which are not as readily available as circumstances warrant (as is probably the case in most provinces) there is no general shortage in the supply of capital such as might account for its much smaller application in Nova Scotia than in the country as a whole. Its smaller application is mainly due to the more limited opportunities to use it profitably, that is, to the province's inferior resources.[48]

THE USE OF ITS RESOURCES

The subject of this section is large enough for several major studies; all that can be attempted here is some generalizations, based partly on informed opinion, which will suggest the types of economic adjustment desirable in Nova Scotia. The method followed is, in the main, in the nature of partial equilibrium analysis in that an attempt is made to determine what economic adjustments should take place within the province, on the assumption that the provincial economy is at least tending towards adjustment with the outside world, particularly with the rest of the country.

Agriculture

Agricultural resources in Nova Scotia are used less effectively than they could be principally because of the small size of the farms, and the low ratio of improved land to total farm area. In 1956 the total

[48]These conclusions by and large correspond with those reached by Professor Cairncross in his report (*Economic Development and the Atlantic Provinces*) to the Atlantic Provinces Research Board, *passim*, and with those in F. E. Lounsbury, *Financing Industrial Development in the Atlantic Provinces* (Halifax and Fredericton: Atlantic Provinces Research Board, 1960), *passim*. The discussion is far more thorough in these two studies than here.

area of farm land in Nova Scotia was 2,775,642 acres of which only 629,874 acres (22.7 per cent) were improved. Woodland accounted for 1,566,071 acres (56.4 per cent) and other land the remaining 579,697 acres (20.9 per cent).[49] The average area of the 21,075 occupied farms in that that year was 131.7 acres and the average improved area 29.9 acres. Ninety per cent of the farms had less than 70 acres of improved land and only .7 per cent of them had 180 or more acres of improved land.[50]

As previously noted, in 1951, 72 per cent of the farms in Nova Scotia sold products of a gross value of less than $1,200.[51] Even allowing for the fact that 22.8 per cent of occupied farms were part-time farms in that year (not all of which would be among the 72 per cent), the low returns are still very striking. The uneconomical aspects of Nova Scotian farms stem from the days of the self-sufficing rural economy which prevailed when the farms were settled (many of them before 1815). Nearness to markets was not then a factor. Nor, of course, was the suitability of the land for the use of agricultural machinery important at that time. As the need for cash income increased and as the competition of better-placed producers in central and western Canada became keen, farms were abandoned. The total farm area in Nova Scotia is now less than half what it was at its peak in 1891.[52] Even over the fairly short period, 1941–56, the number of occupied farms in Nova Scotia fell about 24 per cent.[53] Clearly, there has been considerable adjustment by means of migration from farms. And over the past 35 years there has been some increase in the average size of farms (99.6 acres in 1921 to 131.7 in 1956) and in the area of improved land per farm (20.9 acres in 1921 to 29.9 in 1956).[54] The Royal Commission on Rural Credit observes:

The statistics clearly show . . . that the upward trend [in improved land per farm] has not been great in Nova Scotia and that the area of improved farm land is the smallest of any of the provinces except Newfoundland. The

---

[49]*Census of Canada, 1956,* Bulletin 2-11, calculated from Table 15.

[50]*Ibid.,* calculated from Table 8.

[51]Drummond and Mackenzie, *Progress and Prospects,* p. 154.

[52]*Report of the Royal Commission on Rural Credit,* p. 8.

[53]*Ibid.* Calculated from pp. 11–12, using the commission's adjustment in the figure for the number of farms in 1941 for the changed definition of "farm" first used in the 1951 census.

[54]These increases are somewhat exaggerated because of the change in the definition of a "farm" introduced in the 1951 census. There was a decrease in the average farm size from 1951 to 1956 from 135.0 to 131.7 acres and an increase in area of improved land per farm from 28.0 per cent to 29.9 per cent. (*Ibid.,* pp. 13–14. The average farm size was taken from the *Census of Canada, 1956,* Bulletin 2–3, Table 1.)

Nova Scotia figure is only one-third that of Ontario and slightly less than one-sixth that of Canada. The relative smallness of the area of improved land per farm in Nova Scotia presents problems in connection with the development of certain lines, such as the production of beef which tends to require relatively large acreages, and also contributes to the greater reliance of many farmers on the utilization of their woodlots as a means of augmenting farm income.[55]

Although much of the farmland abandoned is more suitable for forestry than for agricultural use, some of it is quite good land which should be consolidated into larger, more economical units. Unfortunately, consolidation is made difficult because abandoned farms are scattered, because of absentee owners who are unwilling to sell, and by the obscurity and multiple ownership of many titles. The old age pension, which enables old people to live on their farms after they have ceased to work them actively, also leads to a lower average farm income and impedes consolidation. (It is not suggested that these consequences constitute an argument against payment of the old age pensions.)

Table XXXI shows the relative importance of different farm products in contributing to cash income. Dairy products, animals, poultry, eggs, and forest products are the big earners. The woodlots bring in a much smaller proportion of cash income than they bear to total farm area (see "forest products"), but they are a source of extra income and provide off-season work for the farmers on their own land. It is generally agreed that improvements in woodlot management would increase farmers' incomes as well as permit expansion of the forestry industry.

Much of the part-time farming is carried on by fishermen. If the fishing industry was more highly rationalized and if the fishing population was formed into a smaller number of larger communities, there would be larger markets for farm produce which could be more economically supplied. Subsistence operations in fishing, farming, and logging, and frequently in a combination of all three, are no doubt responsible in large part for the low average incomes in Nova Scotia and the other Atlantic Provinces. The Royal Commission on Canada's Economic Prospects in its report observed:

In 1955, the average income for the Atlantic Provinces, including New-foundland, was 37 per cent below the average for the other six provinces. . . . In 1955 income per family for the Atlantic Provinces was 31 per cent below the average of the other six provinces, compared with a disparity of 37 per cent on a per capita basis. . . . In 1955, average family incomes of

---

[55]*Report of the Royal Commission on Rural Credit*, p. 14.

TABLE XXXI

CASH INCOME FROM THE SALE OF FARM PRODUCTS AND NET INCOME
OF FARM OPERATORS FROM FARMING OPERATIONS FOR NOVA SCOTIA, 1959

	($'000)	% distribution of cash income
Oats	51	.1
Potatoes	909	2.1
Vegetables	1,504	3.5
Fruits	1,991	4.6
TOTAL CROPS	4,455	10.3
Cattle and calves	7,501	17.5
Hogs	2,600	6.0
Sheep and lambs	416	1.0
TOTAL LIVESTOCK	10,517	24.5
Dairy products	12,683	30.0
Poultry	3,340	7.8
Eggs	7,567	17.6
Miscellaneous farm products	1,098	2.6
TOTAL LIVESTOCK AND PRODUCTS	35,385	82.5
Forest products	3,101	7.2
TOTAL CASH INCOME FROM SALE OF FARM PRODUCTS	42,941	100.0
Income in kind (including house rent)a	10,856	
Value of inventory change	−460	
GROSS INCOME	53,337	
Operating and depreciation charges	38,706	
TOTAL NET INCOME	14,631	

SOURCE: Government of Nova Scotia, *Annual Report of the Department of Agriculture and Marketing*, for the year ended March 31, 1960 (Halifax: Queen's Printer, 1960), Tables 1, 2, and 4.

aComposition of income in kind ($'000): dairy products ($1,721), poultry and eggs ($923), meat ($603), fruit and vegetables ($2,191), honey and maple products ($9), forest products ($1,357), other products ($11), house rent ($4,041).

people living in metropolitan centres in the three Maritime Provinces were only about 15 per cent below those of the average family incomes of city dwellers in the rest of Canada. (The corresponding figure for Newfoundland was 25 per cent.) . . . The greatest differences in average incomes occur among rural families. People with low incomes who are engaged in subsistence farming combined with part time fishing and logging exist in every province but they are found more commonly in the Atlantic region. This is one of the main reasons for the continued lag in average incomes per capita in that area as compared with other parts of Canada.[56]

[56]*Report of the Royal Commission on Canada's Economic Prospects*, pp. 403–4. In 1956 the two metropolitan areas of Nova Scotia were Halifax and Sydney, which together accounted for 39 per cent of the Province's total population. (*Census of Canada, 1956*, Bulletin 3–2, Table 1; Bulletin 1–1, Table 5.)

Probably about the most Nova Scotia could hope for would be to supply its own needs for agricultural products on a net basis. It is not likely that the Maritime Provinces will become a major exporting area in agricultural commodities although they are presently a surplus area for potatoes, apples, and blueberries. They provide their own requirements of eggs and of some minor products such as strawberries. They import some milk and butter, and production is far short of the region's requirements of animal and usually of poultry meat. Nova Scotia produces only about 35–40 per cent of its red meat.[57] It has an annual deficiency of about 175,000 hogs, 40,000 cattle, and 30,000 calves.[58] There has been considerable expansion in poultry production in Nova Scotia in recent years, based upon federal feed grain subsidies which are paid on freight charges to farmers in eastern Canada and British Columbia. Since 1941, the federal government has paid all but amounts varying from 50 cents to 6 dollars per ton of the freight charges for feed grains shipped to Nova Scotia from the Paririe Provinces. The average subsidy per ton over the period October, 1941, to February 28, 1957, was $10.22. Since March 1, 1957, it has in the three fiscal years ending in 1959–60 averaged over $15. Nova Scotian producers had been subsidized to the extent of over $28 million on over 2.5 million tons of grain up to the end of fiscal year 1959–60.[59] The result is that they receive their feed grain from the Prairie Provinces at the same cost as other producers in eastern Canada receiving feed by rail. One advantage of poultry and egg production under Nova Scotian conditions (of small farms) is that very large operations can be conducted on a few acres of land. The same can be said for hog production if it is based upon purchased feed. At present there are several very large, heavily capitalized, poultry operations in the province.

Grasslands and forage crops grown in the province are suitable for beef cattle production, and reclaimed marshlands are particularly suitable for growing fodder crops for livestock. But here the problem

[57]E. P. Reid and J. M. Fitzpatrick, *Atlantic Provinces Agriculture* (Ottawa: Department of Agriculture, 1957), p. 31.

[58]These estimates were obtained directly from Government of Nova Scotia, Department of Agriculture and Marketing.

[59]Department of Agriculture, Feed Grains Administration, *Statistical Information Relating to the Freight Assistance Policy for Eastern Canada and British Columbia*, compiled on basis of figures available up to November 30, 1958 (Ottawa, 1958). More recent data were supplied by the Department of Agriculture and Marketing, of Nova Scotia. The subsidies began largely as a wartime measure to boost food production, but, as is common with subsidies, they continue to be paid even though the conditions which prompted them are no longer present. As a good deal of agricultural production, especially of eggs, poultry, and hogs, is now dependent upon them, they are probably here to stay.

of size of farm is especially important. For specialization in the production of beef cattle to be profitable, a herd of about 30–50 cattle would be required. Such an operation would require about 250 acres of improved land.[60] In 1956, there were only 61 farms with 240 acres or more of improved land in Nova Scotia, and only 16 with 400 acres or more.[61] The large amount of capital required for an operation of this size is also an obstacle. At present most of the cattle are produced on a small scale in conjunction with a variety of other small-scale operations. Sheep production in most cases is an alternative to cattle production. The provincial government is presently developing community pastures as a means of encouraging cattle and sheep production. The construction of a new abattoir in Halifax, which came into operation in 1960, is encouraging livestock production to an even greater extent than was anticipated, but the limitations on production discussed above can be only slowly overcome, and even then the competition of very efficiently produced and high quality western meat has to be met.

Apple production declined considerably since the loss, after World War II, of most of the United Kingdom markets on which the industry once depended very heavily, although it has recently been increasing slowly. The annual output of just over 2 million bushels is sufficient to supply the domestic demand for fresh apples, the demand for apples for processing, and the slim foreign demand which remains.[62] There has been some improvement in recent years in the growing of vegetables and small fruits and in packaging and processing. While there is further scope for expansion and specialization, the total amount of agricultural resources required to supply the available markets is quite small.

The dairy industry is the largest single contributor to farm cash income. Most dairy farms are located near to their markets in towns and cities. Their production will likely grow with regional population. They too could benefit from an increase in the size of farm.

Experiments, beginning in the summer of 1958, with the growing and curing of tobacco in the Annapolis Valley have shown that good

[60]See Arthur C. Parks, *Beef and Beef Possibilities in the Atlantic Provinces* (Halifax: Atlantic Provinces Economic Council, 1957), p. 4; and Reid and Fitzpatrick, *Atlantic Provinces Agriculture*, p. 17. One expert interviewed set the minimum much higher. He thought the farm would have to produce 75 to 80 head per year to be profitable if beef cattle were the only major product.

[61]*Census of Canada, 1956*, Bulletin 2–11, Table 8.

[62]Government of Nova Scotia, Department of Agriculture and Marketing. About two-thirds of Nova Scotia's apples are processed and more than half of the processed apples are sold in central Canada. (*ibid.*)

grades of tobacco can be produced on some farmland in the province. As a result there might well be some movement into producing that quite profitable crop.

The prescription for improvement in Nova Scotia's agricultural industry is the abandonment of unproductive farms, some of which are suited only to forestry; the consolidation of farmland suitable for dairy farming and cattle and sheep raising; increased specialization in the production of vegetables and small fruits; an extension of the already favourable trends in poultry and egg production until markets are satisfied; the improvement and extension of the use of woodlots as a complementary farm operation; and an extension in the use of capital.[63] The results would be a rise in farm incomes and a reduction in farm population. The displaced population would have to move to other occupations in Nova Scotia or elsewhere. The food processing industry which it is assumed would expand with the anticipated expansion of agricultural production could be a source of employment for a small part of the displaced population. The developments suggested will not come about easily, but they should nevertheless be encouraged as a matter of public policy.

Forestry

Of the forested land in Nova Scotia, the Crown owns about 22 per cent; approximately 200 private companies and individuals with holdings of 1,000 acres or more own about 33 per cent; national parks and Indian reserves account for about 3 per cent; and small woodlots, mostly owned by farmers, account for the balance of about 42 per cent. The small portion owned by the Crown, compared to about 90 per cent for all of Canada,[64] is no doubt largely responsible for the small scale of the logging and saw-milling operations in the province.[65] It also makes it more difficult for the provincial government to foster good conservation practices. The policy of the provincial government

[63]These suggestions are in general similar to those made in Drummond and Mackenzie, *Progress and Prospects*, esp. pp. 157–60. Possibly an expansion in hog raising based on the feed grain subsidy would be appropriate to Nova Scotian conditions, since the size of the farm need not be large. Farmers are being encouraged to expand hog production to supply the new abattoir at Halifax. An increase in the size of the enterprise is generally desirable in other respects as well as with respect to the area of farms. See p. 142, n. 110 for a reference to the new Agricultural Rehabilitation and Development Act.

[64]*Canada Year Book, 1957–8*, p. 473; *Canada Year Book, 1960*, p. 517. These are very rough estimates.

[65]The output of sawn lumber in Nova Scotia per mill reporting was only about one-third that of Canada in 1959. Calculated from D.B.S., *The Lumber Industry, 1959* (Ottawa: Queen's Printer, 1961), Tables 3, 7.

of acquiring forest land as favourable opportunities arise is a wise one, although the speed of acquisition is bound to be slow.[66]

In 1959, lumber and pulpwood accounted for about 91 per cent of Nova Scotia's timber production.[67] Although in recent years lumber has far exceeded pulpwood in terms of volume, at the processing stages paper products (including pulp) and wood products have been of about equal importance in terms of value added by manufacture. In 1958, this value was about $13.4 million for paper products and $12.7 million for wood products.[68] The development of the large new pulp mill at Point Tupper, in the eastern part of the province, will greatly increase the absolute and relative importance of the production of pulpwood and of the value of paper products.

A recent forest inventory of Nova Scotia, *The Forest Resources of Nova Scotia*, indicates that there has been an overcutting of sawlogs for many years and that a substantial reduction in cutting of sawlogs will be necessary if the province's forest resources are to be restored to the state where they will permit maximum annual yields. On the other hand, the cutting of pulpwood and pit props could be sustained at a somewhat higher level than at present without reducing stocks. What will likely happen will be a gradual decline in the sawmill industry and an expansion of the pulpwood industry.

The new mill at Point Tupper will accelerate the shift to the production of pulpwood. One advantage of concentrating on pulpwood production is that it is not necessary to wait so long to utilize new forest growth as in the case of sawlog production, since small trees can be used. Other advantages are that the market for pulpwood is more stable than the export market for sawn lumber, and that modern methods of chemical treatment of pulpwood permit almost complete utilization of the felled trees in obtaining woodpulp. A modern chemical pulp mill can use hardwood and even sick, decadent, and insect-ridden wood. One expert on the province's forestry resources believes that in the near future the value of forest products will increase about 10 per cent, partly because of improved use of resources and partly because of increased yield of pulpwood. He also believes

[66]Most of this is burnt-over or cut-over land. About 587,000 acres were reconveyed to the Crown to March 31, 1960. In the year ending March 31, 1960, 26 parcels of land totalling 6,347 acres were reconveyed. (Government of Nova Scotia, *Annual Report of the Department of Lands and Forests,* for the fiscal year ending March 31, 1960 [Halifax: Queen's Printer, 1960], p. 22.)

[67]*Ibid.,* p. 16.

[68]D.B.S., *The Manufacturing Industries of Canada, 1958.* Section B. *Atlantic Provinces* (Ottawa: Queen's Printer, 1960), pp. 38–9.

that the yield can be doubled over the next 25–50 years.[69] The increased yield depends in large part on the improvement of practices on farm woodlots which, as already noted, account for a large part of forest land. In the past these practices have been notoriously wasteful. The waste has been due to ignorance about good woodlot management, and shortsightedness abetted by property taxation policies which have encouraged stripping of woodlots.[70] Expert opinion has been given that proper forest management on a sustained yield basis can be profitable even to the small woodlot owner.[71]

It appears from this brief discussion that Nova Scotia's forestry resources are not being used to best advantage: that they could yield larger returns with the same amount of or less employment and that some additional capital, especially in the form of a new pulp mill, could be profitably applied. If the consolidation of farms is accelerated then so also will be the consolidation of woodlots, with the likelihood that total income from woodlots will be considerably increased. In general the long-run potential of the forestry industry is quite favourable. Moreover, as the great tracts of virgin forest in other parts of the country become less accessible, Nova Scotia's relative position as a supplier of pulpwood will improve on that account.

Fisheries[72]

There is considerable room for improvement in the way the fisheries resources are used both in primary fishing operations and in processing. With regard to the slowness in the adoption of improved techniques in the fish-catching industry, the authors of one of the special studies for the Royal Commission on Canada's Economic Prospects (Gordon Commission), *The Commercial Fisheries of Canada*, cite the example of the long-standing government restriction on the use of draggers on the Atlantic coast in response to the pressure of inshore fishermen

[69]Information obtained in a confidential interview and letter. The deputy minister of Lands and Forests has stated that the value of output of the industry could even be trebled within a few years, with proper care, conservation, and education. (*Halifax Chronicle-Herald*, February 27, 1959.)

[70]For a good discussion of the harmful effects of property taxation policies on the management of the Province's forests and on municipal finances, see A. Milton Moore, *Forestry Tenures and Taxes in Canada* (Tax Papers, No. 11; Toronto: Canadian Tax Foundation, 1957), pp. 82–3; and the appendix to chap. xvi by R. S. Johnson, "The Forest Tax Situation in Nova Scotia and a Proposed Remedy."

[71]Confidential letter to the writer.

[72]This section is based partly upon confidential interviews with people in the province who are well acquainted with the fishing industry.

who were concerned about the loss of their livelihood. The authors observe further:

As a highly efficient instrument of production, beyond their means to acquire, the dragger seemed to undermine the stability of their [the inshore fishermen's] sales outlets. In response to this opposition, dragging operations were placed under restrictions that, with greater or less severity, persisted for many years. The purpose appears to have been to retain the largest possible labour force in the fishing industry. The effect, however, was to retard the growth of productivity and, consequently, of individual incomes in this industry. The ultimate result, therefore, would be the reverse of that intended. Misguided policy of this nature is a common affliction of the fishing industry.[73]

Recent years have seen a pronounced swing to the use of more efficient and larger boats, especially draggers and the increasingly popular longliners. They have considerable advantages over the small boats of the inshore fishermen in that they can go to where the fishing is best at any particular time, they can be equipped with radar and electronic fish-finding apparatus, they can fish in rougher weather and therefore for more days in the year, and they are more efficient in the actual catching of fish. The result is a larger return to both labour and capital. Since they have a greater range and since they can operate during most of the year, they can assure a more regular supply of fish to the fish plants. More regular employment results in both the primary catching and the processing industries. Another result is that processing operations can be concentrated in a few larger and more efficient plants.[74]

[73]*Commercial Fisheries of Canada*, pp. 4–5. A dragger is a motor-powered boat, about 50–70 feet in length, which catches fish in nets dragged along the ocean floor (as contrasted with the old schooners which carried small dories from which the fishermen fished with baited lines). A dragger carries about 6 men. Trawlers are about 85–100 feet in length. They also use nets, and carry about 18 men.

[74]*Ibid.*, esp. chap. v. See John Proskie, "Operations of Modern Longliners and Draggers Atlantic Seaboard 1952–1957," *Primary Industry Studies*, no. 1, vol. 7, part 1 (Economics Service, Department of Fisheries of Canada; Ottawa: Queen's Printer, 1959), *passim*, for an excellent analysis of the experience with draggers and longliners. Where the size and type of the vessel are well-adapted to the types of fishing operations and where the vessel is used skilfully and with an awareness of cost-revenue relationships, returns to capital have been sufficient to justify the investment and the returns to labour have compared favourably with those in alternative occupations. There have been a number of instances, however, where the above conditions have not been met, and where the operation of the vessels has therefore not been profitable. See also, by the same author, "An Appraisal of the Atlantic Fishing Craft Modernization Programme and the Otter Trawling Fleet" (Economics Service, Department of Fisheries; Ottawa: 1960), *passim*.

Experience in British Columbia, where the industry is much more heavily capitalized than in the Atlantic Provinces, and in the more heavily capitalized parts of the industry in Nova Scotia shows that good returns can be had from efficient operations. In British Columbia the average annual income of salmon fishermen from all sources in 1954 was $3,056, only one dollar less than the average earnings of all paid workers in the Canadian labour force. The skipper of an Atlantic Coast dragger might make $5,000 while an inshore fisherman with a small boat might make only a few hundred dollars.[75]

In 1956, of 14,379 fishermen in Nova Scotia, only 944 (6.6 per cent) worked on draggers and trawlers; 2,762 (19.3 per cent) on other vessels of 10–40 tons; and 9,947 (69.4 per cent) on small inshore boats. The balance of 726 (5.1 per cent) worked on carrying smacks, or fished without boats. These figures indicate that there is still room for a great deal of adjustment in the fishing operations. In 1955, for all five provinces with fishing operations on the Atlantic coast, over 50 per cent of the total catch by weight was landed by trawlers, draggers, schooners, and longliners, which carried only about 20 per cent of the fishermen.[76] The comparison would likely be even more striking for Nova Scotia alone, since its fishing operations are more heavily capitalized and more progressive than those of the other Atlantic Provinces.[77]

Although the use of larger boats has produced some tendency for the catching and processing industries to concentrate at a few large centres, there are still numerous fishing villages scattered around the province. Many of these villages are quite isolated, with few alternative occupations to fishing and few social amenities. There would appear to be much merit in the concentration of fishing families in a smaller number of larger communities. Such amalgamation would facilitate the use of larger boats and of larger, more efficient, processing plants; and the wider range of employment opportunities of a larger centre would alleviate the underemployment of labour which prevails in many villages. Amalgamation would also reduce the wasteful erection and maintenance of wharves in the many small villages, to which the federal government is presently committed. The released funds

[75]*Commercial Fisheries of Canada*, pp. 112, 124.

[76]Calculated from D.B.S., *Fisheries Statistics of Canada, 1956, Nova Scotia* (Ottawa: Queen's Printer, 1958), Table 5; and D.B.S., *Fisheries Statistics of Canada, 1955* (Ottawa: Queen's Printer, 1958), Tables 5 and 7. Quebec is the fifth province. Data for number of men working on different types of vessel are not given in later editions.

[77]The amount of fish landed in terms of tons per man per year in Nova Scotia has increased from 9 tons in 1941 to about 18 tons in 1958. (Government of Nova Scotia, Department of Trade and Industry.)

could be used to much better effect to supply some of the large amounts of capital required to increase the productivity of the industry, and social capital such as roads and schools could be more economically provided.[78]

Cogent though these arguments are, the strong attachment of fishermen to their villages is an inhibiting force to be reckoned with. The experiences at Louisburg and Petit de Grat, where large new processing plants have been established since the Second World War, underline the difficulties of inducing people to move. The Louisburg plant failed to attract the fishermen and good labour force it hoped for. As a result some retrenchment and consolidation have been necessary. At Petit de Grat the plant employees are commuting from some distance rather than moving into the village. In time they might move; but their reluctance to do so is illustrated by the plaintive words of an old Newfoundlander who wanted to return to the village his government had induced the inhabitants to abandon: "Who will take care of the cemetery?" Furthermore, the flexibility of the longliner does enable a fisherman to live in a small village and yet market his catch at fish plants in larger centres. He can radio to a number of plants and pick the one offering the best price even though it may be far from his "home port." Where small boats which cannot fish in the winter are still used, unemployment insurance and family allowances carry many of the fishermen over the winter and will prolong the life of the small communities. Thirty dollars per month, say, in one of these villages, where the fisherman owns his own home, will go further than one hundred dollars in Halifax. Small-scale subsistence farming in conjunction with fishing is very common where the quality of the soil permits it and helps the people to get along.[79] Moreover, even if fishermen are unwilling to move to larger centres, much can still be and is being done, as a second best alternative, by improving equipment and organization, to raise incomes in the small villages, as successful attempts in a few of them have demonstrated.

One of the problems in introducing larger boats is the unwillingness

[78]One person well-acquainted with the industry said that many of the small places are doomed because facilities such as freezing plants, cold storage plants, electricity, a good water supply, and good roads, all of which are essential to the modern fishing industry, cannot be economically provided in a small community. He added as an illustration that east of Port Bickerton a dozen communities, with about 30–40 fishermen each, are trying to eke out a living, whereas there is room for only about two centres with good harbour facilities, which could sustain communities of about 1,200 to 1,500 people with good roads and with cold storage and other facilities. (Interview.)

[79]The last three sentences are based upon a personal interview.

of the fishermen in many sections of the province to stay away from port for many days. As a result, many of the fishermen on trawlers and draggers are Newfoundlanders. The longliner, or some similar craft, may turn out to be the main instrument for revolutionizing the catching industry. Also, this sort of boat appeals more to the independent character of the Nova Scotian fisherman. A competent skipper with the financial aid mentioned earlier can acquire his own vessel; and the better working conditions on a longliner than on a small boat, and the greater net earnings it makes possible, make fishermen's sons aspire to become skipper-owners.[80]

It is not argued here that inshore fishing should be abandoned. Far from it. The valuable lobster fishery, for example, is dependent upon inshore operations. It is where fishing from the larger vessels is a more profitable substitute for fishing from small boats that the change should be encouraged.

The Gordon Commission study concludes that increased capital per man in the primary fishing industry should be accompanied by a reduction in the number of fishermen employed. It envisages "an increase in investment per fisherman rather than an increase in overall capital."[81] In support of these views it points to the small increase in the landings which the resources will sustain and to the underemployment of labour currently in the industry's labour force.[82]

To a considerable extent the future of the industry is dependent upon American markets which in turn depend upon American tariff policy. In 1958 total Canadian production of all fishery products was about $231 million, total exports were $152 million, and exports to the United States were $102 million (44 per cent of total production and 67 per cent of total exports).[83] Tariff policy is especially relevant to the degree of processing which can take place in Canadian plants. At present, for example, the higher tariff on pre-cooked frozen fish sticks than on the frozen fish blocks from which the fish sticks are made permits the export of the blocks but not of the sticks. A lowering of the tariff on fish sticks would permit further processing in Canada. An increase in the tariff on fish blocks would reduce the extent to

[80]The longliner can be used for catching ground fish like cod and haddock, on the banks, or elsewhere; for catching halibut, which must be followed around; for dragging for deep sea scallops; for dragging smooth bottoms for high-priced flat fish (an operation new to the province, known as "Danish seining"); and for swordfishing. Swordfishing is not only profitable, but is a source of excitement and recreation to the fisherman, like deer hunting to the farmer.

[81]*Commercial Fisheries of Canada*, p. 117.

[82]*Ibid.*, pp. 124–5.

[83]*Canada Year Book, 1960*, pp. 644, 1031.

which even that product could be sold to the United States. As one observer pointed out,[84] the fishing industry in Nova Scotia characteristically depends on a large volume of fish with small margins of profit. Consequently, any drastic upward movement of tariffs by the United States would quickly close the less efficient plants and cut into fishermen's already low incomes. Rationalization is therefore all the more important, to develop a more resilient industry.

It would seem, moreover, that, within the limits imposed by markets, it is in the Nova Scotian industry's interest to concentrate on producing high-value fish products. Such a trend has been very pronounced in recent years in the swing from low-value, salted fish to the higher-value fresh and frozen forms. Greater emphasis on marketing fresh and frozen lobster and less on marketing the somewhat less palatable canned lobster would also seem to be desirable.

The part-time nature of much of the fishing industry, as in the case of farming and logging, is no doubt partly responsible for the low average productivity in the industry. The amount of capital used in part-time fishing is generally very small. The common situation is for the part-time activities in all three industries to be quite primitive. This is not to say that part-time occupations are necessarily undesirable. Properly co-ordinated they can provide more sustained use of the rural labour force and higher average earnings than would otherwise be possible in such highly seasonal industries as farming, fishing, and logging. But a greater degree of specialization than at present should be possible, with concomitant improvements in the use of capital and in earnings.

This discussion indicates that there is much room for improvement in the use of the province's fisheries resources—that an increase in the use of capital per man combined with a reduction of the labour force could substantially raise the earnings of those remaining in the industry, with some increase in production.

The prescriptions for adjustments in agriculture, forestry, and fishing are similar in that they call for higher ratios of capital per man without sufficient expansion of production to absorb all of the labour force presently in these sectors. As these adjustments are gradually made, improvements in income in the primary and primary processing sectors will widen the base for the rest of the provincial economy, so that a large part of the population that moves out of the primary industries will find employment in manufacturing geared mainly to the provincial and regional markets, in distributing the larger volume

[84]In a letter to the writer.

of primary products, in construction, in retailing, and in the other service industries.

Mining

A good deal has already been said about Nova Scotia's mining industry, in particular about its domination by high-cost coal mining which is sustained at the present level of output only by large federal freight subventions designed to permit the coal to enter central Canadian markets in competition with low-cost American coal.

In 1960 Nova Scotia produced 4,567,000 short tons of coal, 52 per cent of which was shipped to other provinces. All of the rest, except a very small quantity exported to other countries (less than one per cent), was used locally. Quebec takes about a third of total output.[85] Until recently, the maximum subvention was $4.50 per ton for Nova Scotian coal moving into the subvention area (western Quebec and Ontario) by rail, $3.00 per ton by water, and $5.25 per ton by rail and water. A graduated rate was paid, up to the maxima, ranging from 25 per cent to 60 per cent of freight rates depending on the distance the coal was moved. In several recent years the subvention on Nova Scotian coal has been over $8 million annually and usually over $3 per ton of coal moved under subvention.[86] Because of severe marketing difficulties which have been worldwide, and which required long lay-offs of many miners, the federal government in 1959 announced an additional emergency freight subvention of $4,340,000 for the fiscal year 1959–60, the provincial government to pay up to $500,000 of it. It was designed to sell 700,000 tons in new markets in Ontario. At the same time, the existing subvention scheme was made more flexible so that a larger subvention per ton could be paid than before, in particular markets, to meet competition without increasing the over-all total. In 1959–60 the subvention rose to $13.5 million and was $5.60 per ton.[87] Practically all of the coal sold in the subvention area is sold by Dosco subsidiaries, which account for over 90 per cent of the coal mined in Nova Scotia. The small independent companies are mainly dependent upon local markets, including railway purchases. These markets have been hurt by the use of fuel oil for some heating and power generation and by the conversion of the railways to diesel locomotives.

[85]Government of Nova Scotia, *Annual Report on Mines, 1960* (Halifax: Queen's Printer, 1961), calculated from Table 9.
[86]*Report of the Royal Commission on Coal* (Ottawa: Queen's Printer, 1960), p. 78.
[87]*Ibid.*, p. 78.

A current programme of mechanization of some of Dosco's Cape Breton mines,[88] begun in 1950, has resulted in some increase in productivity per man-day. However, productivity in American mines has been increasing even more rapidly than in Nova Scotia. The Royal Commission on Coal states: "For 1958 the average cost at the pit-head of Nova Scotia coal was $10.72 against prices at the mines of United States coal shipped into Canada ranging from $3.60 to $5.33. A similar contrast shows in the average output per man-day. The average in 1958 at the Nova Scotia mines was 2.66 tons; in the United States it was over 11 tons and is steadily rising."[89]

Although increased productivity is desirable in itself, it is bound to reduce employment in view of the acute marketing problems, in addition to the unemployment resulting from the closure of high-cost mines. In fact, mines *have* been closing in recent years (two of them in Springhill as a result of terrible disasters in 1956 and 1958). In 1948, there were 43 mines employing 12,044 men, which produced 6,412,000 tons of coal. In 1960, there were 27 mines employing 8,073 men, which produced 4,567,000 tons.[90] Further reductions in production and employment have occurred with the more recent closures.

A federal Royal Commission on Coal was appointed in October, 1959, with Justice I. C. Rand as sole commissioner. It reported in August, 1960, and made sixteen recommendations concerning subsidies, development of the tourist industry in Cape Breton, productivity of mines, utilization of coal, the setting up of trade and vocational schools, and reconstitution of the Dominion Coal Board. Most of the report is concerned with Nova Scotia, particularly Cape Breton Island. While taking cognizance of the likelihood that the competitive position of coal in relation to other fuels will improve in about 25–35 years, possibly sooner, the commission argued that the high costs of mining coal in Cape Breton necessitated the closure of three mines within five years and a fourth within ten years, with the possibility of further closures if the costs of the remaining mines were far out of line with market value. At the same time, it mentioned the possibility of opening up somewhat lower-cost mines in the Lingan area. The commission found that such measures were essential to bring production into line

[88]Dosco's Cape Breton mines accounted for 95 per cent of that company's production in 1960. (*Annual Report on Mines, 1960*, calculated from Tables 7 and 8.)

[89]*Report of the Royal Commission on Coal*, p. 17.

[90]*Annual Report on Mines, 1957* (Halifax: Queen's Printer, 1958), Table 11; *ibid.*, 1960, Table 7; and Urwick Currie, Limited, *The Nova Scotia Coal Industry* (A study for the Royal Commission on Canada's Economic Prospects; Ottawa: Queen's Printer, 1957), p. 19.

with market demand and that even the reduced production would
require a subsidy. Although regretting the necessity of such drastic
measures, the Commission stated:

. . . there is no purpose in bewailing the failure of the impossible. Not to
emphasize this is to encourage deception; and the absurdity for the next
ten years to continue, without other action, a subsidy of over $13 million
a year is made obvious by considering what $130 million, within that time,
could bring about if put to a different purpose. What is there now of
permanent sources of new productive wealth from the $100 million paid
out over the last 30 years? These are the naked facts and they cannot be
evaded.[91]

The commission called for a new set of subsidies to the mine
operators, to be paid on coal other than that mined for the primary use
of the owner, to replace the freight subventions. For Nova Scotia it
proposed a basic subsidy of 50 cents per ton "to assist mines to maintain at least skeletal operations and in some degree to conserve existing
mine investment values,"[92] and a social subsidy of $2.00 per ton on
sales in the Atlantic Provinces and defined parts of eastern Quebec, or
$4.00 per ton in those parts of Quebec for which the current freight
subvention was 35 per cent of the rail freight rate, and $5.00 per ton in
other parts of Quebec and Ontario, to conserve "for future use the
economic values [social capital] of the local population which have
grown up dependent on the mining industry."[93] It proposed that these
subsidies be paid for ten years so that the industry and communities
would know where they stood, during which time the production of
Dosco eligible for subsidies should be reduced to not more than three
million tons to bring it into line with market demand. The total annual
subsidy to be paid to Dosco was to be limited to the subventions paid
for its coal in the fiscal year 1959–60. In support of these proposals,
the commission argued:

The main object is to assist coal production to a better competitive position in its own market. In that the carriage charges are such that a greater
unit profit should result than on remote marketing; and except where the
absolute limits of local consumption are reached, to send fuel, at the general
government's expense, a thousand miles for consumption for purposes which
are present locally but are served by a foreign fuel, appears to be an ultimate
in absurdity. The paramount objective is to ease the present straits, not to
aggravate them.[94]

Although the commission took a refreshingly realistic view of the

[91]*Report of the Royal Commission on Coal*, p. 25.
[92]*Ibid.*, pp. 32, 51.
[93]*Ibid.*   [94]*Ibid.*, p. 34.

economic prospects of the coal industry in Nova Scotia and a commendably humane attitude towards the members of the communities afflicted by closures of mines, its report was disappointing in that it made no comprehensive provision for the economic and social rehabilitation of the members of the mining communities experiencing closures. It did propose reconstruction of the fortress of Louisburg, completion of a modern highway from Point Tupper to Louisburg, and further development of Cape Breton Highlands National Park as projects which would both provide direct employment and help to develop the tourist industry, but the seasonal employment on these projects and in the tourist industry are by no means an adequate substitute for the year-around employment that is sorely needed. Another recommendation urges the immediate establishment of a vocational and a trade school near Sydney. While such schools are highly desirable, even in themselves, their development should be related as far as possible to employment opportunities in Cape Breton or elsewhere. Here is still another instance that underlines the urgent need for a well-thought-out programme of economic and social rehabilitation. The history of federal and provincial policies with respect to the coal industry and with respect to the economic policies for the Atlantic region in general has been characterized by excessive amounts of generally well meaning but bungling "ad hockery" and by far too little thoughtful long-range planning.

In June, 1961, the federal government announced its intention to proceed with the Louisburg restoration, to begin a programme of improvement of forest stands in Cape Breton, to accelerate projects that were already parts of departmental programmes, and to consider several other unnamed projects.[95] At the time of writing the federal government had not acted further on the recommendations of the commission. A new vocational high school at Sydney and a trade and technical institute in Halifax, the latter to serve the whole province, are slated for completion late in 1962.

Because of shrinking markets and recurring losses on its coal operations, Dosco, in October, 1960, announced that three mines would be closed in 1961. They are the mines the Royal Commission suggested would have to be closed within five years; they had all been marked for closure in the fall of 1959, but had been kept open by the emergency subventions already referred to. Caledonia colliery at Glace Bay was scheduled for closure January 14, 1961, but was kept open by additional subsidies until May 31. Florence colliery was closed July 1,

[95]*Halifax Chronicle-Herald,* June 19, 1961.

1961, but it was decided that No. 16 at New Waterford, scheduled for closure August 12, 1961, should be kept open another year, with the government underwriting its losses. No. 16 was closed August 4, 1962. The special subsidy was set at one dollar per ton sold in the non-subvention area, that is, in the Atlantic Provinces and in Quebec east of Lévis, and was made retroactive to April 1, 1960. It was intended to compensate Dosco for losses incurred in the three mines. The province agreed to pay 20 per cent of this subsidy up to $300,000, the federal government paying the balance.[96] In 1960, the Caledonia and Florence collieries produced about 644,000 tons and employed about 1,300 men; No. 16 at New Waterford produced about 510,000 tons and employed about 1,000 men.[97] The Louisburg restoration and other projects mentioned above were initiated largely to provide at least interim employment for the released miners.

It seems clear that with respect to the national economy much of the capital and labour employed in the Nova Scotian coal mines has been uneconomically used and that the federal government should gradually reduce its subventions. At the same time it should underwrite some of the painful reallocation of factors and other adjustments which are required and apply its aid to the province in more fruitful ways. The subventions are often defended with the argument that the Canadian tariff on American coal of 50 cents per ton gives ineffective protection compared to that given industries like the automobile industry in Ontario. (A drawback of this duty is paid to Canadian producers using this coal to produce goods for export.[98]) This argument has some weight, but becomes flimsier as subventions have to be increased further and further to provide markets. The slogan of the advocates of subventions seems to be "sell Nova Scotian coal in central Canada regardless of cost."

Nevertheless, from Nova Scotia's point of view, to the extent that the federal government is prepared to pay subventions and subsidies sufficient to keep the mines open, most of the resources employed in the coal-mining industry will probably be at least as productive where they are as they would be elsewhere in the province. In the case of labour, for example, in 1959 average weekly earnings in coal mining in

[96]Department of Trade and Industry.
[97]*Annual Report on Mines, 1960*, Table 7.
[98]A drawback of 99 per cent of the duty is paid for imported coal used in the making of steel. The Canadian Coal Equality Act provides for payment by the federal government of 49.5 cents per ton on Canadian bituminous coal used by the Canadian iron and steel industry to produce coke. Dosco's iron and steel operations are the main beneficiary. (*Report of Royal Commission on Coal*, p. 85.)

Nova Scotia of $68.90 compared favourably with $60.17 for the industrial composite for the province and not very unfavourably with the industrial composite for Canada of $73.47.[99] After all, if the federal government were willing to subsidize banana production in hot houses in the province at higher returns than the factors of production employed in it could obtain in other occupations in the province, it would be in the province's, although of course not in the nation's, economic interest to have them so employed.

The Tourist Industry

The general consensus seems to be that the tourist industry is capable of considerable expansion. At present the annual expenditure of tourists in the province is about $45–$50 million a year.[100] A recent survey indicated that few regular tourists return to the province for repeat visits: "Although our study confirmed the opinion that Nova Scotia's natural scenic beauty was a great attraction to tourists, it also revealed that the tourist industry failed to supplement natural attractions with adequate facilities, which might encourage the tourist to extend his stay or return for future visits."[101]

Although there are places where a tourist can get good comfortable accommodations and excellent food under congenial conditions, these are few and far between. The province cannot expect to make best use of its excellent natural attractions as long as most accommodations and restaurants are mediocre or worse. Even the dining rooms in some of the larger hotels and inns are very disappointing. And in a province abounding with excellent seafood, it is amazing how few restaurants cook it appetizingly and how many offer little of it on their menus. The provincial government is aware of these shortcomings and is continually working to remedy them. But since in many cases the people catering to tourists are not very imaginative and moreover are not accustomed to attach much importance to these matters in their own lives, progress is likely to be slow. What is more difficult to explain is that even areas in the province that have traditions of excellent home cooking have poor public eating places. Unfortunately, if one can judge from the defensive reactions of some proprietors to inoffensively expressed complaints of a constructive nature, some of the poor food

[99]D.B.S., *Review of Employment and Payrolls, 1959*, pp. 38, 47.
[100]Department of Trade and Industry.
[101]Arthur D. Little, Inc., *A Statistical Analysis of Tourists Visiting Nova Scotia in 1956* (A report to the Department of Trade and Industry, Government of Nova Scotia; 1957), p. 1. See also Irene E. Johnson, *Tourist Survey, Nova Scotia, 1960* (Halifax: Department of Trade and Industry, 1960).

and service can be attributed to stubborn indifference. It is hoped that the provincial government's new policy of granting licences to some of the better hotels, inns, and restaurants to serve beer, wine, and spirits will result in a substantial improvement in the quality of meals. Previously, only beer and wine were served with meals and these only in a few hotels, most of which were in Halifax.

The province's main attractions would appear to be its rustic aspects and its pleasant summer climate, that is, its opportunities for wholesome outdoor activity. The straightforward friendliness of the people, especially in the rural areas, is another asset. These are features which appeal to city dwellers who wish to get away from the pressures and confines of city life. Care must be taken in developing the industry not to destroy these attractions. Rather they should be enhanced and made more accessible to tourists. Apart from improving accommodations and eating facilities, emphasis should be on such things as mapping out pleasant walks, developing campsites, the packing of tasty picnic lunches by restaurants, and providing more opportunities for people to go out with local fishermen. The provincial government is presently engaged in a vigorous programme along these lines.

One problem in developing the tourist industry is that the season is very short, being confined virtually to July and August. The fact that many facilities are used only in these months limits the amount of capital it is profitable to invest in them. September and October are very pleasant months in Nova Scotia and are the most reliable as far as good weather is concerned, although somewhat cooler than July and August. If the season could be extended into these months, the longer season would warrant improvements in accommodations that are presently uneconomical.

It appears that the province's resources in the tourist industry are not being as effectively used as they could be and that provincial incomes could be raised by an improvement in their use, although a serious drawback of the industry is that, because of its seasonal nature, it does not provide the year-around employment that is sorely needed in the province.

Manufacturing

"Manufacturing" is a very heterogeneous category. Since some primary manufacturing has been touched upon in the preceding parts of this section, the emphasis here will be on secondary manufacturing. But it is also of some value to get an over-all general picture of both primary and secondary manufacturing. As might be expected, since the province is not well situated with respect to markets for products of secondary manufacturing, most of the important manufacturing in Nova Scotia is of the primary sort, directly related to local natural resources.[102] Table XXXII bears this out. The industries in the table are arranged in order of net value added by manufacture. Of the first five industries, all except shipbuilding may be classed as primary industries. If the industries were arranged according to gross value of factory shipments, these five industries would still head the list. If the figures for oil refining were given separately, that industry would likely rank high on the list; but since there is only one firm in the industry, the Dominion Bureau of Statistics is not permitted to show it separately and so has put it in "all other leading industries." Most of the secondary industries in the list are of the sort that are usually established to supply local markets, for example, printing and publishing, baking, and the making of carbonated beverages. They require no special comment. Exceptions are shipbuilding, perhaps confectionery, and some of the items in the catch-all category "all other leading industries" at the end of the list, such as cotton yarn and cloth, aircraft and parts, and railway rolling stock.

It is interesting to note that among the industries listed, with no important exceptions, value added by manufacturing per employee is lower for Nova Scotia than for Canada. And in most cases value added as a ratio of selling value is lower for Nova Scotia. An important exception is the pulp and paper industry which has been dominated by the Mersey Paper Company at Liverpool (now owned by the Bowaters Paper Company). This firm is advantageously situated with regard to natural resources and is well located at tidewater to supply its foreign markets. The large new pulp mill at Point Tupper is also favourably situated.

Table XXXII shows that primary iron and steel production is Nova Scotia's leading industry in terms of value added by manufacture. Some of the advantages and disadvantages of Dosco's primary iron and steel operations have already been referred to in chapter II. While it is probably true that if the company were making a new start, it would not locate at Sydney, it is likely that it will continue its operations there for some time to come, especially in view of the large amount of capital spent in modernizing both steel and coal operations since the end of World War II. As the Maritime market can absorb

102As already mentioned, developments of the kind which took place in Switzerland are not out of the question, although conditions do not seem propitious for them at present.

TABLE XXXII

LEADING MANUFACTURING INDUSTRIES OF NOVA SCOTIA, 1958

Industry	Number of establishments	Number of employees	Value added by manufacture ($'000,000)	Value added by manufacture per employee		Value added as ratio of selling value of factory shipments	
				Nova Scotia	Canada	Nova Scotia	Canada
Primary iron and steel	3	3,999	24.3	6,080	10,080	.44	.52
Fish processing	138	4,015	15.3	3,810	4,580	.32	.33
Pulp and paper	3	1,227	11.7	9,540	10,970	.54	.50
Shipbuilding	17	2,470	10.5	4,250	5,930	.61	.64
Sawmills	467	2,055	5.8	2,820	4,960	.41	.43
Printing and publishing	26	878	5.7	6,490	7,810	.75	.73
Bread and other bakery products	76	867	4.4	5,070	4,840	.47	.51
Sash, door, and planing mills	51	712	4.4	6,180	5,170	.53	.39
Butter and cheese	21	701	3.6	5,140	5,660	.31	.22
Carbonated beverages	27	260	3.2	12,310	13,660	.65	.68
Knitted goods, not including hosiery	3	731	2.7	3,690	3,970	.46	.44
Confectionery	6	904	2.4	2,650	6,760	.41	.47
Miscellaneous food preparations	11	240	2.2	9,170	12,420	.42	.35
Fruit and vegetable preparation	17	515	1.9	3,690	6,060	.37	.35
Milk pasteurizing	30	453	1.8	3,970	5,540	.27	.33
Miscellaneous wood products, n.e.s.	7	118	1.0	8,470	5,620	.45	.46
Prepared stock and poultry feeds	16	121	1.0	8,260	8,310	.20	.22
All other leading industries[a]	18	4,338	54.9	12,660	b	.39	b
TOTAL, LEADING INDUSTRIES	937	24,604	156.9	6,380	b	.42	b
TOTAL, ALL INDUSTRIES	1,297	29,010	177.0	6,100	7,590	.43	.46

SOURCE: D.B.S., *General Review of the Manufacturing Industries of Canada, 1958* (Ottawa: Queen's Printer, 1961), calculated from Part I, Table 1, Table 2, and Part II, Table 7.

[a]Includes: breweries, cotton yarn and cloth, boxes and bags, paper, bridge and structural steel work, wire and wire goods, miscellaneous iron and steel products, aircraft and parts, railway rolling stock, coke and gas, and petroleum products.

[b]Not available.

only a few weeks' production of steel, the central Canadian market is very important. As a result, the company's fabricating facilities are located mainly at Montreal, the Sydney plant serving as the supplier of semi-finished steel. It is in the province's long-run interests that the company's over-all coal, iron, and steel operations be conducted to make its Nova Scotian operations as productive as possible. It is better to have an efficient secure operation employing fewer men than a weak operation, with a larger labour force. As the company's fabricating operations expand, so should its needs for the products of the Sydney plant.[103]

The steel shipbuilding industry in which there are four firms is dominated by the Halifax Shipyards Limited, a subsidiary of Dosco. This company works mainly on naval and other government orders, mostly repairs, on what amounts to a subsidized basis, as part of the federal government's policy of maintaining shipbuilding facilities, largely for reasons of security. Most of the other steel and wooden shipbuilding and numerous wooden boatbuilding companies make fishing boats and pleasure boats of various kinds.[104] Certainly boatbuilding is an activity indigenous to Nova Scotia, and one for which there is long tradition of skill and technical knowledge. There should be a continued basis for a sound industry, dependent largely, but by no means entirely, on regional markets.

Most towns have some woodwork manufacturing industry, mainly handling factory millwork, such as windows, door frames, kitchen cabinets, and institutional built-in furniture, geared mainly to local needs.

As a great deal of emphasis has in recent years been placed by the provincial government and by other groups on encouraging the development of new secondary manufacturing industries in the province, it is of interest to ask what the prospects are. It would appear that the types of secondary industry the province might expect to develop, apart from industries based on regional markets, are those of a specialized sort for which raw materials are obtainable cheaply and whose products are high in value in proportion to bulk, so that trans-

[103]A good discussion of the nature and problems of Nova Scotia's steel industry is contained in L. A. Forsyth, "Memorandum in Connection with the Primary Iron and Steel Industry of Nova Scotia" (A submission to the Commission on Canada's Economic Prospects; Halifax, 1955).

[104]In 1960 there were over eighty wooden shipbuilding and boatbuilding firms scattered throughout Nova Scotia (Government of Nova Scotia, Department of Trade and Industry, *Directory of Manufactures, 1960* [Halifax, 1960], pp. 4–6, 41–2.)

portation costs would not be a serious hindrance to competing in the central Canadian market and perhaps even in foreign markets. An intensive programme of technical training to provide a highly skilled labour force might also be desirable, although the reservations expressed earlier about the prospects of developments similar to those in Switzerland are relevant here.

Certainly firms of the type just described should be encouraged (as they are being) to locate in Nova Scotia if they have profitable prospects. Possibly at some time in the future enough such firms will locate there to generate external economies of production which will make the province more than just marginally attractive to them. But soundly based opinions have been expressed that conditions are not at present propitious for extensive developments, even of the most appropriate type.[105] An illustration used by one informant was the frequently mentioned possibility of producing high-quality, well-designed furniture, using local wood. With a superior designer an aggressive manufacturer could probably make a living in the furniture industry in Nova Scotia, but would be better off with the same capital and technical knowledge in, say, Hamilton, Ontario, where he would have the advantage of nearness to customers (including the opportunity to deal expeditiously with problems arising from goods damaged in transit), quickness of delivery, lower freight costs, and a good labour supply. Since this kind of business is highly specialized, it is an advantage to a manufacturer to be in close contact with developments in techniques, materials, and styles. He can do this most easily if he is located near his competitors and near the manufacturers of materials. Moreover, in some instances, furniture shipped from Montreal can be delivered to some points in Nova Scotia more cheaply than furniture shipped accross the province by a Nova Scotian producer. Perhaps these considerations explain why the furniture made in Nova Scotia, most of it by three firms, is largely of an institutional sort and is sold mainly but not wholly in the Atlantic region.

In instances where secondary manufacturing industries are supplying markets outside of the region, there are usually special circumstances to account for them. In one case of an old textile firm, the special circumstances are a well-established name and a long history of good management combined, it is likely, with financial resources built up over the years sufficient to cope with temporary setbacks. In another case, an Englishman with a good knowledge of textiles and of the Canadian industry obtained the plant of a defunct firm very

[105]In confidential interviews.

cheaply, permitting him to use most of his financial resources for product development and marketing. It would be extremely difficult for new firms of this kind to establish themselves, especially in view of the generally weak position of the textile industry in Canada arising from stiff foreign competition. A similar instance is that of the manufacturers of a moulded plywood pleasure boat. They had a good process, were imaginative and aggressive, and were able to build up good markets in the United States and Canada. But they also obtained a surplus war plant for very little and so had little overhead to begin with. Even for their type of production, there were no great advantages to locating in Nova Scotia and, as a result of a combination of unfavourable events, the firm went bankrupt and had to be reorganized. There was a swing in the industry from moulded plywood to fibre glass hulls, a senior sales representative went into the business himself taking with him much of the firm's custom that he had developed, and the organizer and main driving force of the firm died.

In all three instances cited, the firms were able to do well in Nova Scotia, at least for a time, but with the same entrepreneurship and capital they could probably have done even better elsewhere. A large confectionery firm in Halifax which sells in the national market is another example of a firm which might have higher potential earnings elsewhere in Canada, but which has remained where it got started. Certainly such firms are an asset to the province. Entrepreneurs of unusual abilities who are willing to operate in Nova Scotia, possibly for non-monetary reasons, may do much to raise its economic level. But at the same time the fact must be faced that Nova Scotia in the near future is not likely to attract very much secondary manufacturing industry, geared to markets outside of the Atlantic region, although some will develop gradually in response to growth in the regional market. For example, a chemical plant producing chlorine and caustic soda, based on the salt deposits at Pugwash or elsewhere in the province, is a possibility if the market in the pulp and paper industry in the Atlantic region expands sufficiently, although the need for cheap power for this kind of plant might be an obstacle. The proposed new chemical pulp mill in eastern Nova Scotia might make the plant feasible. A similar type of plant will likely be built in Saint John, New Brunswick. If it is, it may put the building of a plant in Nova Scotia further into the future.

While no evidence has been found of current misuse of resources in secondary manufacturing in Nova Scotia which might contribute to the lowering of the province's per capita income, it does appear that the major emphasis of the government should be placed on correcting maladjustments in the primary industries.[106]

This description of the economic prospects for development of secondary manufacturing is probably fairly accurate given the present economic structure of the country and the existing framework of public, especially federal, policies. The question arises, however, as to whether the resulting development would be conducive to the best use of the province's resources, in particular its labour. The population of the province and the labour force are likely to continue increasing at a fairly rapid rate. At the same time employment opportunities have been declining in the primary industries and will likely continue to decline if these industries become more highly rationalized as it is urged here they should. Coal mining is a special case; not only is the cause of unemployment different than in the other primary industries, but the men released by closures of mines do not have the opportunity to subsist on the land or the sea until they can transfer to other occupations as have those preparing to leave farming, fishing, or forestry. Expansion of the service and construction industries can probably at best only compensate for the reduction of employment in the primary industries.

There are only two avenues for preventing a large and persistent surplus of labour: (1) even larger movements of population from the province than have been taking place in recent years, or (2) a considerable expansion of secondary manufacturing industries. (Some combination of the two avenues is the most likely outcome.) Ordinarily the first alternative would seem to be the obvious economic solution, assuming that the large-scale unemployment that has been plaguing the rest of the country is eliminated, and perhaps the rate of migration of people to more productive pursuits elsewhere could be accelerated by financial assistance to those prepared to move; and yet, experience suggests that after allowing for all of the migration that can be expected to take place, even with the most prosperous of conditions in

106A study for the Royal Commission on Canada's Economic Prospects (D. H. Fullerton and H. A. Hampson, *Canadian Secondary Manufacturing Industry* [Ottawa: Queen's Printer, 1957]) shows that the degree of concentration of secondary manufacturing in Ontario and Quebec has been substantially unchanged since 1926 (Table 27) and adds: "In fact, no provincial decentralization of domestic manufacturing has taken place since before the turn of the century when first the development of a single Canadian market and later the growth of mass production industries made such a move economically unsound" (p. 46). The study is not optimistic about the prospects of expansion of secondary industry in the Maritimes, "in view of the slower rate of growth . . . and their relative proximity to Ontario and Quebec manufacturers" (p. 199).

other parts of the country, there will still be a large residue of unemployed and underemployed labour. If such a surplus is in fact
inevitable, there is a strong argument on economic grounds for the
use of federal subsidies for a limited duration in such forms as low-
interest loans, grants, tax concessions of various sorts, and transportation adjustments to encourage the expansion of secondary manufacturing
industries, provided the value of the contribution to production of the
otherwise unemployed and therefore completely wasted labour exceeds
the cost of the subsidies (including, of course, the subsidies with
respect to the cost of capital). The success of such a programme would
still depend upon a considerable degree of occupational adaptability
of the Nova Scotian people and a willingness to move at least within
the province to those localities where new industries can be established
with the best prospects for success. Since most of the conditions
described apply to all of the Atlantic Provinces, these statements are
applicable to the whole region. It is likely that any expansion that
could be induced would be geared mainly to regional markets, although
some industries, especially those producing specialties of a unique
character, might be able to enter national markets as well.

This line of argument follows that developed by Mr. A. C. Parks,
Director of Research for the Atlantic Provinces Economic Council, in
The Economy of the Atlantic Provinces, 1940–1958, and by Professor
A. K. Cairncross in *Economic Development of the Atlantic Provinces*,
his report for the Atlantic Provinces Research Board, as the following
quotations indicate.

Although employment opportunities in the resource-based industries, and
in the service trades of higher labour intensity . . . are expected to increase,
these additional opportunities can not be relied upon to be sufficient to
remove the chronic situation of unemployment and underemployment in
low-income sectors. For this purpose further development of industry with
relatively higher labour intensity, such as other manufacturing or manufacturing of a secondary nature based on the resources of the region, must
be anticipated. But such industry by and large, faces serious locational
disadvantages in the Atlantic region. These disadvantages must then be
sufficiently overcome to make such development more attractive. This
would involve the introduction of public policies to compensate for the
natural disadvantages of the area and might, for example, be in the field of
cheaper transportation to central Canadian markets, in the area of regional
taxation concessions, or in a combination of these and other policies.[107]

I start from the evidence that the Atlantic Provinces are lagging behind

---

[107]Arthur C. Parks, *The Economy of the Atlantic Provinces* (Halifax: Atlantic
Provinces Economic Council, 1960), p. 154.

the rest of the country. I then go on to discuss the reasons for this lag, emphasizing the downward trend in employment in each of the primary activities of the region—the activities that endow it with an economic purpose and are the principal source of its prosperity. Thereafter, I discuss the handicaps to which manufacturing industry in the Atlantic Provinces is subject and the dimensions which, given those handicaps, a realistic programme of industrial development might assume. Although I have not set out in detail the grounds upon which it would be justifiable to seek federal help in carrying out such a programme, it will be apparent from the line of argument pursued that those grounds are twofold: the probability of a labour surplus after allowing for migration to other parts of Canada; and the probability that, for a limited range of industries, costs of production would not rise perceptibly (except perhaps in the first year or two) if a location in the Atlantic Provinces were selected in preference to a location in central Canada. It does *not* appear to me that the proper criterion by which federal aid for this purpose should be governed is the disparity in income levels or in rates of growth but rather the waste of man-power and the loss of production resulting from local underemployment. I fully accept the need to push ahead with the development of those areas of Canada that have the greatest growth potential, and I see long term advantages in encouraging the movement of labour from declining to expanding areas. But I recognise that there are limits to the scale on which labour transfers are possible without inflicting lasting damage on the economic and social life of both types of area; and there appears to me a serious danger that, at current rates of population growth, these limits would have to be exceeded if no special efforts were made to develop new industries in the Atlantic Provinces.[108]

Even with an imaginative, well-conceived, and well-administered programme of economic development for Nova Scotia and the other Atlantic Provinces, it is unlikely that substantial economic improvement will take place quickly. The experience of Britain and Italy with their redevelopment programmes and knowledge of the time it takes for new industries to get established and to grow support this view. It will probably take a decade, perhaps even a generation, before one can hope to see a substantial expansion of secondary industry from its present narrow base, or improvements in agriculture, fishing, and forestry on the scale envisaged here. Sociological factors appear to be generally not conducive to rapid economic change; but, again, if change is considered in terms of taking place over the next generation, the prospects for economic improvement are quite bright. These considerations make careful long-range planning more rather than less important; for without such planning the province and the rest of the region may be little further ahead in ten years time than they are now.[109]

---

[108]Cairncross, *Economic Development of the Atlantic Provinces*, p. 19.

[109]In May, 1962, after this study was finished, the Government of Nova Scotia

With respect to secondary manufacturing, probably the best that can be hoped for, even with powerful inducements, is to attract new industries for which the conditions are at least marginally favourable. The forcing of types of economic development for which conditions are clearly unfavourable is likely to result in considerable waste of resources over long periods of time and a concomitant depressed psychological state of the people.

Many reasons for Nova Scotia's being a low-income province have been given relating both to the nature of its resources and to their utilization. While it is unlikely that the over-all average productivity of the provincial economy can rise to the average level of the richest provinces, there are nevertheless considerable opportunities for economic adjustments that could raise its over-all productivity considerably above the present level.[110] In any case, the long-run objective should be to put the economy of the province on a sound economic footing, not only so that it can make the maximum contribution to the welfare of its people, but also so that it will be more attractive to the vigorous and able men and women upon whom the level of economic development and the quality of society largely depend than would a basically sick economy that must be perpetually bolstered by subsidies.

---

established a Department of Finance and Economics, which has embarked upon a programme of voluntary economic planning, on a sectoral basis, beginning with the agricultural sector. The government intends to co-ordinate and integrate the provincial planning with any planning that develops at the regional and federal levels. It is too early to assess this programme. Its success will depend to a large extent upon federal policies and the degree of direction the federal government is prepared to give and the strength of the inducements it is prepared to use. A necessary condition for its success is the acquisition of a staff of highly competent economists at the outset, for the formulation of such a programme is a highly technical task; it is no job for amateurs, however capable they may be in their own particular professions or businesses.

[110]The federal Agricultural Rehabilitation and Development Act of 1961 provides for joint federal-provincial projects for converting unproductive cultivated land into more appropriate uses, for raising the level of incomes and employment in rival agricultural areas, for the development and conservation of soil and water resources, and for research on land use and rural economic adjustment. While it is too early to assess this new act, it does seem to have considerable bearing on the type of programme for agriculture envisaged here.

The Pattern for
Optimum Economic Adjustment:
Further Analysis in the
Nova Scotian Context

SOME SOCIOLOGICAL FACTORS IN ECONOMIC CHANGE

The Paradox of Emigration Accompanied by Lack of Adjustment

SOME INDICATION of the degree of emigration from Nova Scotia has already been given (chapter II, Table I). There was particularly heavy emigration over the period 1871–1931 and, apart from a slight interruption in the decade 1931–41, the trend of emigration has continued to the present. In view of this long period of heavy emigration from the province it is surprising that so much economic adjustment remains to be made in the primary industries, especially agriculture and fishing. It may be that the great emphasis which has long been placed on migration from the province as a means of economic adjustment has obscured and slowed down the very considerable adjustments which could profitably be made *within* the province. Lack of sufficient capital to move by those with very low incomes in the rural areas is also partly responsible for the slowness of adjustment.[1] And no doubt con-

[1]Howland gives considerable weight to poverty as an explanation of immobility in his discussion of economic rigidity in the Atlantic Provinces. He does not overlook the strength of tradition as an explanation of immobility, but at the same time points to the adventurous seafaring tradition as being conducive to mobility. (*Some Regional Aspects of Canada's Economic Development* [A study for the Royal Commission on Canada's Economic Prospects; Ottawa: Queen's Printer, 1958], pp. 194–200.)

tinual emigration of the more vigorous and ambitious members of the communities has tended to leave people behind who were slow to effect adjustments within the province. Strong though these two factors may be in impeding economic adjustment, what seems to be an even stronger factor is the intense attachment that many rural Nova Scotians have to their homes, and their tenacious desire to stay where they are. This sort of attachment is also characteristic of the Nova Scotian towns-folk. There is a very pronounced insistence in the declining coal mining towns, for instance, that economic opportunities in the form of new industries be developed in these towns and that the people should not be expected to seek new opportunities elsewhere. This is the case even in towns that would not appear to be very attractive to the outsider. Naturally, personal friendships play a big part in the reluctance of people to move. But whatever the reason, the reluctance to move seems unusually strong in Nova Scotia and is a factor to be reckoned with in considering improvements in the use of Nova Scotia's resources.

One further point is worth mentioning here. When there is a large amount of emigration from a region over a long period of time for economic reasons, it is bound to mean that many of those who stay do so for sentimental reasons with full knowledge of higher mone-tary rewards elsewhere. As a result, the population left behind becomes heavily weighted with people who may be proficient and may work very diligently at their occupations, but who are not much moved by the lure of higher incomes—people who are "unproductive" because they choose to be. This will not often be true where unemployment is the alternative to moving but it may well be where people can eke out a living in the farming, fishing, and logging sectors. To the extent that this is true, changes will not come easily and it is arguable whether they should be deliberately forced by public policy.

The Happy Low-Income Casual Worker

Those government officials and others interviewed who are well acquainted with the province's economy and its people agreed that a fairly substantial part of the labour force, particularly in the rural areas, consists of men who work occasionally at a number of different jobs and who show no apparent desire to acquire full-time occupations even when they are available.[2] They do not want to be pinned down.

[2]It is difficult to get any precise measurement of the number in this group. Only a rough guess is possible. The large number of low-income farming operators, already referred to in chapter v (16,926 out of 23,496 farms in 1951), is in part attributable to this group. The fact that the non-farm rural population of 200,242 was 68 per cent of the rural population in Nova Scotia in 1956, compared to

They seem to have no desire to move to where permanent employment is available within the province or elsewhere. No doubt all provinces in Canada and most other countries have men of this sort. But the group seems to be relatively larger in the Atlantic Provinces than elsewhere in Canada. The prevalence of part-time work in fishing, logging, and farming was probably mainly responsible for the development of this situation and no doubt has made its perpetuation possible. Perhaps the long history of emigration of some of the vigorous elements from the province has helped to create a disproportionally large residue of these people. Many in the group have a great liking for their way of life. Many are also very much aware of and glad to receive benefits from social assistance measures. If they succeed in building up unemployment insurance benefits they are content to coast along with their payments through their entitlement period, without looking for or wanting work. One might argue that as long as such people are satisfied with their lives and do not wish to change, they should be left alone, but their existence is to some extent parasitic in that they are a burden on their fellow citizens who must pay the taxes for the public benefits they are glad to receive.

Of those interviewed, the person who was best informed on such questions was not optimistic about reducing this kind of casual working, especially since there is little desire on the part of these people to change their ways. He expects the present proportion of rural to total population, 42.6 per cent in 1956,[3] to decline very slowly, and itinerant operations to continue for a long time. He emphasized that rural patterns in Nova Scotia are very slow to change and offered as an illustration the case of Queens County where the Mersey Paper Company is located. When the Mersey mill was established at Liverpool in 1928, there were general predictions that great social changes would ensue in the surrounding rural area as a result of this major industrial development. In fact the changes have been very slight in terms of the way people conduct their lives.

It is possible that the low-income casual worker is not really misallocated, in that he and his family may be less of a charge on the rest of the community if he is left where he is, where, one way or another,

---

49 per cent for Canada, may be another indication of its presence and of its size. As a rough guess, the number in this group is probably of the order of 10,000 male members of the labour force, or about 6 per cent of the size of the male labour force in 1951. (D.B.S., *Ninth Census of Canada, 1951* [Ottawa: Queen's Printer, 1956], X, Part II, Table 65; and D.B.S., *Census of Canada, 1956* [Ottawa: Queen's Printer, 1958], Bulletin 3-2, Table XI.)

[3]D.B.S., *Census of Canada, 1956*, Bulletin 3-2, Table IV.

he provides for most of their needs; whereas if moved to an urban area, he might not be fit for steady work and might even become a complete charge on the community. In any case his presence in the province poses a socio-economic problem which should not be overlooked.

The type of worker discussed here should not be confused with the diligent worker who works in a sustained way at a combination of, say, running his farm and a woodlot and engaging in lobstering. Perhaps his activity, too, could be more productive, but there is in his case no lack of application.

Although sociological factors discussed briefly above seem to have been a deterrent to economic development in Nova Scotia, it is difficult to assess their importance. Moreover, one should not overlook the fact that provinces outside of the Atlantic region, rural Quebec, for example, also face sociological impediments to economic development.

THE PROBLEM OF THE DECLINING COMMUNITY

The Ghost Town as an Objective

Ghost towns are not attractive things; but neither is poverty. Making a town a ghost town is certainly not a desirable thing in itself. But if a town experiences a gradual or sudden loss of the economic basis for its existence and if there is no sound alternative in the offing, the acceptance of these objective facts and adjustment to them will likely produce results more conducive to the long-run interests of the province than an attempt to ignore them.

It is in the economic interest of any province as a whole, and especially of one with a low average income, that its resources be put to their most productive uses. If a town which would otherwise decline is prevented from declining by the support of old or new industry by perpetual provincial subsidies,[4] it may be in the town's interests to receive the support, but not likely in the general provincial interest to give it. Since the town's interest is usually more sharply focused than

[4] Such subsidies may be in many forms, such as low-interest loans to industry, the writing-down or writing-off of loans to industry, tax concessions, or direct payments to industries. Federal subsidies might also be used and may be, as already suggested, a desirable part of a programme of redevelopment, providing they are designed to attract new industry into the parts of the province most suitable for them; but such locations may not be in distressed areas. It may, however, be easier for people to move from declining localities to expanding localities within the province, or region, than to move to other parts of Canada or to the United States. Provincial subsidies are stressed here since this study is primarily concerned with provincial-municipal fiscal relations.

the provincial interest, the concentrated efforts of a town to promote its interests may result in the more diffused and less easily understood over-all provincial interests being neglected.

Although the idea of their town becoming a ghost town is bound to be a cruel one to the townsfolk, acceptance of such a fate and adjustment to it may be kinder than the discouraging one of economic stagnation, as well as being more just to the people of the province as a whole. It is unlikely that a town that accepts such a fate will pass out of existence immediately or fully. Retired people may continue to live there and the town may continue to serve, if it did in the past, as a marketing centre for the surrounding rural area. Rather than becoming a ghost town it might level off and thrive with a much reduced population and with its commercial and other servicing establishments reduced in proportion. Such an adjustment of course creates serious problems in maintaining public services, and points up the need for determining how the financial responsibility for municipal services can best be divided between the province and the municipalities. The problem of how such services can best be provided is central to this study and will be taken up in later chapters.

In Nova Scotia at present the question of the declining town is especially relevant to those towns depending upon the coal industry. For a time Port Hawkesbury and Mulgrave, which developed as termini for the Strait of Canso ferry and are now by-passed by the causeway replacing it, also faced serious adjustment problems. The construction at Point Tupper on Cape Breton Island of a new $40,000,000 pulp mill by Nova Scotia Pulp Limited, a subsidiary of the Swedish firm, Stora Kopparberg, is now revivifying Port Hawkesbury which is nearby; Mulgrave may also benefit.

At the time the Urwick, Currie study was made for the Gordon Commission in 1956, Dosco estimated that about 120,000 persons in Nova Scotia were dependent upon the coal industry as an industrial base. Urwick, Currie favoured a more conservative estimate of about 90,000 persons. The number will have declined considerably with the shrinkage of the industry since that date, when about 11,000 men were directly employed in coal mining.[5] From 1956 to 1960, the production of coal declined by 20 per cent, from 5,731,000 to 4,567,000 tons. If allowance is made, on the basis of 1960 data, for the closure of three of the mines in Cape Breton County, production will be

---

[5]Urwick, Currie Limited, *The Nova Scotia Coal Industry* (A study for the Royal Commission on Canada's Economic Prospects; Ottawa: Queen's Printer, 1957), pp. 20, 32.

reduced by another 1,155,000 tons to 3,412,000 tons, a total reduction since 1956 of 2,319,000 tons or 40 per cent. Over the same period, the number of men directly employed in coal mining declined to about 8,000, a reduction of 27 per cent. The three Cape Breton closures will reduce the number employed by another 2,000 to 6,000 men, a total reduction since 1956 of 45 per cent.[6] If the Urwick, Currie basis of estimate is used, it is likely that this amount of direct employment can provide the basis for a population of only about 40,000 persons.

Coal-mining towns, based as they are upon exploiting a depleting resource, have eventually to face the problem of reallocation of movable resources and should prepare themselves for the eventuality, unless the community in the meantime attracts other industry which takes up the slack. In the case of Springhill, for example, no such industry developed. When its last mine closed, following the 1958 disaster, the town and the provincial and federal governments combined forces to persuade new industry to locate there. The province set up the Springhill Development Corporation Limited (as a subsidiary of its Industrial Estates Limited), capitalized at one million dollars, to induce industry to locate at Springhill. While it seemed possible that the unemployed labour force of 850–900 men would be attractive to new industry, no new industry was attracted there by the surplus labour resulting from the closing of the town's other mine after the 1956 disaster. A small woodworking plant and the federal government's new prison farm have been located at Springhill since 1958 in response to the efforts to attract new industry; they do not absorb a very large part of the labour force. A new, smaller coal mine opened by private interests with provincial assistance provides employment for about 100 men.

The emotional element is understandably strong, in the desire to help the town to survive. The very thought of the horror of men imprisoned and dying underground is enough to cause those concerned to overlook hard economic realities. But even so, as a more enduring solution, it might be better, where a town is not suitable for the location of new industry, to place the emphasis on emigration of labour and capital. The province will be hard put to resist the demands from other declining towns for similar treatment and, if it yields, may only accentuate the already considerable maladjustment of the provincial economy.

[6]*Ibid.*, p. 19; Government of Nova Scotia, *Annual Report on Mines, 1960* (Halifax: Queen's Printer, 1961), Table 9; and Department of Trade and Industry.

The problem of the declining community is a real one in Nova Scotia and it must be taken into account in any discussion of influencing economic development by adjustments in provincial-municipal fiscal relations.

Some Secondary Effects of Factor Migration

According to the marginal productivity principle of economic adjustment, factors of production should move from where their marginal productivity is low to where it is high, allowing for the costs of moving. For example, when a locality loses the industry which had been its economic base, the part of the population directly dependent upon it should leave the locality for employment elsewhere. But the resulting loss of this part of the population and its expenditures will bring a reduction in the service industries since the population base on which these industries depended will have narrowed. As a result, labour and movable capital employed in the service industries will be induced to leave; much of the social capital, such as houses, schools, churches, streets, sewers, and the water supply system, will go unused; the extreme case is where all of the population is induced to leave.

Here is simply a partial description of the economic process by which a town becomes a ghost town, or at least shrinks in size. The object in describing this process is to emphasize that all of the productive resources of a locality are affected by the loss of its industrial base and in particular that the value of its immovable capital will be much reduced, if not wiped out entirely, even though only a relatively small part of the population, perhaps only 10–20 per cent,[7] may have been employed by the basic industry. Much social and private immovable capital that still has many years of potential use will be abandoned and will be lost in this sense as well as resulting in losses to its owners in terms of money value.

If the movement of population out of the community is gradual and is anticipated, no serious consequences need ensue with respect to the service industries and social capital; for adjustments in the resources employed in these sectors can also be made gradually without great loss of capital either in terms of its potential usefulness or in terms of its monetary value. But when the population movement is rapid, the undermining of the economic base of the community is a more serious matter, for large amounts of social capital and capital in the service industries will be lost in the ways described. The productive potential of both types of capital will be as great as ever in real

[7]Compare Urwick, Currie Limited, *Nova Scotia Coal Industry*, p. 20.

terms, but the value of their marginal products will be drastically reduced and may even become zero.

It may well be that it is still desirable for the painful adjustments in the form of large-scale migration of population and capital to be made. Certainly they are preferable to the economic waste which would result from unproductive use of labour and capital in sick industries indefinitely maintained by subsidies. But in prescribing, in terms of the marginal productivity principle, the types of economic adjustment which should be made in a locality that has a declining industrial base, one cannot concern himself only with the resources employed in the basic industry. Only when there is no alternative which is consistent with economic realities should the conclusion that factor migration is desirable be accepted. Such an alternative would be some viable new industry or industries to take the place of the old one, or the revival of the old one by developing hitherto unexplored potentialities.

In sum, what might be called the secondary effects of the reallocation of resources must be taken into account in weighing the desirability of the reallocation. The effect of this argument is to modify somewhat, but not to negate, the conclusions of the preceding section.

Implications of a Declining Farm Population

One of the objectives proposed in the discussion of agriculture in chapter v is the elimination of subsistence farming operations, especially of those farmers whose main source of income is farming. If they transfer to other occupations in Nova Scotia, one result will be better markets for the farmers who remain. The rationalization of the fishing industry into a smaller number of communities, with a concomitant reduction in the subsistence farming operations of fishermen, would have the same effect.

On the other hand, even if the subsistence farmers were to leave the province, the effect of their departure would not be very serious, since at present, with their very low incomes, they do not have much impact on the rest of the economy. The same could be said about those engaged in submarginal fishing operations.

A big reduction in low-income farms would mean the abandonment of a considerable amount of capital such as buildings and electrical and telephone installations, but in view of the very small returns on these farms at present, the abandonment would be more than warranted by gains from more remunerative employment of the relocated farm population, and from superior use of the freed land by consolidation into larger farm units or conversion into forest tracts. Some of the farmhouses would not be abandoned but would be used by hired help, by retired people, and as summer homes by city and town dwellers; however, experience has shown that when dwellings and outbuildings are abandoned after consolidation, they are usually too old and dilapidated for use and so are of little value anyhow.

The rural municipalities would benefit by being able to extract more taxes because of the appreciation in land values resulting from improvement in land use, and by having fewer people to serve. The reduction in assessment resulting from the abandonment of buildings which did take place would be in part made up by better buildings on the larger, more profitable farms. Furthermore, in the case of many submarginal farms in the more remote rural areas, the value of buildings is so small that their loss through abandonment makes very little difference to municipal assessment rolls. The net over-all effect of consolidation would almost certainly be an increase in property values and therefore also in assessments and taxes.[8]

THE HALIFAX AREA: A SPECIAL CASE

The population of the Halifax metropolitan area grew by 66.5 per cent over the period 1941–56 (from 98,636 to 164,200) and by 22.6 per cent over the period 1951–6. Among the fifteen Canadian metropolitan areas listed in the census of 1956, its rate of growth over the longer period was exceeded only by Edmonton, Calgary, and Vancouver, and over the shorter period, by Edmonton and Calgary. For fourteen of the areas taken together (St. John's being the one excluded from the fifteen), the rate of growth was 52.1 per cent for 1941–56, and for all fifteen areas, 19.3 per cent for 1951–6.[9] Yet, Halifax has not been the centre of an industrial boom linked to the general postwar expansion of the Canadian economy, as have nearly all of the other areas on the list.

There is no doubt that the expanded defence installations in and around Halifax have been the predominant dynamic factor in generating the extraordinary expansion of that city, especially since 1950.

[8]An assessor, with much experience with assessment in Nova Scotia, expressed general agreement with this paragraph and the previous one and added: "In the *rural* areas of Nova Scotia I know of no case where a Municipality lost assessment by consolidation. As to what increase in value will result over the years I could not guess." (Letter to the author.) He also noted that where abandonment of land occurs without consolidation there is nearly always a drastic loss of value.

[9]*Census of Canada, 1956*, Bulletin 3-2, Table VII.

Halifax is the eastern base for the Royal Canadian Navy; the large dockyard and other large naval establishments in Halifax, the naval airbase across the harbour, and the naval research laboratory give considerable direct employment. There are also much smaller army and air force contingents.[10] The Halifax Shipyards Limited is largely dependent on defence contracts. Fairey Aviation Company of Canada Limited, which repairs aircraft and makes aircraft parts, and Cossor (Canada) Limited, a branch of a British firm which makes and designs electronic equipment,[11] both located in the area since World War II because of the opportunity for defence contracts and both are still heavily dependent on them. Even the large, recently expanded Imperial Oil Company refinery in Dartmouth receives much of its business from the naval establishment. The defence establishment and the industries directly serving it have together provided a base for expansion of construction and service industries in the area.[12]

There is also a large civil service establishment in Halifax, since it is the seat of the provincial government and is a regional centre for many federal civil service activities. Four universities, general hospitals accounting for a third of the province's patient-days, and the provincial mental hospital add further to the institutional activities of the area. Its function as the commercial and financial centre of the province, commercial port activity, Moirs Limited (a large confectionery, box, and bakery concern), and fish processing account for much of the remaining industrial base of the Halifax area. And in the case of port activity, the National Harbours Board, a federal Crown corporation, plays an important rôle.

To the considerable extent that the Halifax area is dependent upon governmental and other institutional activities, the ordinary theory of allocation of resources according to the marginal productivity rule is not relevant as an explanation of economic development.[13] It is in this

[10]For security reasons, data are lacking on the size of defence establishments.

[11]In 1958, Cossor (Canada) Limited merged with the large British firm, Electrical Musical Industries Limited (which controls Capitol Records, Inc., in the United States), to form EMI-Cossor Electronics Limited. It is hoped that the merger will eventually result in a considerable extension of products and activities, which would make the company less dependent on defence contracts.

[12]In the opinion of one informant, who has observed the growth of the area very closely, the big growth generated by the defence establishment is now about over, although there will continue to be some gradual growth of the service industries.

[13]Marginal productivity theory is, of course, applicable to the public sector in the sense and to the extent that the governmental and other institutional activities are carried on in the Halifax area because of the superiority of that location for these activities, but such decisions are not guided by market forces. The marginal

important sense that Halifax is a special case. As a result, the influence of fiscal adjustment on economic development in the Halifax area will be less than where development is more dependent upon market forces. This conclusion also holds in large part for the vicinities of the air force base at Greenwood in the Annapolis Valley and the Cornwallis naval installation near Digby.

FACTOR ADJUSTMENTS APPROPRIATE TO NOVA SCOTIA AND THE SCOTT-BUCHANAN CONTROVERSY

It was argued in chapter v that Nova Scotia is a low-income province partly because it is not so well endowed with resources as the wealthier provinces and partly because its resources are not being put to their most effective use. The question of adjustment in the Nova Scotian economy will now be examined in the framework of a debate between A. D. Scott and J. M. Buchanan,[14] a debate that is particularly useful for the purpose because of the way in which it illuminates much that is of primary concern in this study.

Two aspects of the debate are of interest here, and it is important to distinguish clearly between them. One is concerned with the reasons for a province in a federal country being a low-income province,[15] and with the types of economic adjustment appropriate to such a province *vis-à-vis* the rest of the country. The other is concerned, within this context, with whether federal grants tend to stimulate the appropriate economic adjustments or tend to distort the allocation of resources from the optimum. Essentially, Scott argues that they have a distortive effect; Buchanan, that grants for some services are distortive, for others, corrective, and that their net effect is not easily determined. He also argues that, in general, federal transfers are needed to equalize fiscal pressure on similarly situated individuals in rich and poor

---

productivity rule is applicable in a market framework to the considerable economic activity generated by the institutional base. The point is that it is not applicable in that framework to much of the base itself. One result is that this important area of the province is largely insulated from the vicissitudes of market forces. It is, however, subject to the insecurity resulting from the uncertainty of future defence policy.

[14]The relevant articles are: A. D. Scott, "A Note on Grants in Federal Countries," *Economica*, XVII (November, 1950); J. M. Buchanan, "Federal Grants and Resource Allocation," *Journal of Political Economy*, LX (June, 1952), a criticism of Scott's analysis in the above article and that of other authors with similar viewpoints; A. D. Scott, "Federal Grants and Resource Allocation," *Journal of Political Economy*, LX (December, 1952), a criticism of Buchanan's article; and in the same issue, "A Reply," Buchanan's reply to Scott's criticism.

[15]The term "province" is substituted for "state," which is used in the debate, because the context of this study is that of a Canadian province.

provinces. The second aspect of the debate will be considered later; the first will be examined now.

Buchanan maintains that to the extent that a poor area is poor in relation to other areas on account of misallocation of resources[16] it is:

. . . largely attributable to the comparative abundance of unskilled labor in relation to capital, skilled labor, and entrepreneurship. Thus, the returns to capital and entrepreneurship tend to be higher, the returns to unskilled labor lower, than the corresponding rates of return in the richer sections. Income differences among regions will tend to be reduced by an out-migration of the relatively abundant resources and an in-migration of the relatively scarce resources in all areas.[17]

Scott argues that natural resources may not be in good supply or of high quality in a poor area, in which case there should be an out-migration of the other factors of production, that is, of both labour and capital.[18] Scott's point is well taken. In his reply to Scott, Buchanan attempts to hold his ground by minimizing the importance of natural resources, which he regards (in "Knightian" terms) as a subdivision of capital; and by stressing the importance of an excess labour supply in attracting capital. He argues that natural resources are not of great importance because of the increasing extent to which they can be "manufactured." "Invested capital seems clearly to be a more important subdivision [than natural resources] in the consideration of most economic problems. There are few resources which cannot be produced and destroyed in an economic sense; investment can produce soil and even climate to a degree." He adds that with technological advances natural resources will become less and less distinguishable from capital.[19]

If such contentions were valid to the extremes to which Buchanan carries them, it would make a very nebulous thing of location theory. It would virtually eliminate natural resources as a factor influencing industrial location and would make irrelevant most of the theory of

[16]It will be poor even with no misallocation of resources if it has in economic equilibrium a higher proportion than other areas of factors of production that are relatively unproductive.

[17]Buchanan, "Federal Grants," p. 209. He is arguing in terms of *marginal* returns.

[18]Scott, "Federal Grants," p. 536. He refers to "Buchanan's implicit assumptions that natural resources are adequate, awaiting only development, and that labor in poor areas requires only training and experience for its efficient utilization" and adds "my own assumption was that *both* natural resources *and* the other factors are scarce and that national product will be highest when the scarce labor, capital, and enterprise are attracted to the best soil, ports, mines, sites, etc." (*Ibid.*)

[19]Buchanan, "A Reply," p. 538.

international and interregional trade. He also seems to be overlooking transportation costs as a factor in location. There is no particular reason why the marginal productivity of skilled and professional labour, enterprise, and capital should be high where that of unskilled and semi-skilled labour is low. It is quite possible for the marginal productivity of any or all of these factors to be low compared to other provinces if natural resources are poor or if transportation costs are an important factor. Buchanan, in thinking particularly in terms of the southern American states, seems to be led to adopt as generally valid, premises which may well be applicable to these states.

So much for the debate in terms of the abstract. What is in fact Nova Scotia's situation? Nova Scotia is an economically mature region in terms of exploitation of natural resources, and is consequently not now abundantly endowed with natural resources relative to the wealthier provinces. This shortcoming is particularly serious in view of the preponderance of the development of natural resources and the production of primary commodities in Canada's economic growth, an aspect of Canada's growth that makes this part of Buchanan's analysis less applicable in Canada than in the United States. The province is poorly located to compete, in most industries, in the large central Canadian markets, and has in recent years continued a long-period trend of developing at a slower pace than the country as a whole. As a result, the marginal productivity of both capital and labour has been persistently lower than in some other parts of the country, as evidenced by the chronic drain of labour and capital funds from the province.

The province has for many years experienced emigration of labour of nearly all sorts. Skilled and professional labour and entrepreneurs have been exported in large numbers,[20] quite contrary to Buchanan's prescription. As already observed, it seems clear that there is a heavy net drain of capital out of the region.[21] It does appear, although it is difficult to substantiate, that Nova Scotia's labour force is weighted more heavily with semi-skilled and unskilled labour than in other

[20]It is a common saying in the Maritime Provinces that one of the area's main exports is brains. Every year the Nova Scotian universities see many of their best students leave the province in response to better economic opportunities elsewhere. Howland refers to the training of these people as an "unrequited export" (*Some Regional Aspects of Canada's Economic Development*, p. 199). This is not to say that there is necessarily direct correlation between amount of education and the propensity to migrate. Mrs. K. Levitt found no evidence of such correlation in the Atlantic Provinces. (*Population Movements in the Atlantic Provinces* [Halifax and Fredericton: Atlantic Provinces Economic Council, 1960], pp. 30–8.)

[21]See chapter v. It is true that some capital and some types of labour have moved into the province, but the outward movements have predominated.

regions. To the extent such weighting exists, it is likely partly due to the relatively heavy emigration of trained labour, partly to the more limited opportunities to apply skills in Nova Scotia, and partly to the greater inertia and greater poverty of the untrained group.

In his reply to Scott, Buchanan, while conceding that "investment in heavy industry would be inefficient in regions deficient in power potential regardless of the degree of labor surplus," argues that "investment in light industry requiring little capital equipment per worker would probably be efficient in regions possessing surplus population no matter how inadequate the resource base."[22] This argument has really already been dealt with in chapter v, in connection with the question of whether or not light industries similar to some of those in Switzerland could be established in Nova Scotia. While it is conceivable that they could, it was pointed out that Nova Scotia's location in relation to markets, and the pulls on labour and capital from elsewhere, do not favour their establishment at present. With regard to heavy industry, it is of interest that Dosco would like to expand its fabricating operations in Montreal rather than Sydney, not because of lack of power resources, but partly because of the cost of transportation and mainly because of the crucial importance in other respects of nearness to markets. As was observed in chapter v, not only is light industry not strongly attracted to Nova Scotia under present circumstances, but at least some of the capital and entrepreneurship successfully employed in such industries in the province would be even more productive if employed elsewhere, again largely because of reduced transportation costs and other advantages of nearness to markets.

While it is argued in chapter v that certain industries in Nova Scotia, especially fishing and agriculture, would become more productive with the further use of capital, the situation is essentially not the kind which Buchanan envisages when he talks about factor adjustment in a poor area. What is called for in Nova Scotia is mainly a consolidation of and concentration (but also some expansion) in the use of capital and, possibly, even some decrease in population in some areas. For example, if two or more farms are combined, the total amount of capital used on these farms may be little more than before (although the capital per farm will be much more), but its use may be much more effective and the capital equipment itself may be of a different sort. Similarly, in the fishing industry, five men can work on one longliner rather than on five separate small boats, with a concomitant reduction in the total number of fishermen. Rationalization in fish processing will have

22Buchanan, "A Reply," pp. 537–8.

analogous effects. What is likely to come about is a higher ratio of capital per man, and consequently greater productivity, greater earnings per man, and also greater total production. Recent mechanization of some of the coal mines is having the same kind of effect. This kind of rationalization is rather different from Buchanan's prescription for a poor area of importing capital in relation to labour and natural resources. For Buchanan envisages the establishment of new manufacturing industries rather than adjustments in old primary ones, as are particularly called for in Nova Scotia. To the extent these adjustments call for some additional use of capital and for some emigration of labour, they do bear some semblance of Buchanan's prescription. Even the suggestion made earlier that the establishment of new secondary industries with the help of subsidies may be economically sound is at variance with Buchanan's analysis because it is based upon immobility of labour, whereas Buchanan's analysis provides for mobility, that is, it is essentially an efficiency argument in the conventional sense.

It is important to distinguish clearly between the two aspects of adjustment in allocation of resources discussed above. (1) Adjustment of the provincial economy *vis-à-vis* the rest of the country. This adjustment calls for some movement of both labour and capital out of the province as a result of higher marginal productivity of these factors elsewhere. This movement is a balancing one in that it tends to maintain the marginal productivity of labour and capital in Nova Scotia at higher levels than would otherwise obtain, although, because of some resistance to moving, probably still at lower levels than in other parts of the country. (2) Internal adjustments to effect more productive use of the factors of production within the province. These are the kind of adjustments discussed in chapter v and just referred to in the discussion above.

The two kinds of adjustment are related. The internal adjustments of the kind advocated will likely call for some addition to total capital, especially if they are accelerated. One effect, then, will be to reduce, at least temporarily, the net outflow of capital from the province, because of recognition of the opportunity to put it to better use than before in the province. Another effect will likely be to release labour, some of which will find employment in other occupations in the province as a result of the improvement in the economic base, and some of which will swell the tide of emigration.

Is a reduction of the net outflow of capital, assuming it does occur, the same thing in Buchanan's terms as the importation of capital?

Ostensibly it is. But the fact remains that the outward movements of capital (and labour) which have persisted for many years, and which are expected to continue, reflect a tendency for the marginal productivities of labour and capital to be greater in some other parts of Canada. While this traditional adjustment may be modified slightly in extent, it is not expected that it will be in its nature. And so Scott's argument that poor endowment with natural resources in a poor area may mean that both labour and capital have higher marginal productivities elsewhere will likely continue to be valid for Nova Scotia for some time in the future as it has been in the past.

Both Scott and Buchanan were preoccupied with the problem of economic adjustment of a province with respect to the rest of the country; neither concerned himself with the question of internal adjustment. It is now clear that the question of internal adjustment is a highly significant one in Nova Scotia. Traditional patterns of resource use have proven intractable even though they are glaringly inappropriate to the conditions of the present day. Even heavy emigration has had surprisingly little effect. It is these internal adjustments that are of particular interest to this study. In general the adjustments called for in the rural municipalities are those which have been described, relating to farming, fishing, and logging operations. The adjustments in the fishing industry will probably cause the towns depending in whole or in part upon fishing to increase in importance as the industry's operations become more concentrated in the larger centres. To the extent that towns are marketing centres in rural areas they will benefit from the higher incomes which will ensue from improved use of agricultural and forest land and will attract some of the displaced rural population. Declining coal-mining and other towns that have lost part of their industrial base will probably lose population to other towns and cities and to other parts of Canada. Although some secondary industry might move into towns having a surplus labour supply, such movement is likely to be concentrated in a few of the larger centres where ancillary industries can also develop and where there is a sizable local market, and will be geared mainly to supplying markets in the Atlantic Provinces, which will expand slowly with population, rather than to supplying markets in central Canada. As in the case of the province *vis-à-vis* the rest of the country, much of the required adjustment stems from poor natural resources which result in low marginal returns to both labour and capital (the kind of adjustment emphasized by Scott). Where increased capital is required, it is mainly for rationalizing existing industries, with the effect of releasing labour, although some industries based upon an influx of capital and a surplus labour force might be initiated as part of a publicly sponsored programme of development.

Since this study is concerned with the effects of provincial grants, or other forms of provincial-municipal fiscal adjustment, on allocation of resources, and since fiscal adjustment is likely to affect the level of certain public services (especially the general services) in the poorer areas, it is relevant to ask what effects the level of the general public services has on factor movement in Nova Scotia. This question will in part be discussed with reference to the second aspect of the debate between Scott and Buchanan—that concerned with the effect of federal grants on the allocation of resources.

Scott argues that federal transfers from rich to poor provinces, providing as they do additional services in poor provinces, impede the migration of labour out of the poor provinces, according to the marginal productivity rule, and so lower the level of production of the nation as a whole. He also argues that since such services form a larger part of income of poor people than of rich people, they will particularly impede the movement of low-income groups.[23]

Buchanan argues that Scott's generalizations are not necessarily valid. To support his argument he examines the effects on factor mobility of increases in the level of certain services. His conclusions will be of some interest here. He relates his argument to his premises about the desirable directions of factor movements for a poor area, already critically dealt with in the previous section; the following analysis will instead be related to the types of internal adjustments which it has just been argued are appropriate to Nova Scotia. Although his discussion (and Scott's) is concerned with changes in the level of services and their effects arising from federal transfers to poor provinces, it is also relevant to the effects of provincial transfers to poor localities.

Highways and Roads

Although in Nova Scotia all public roads except those in towns and cities are already provided by the provincial government, they do have

[23]Scott, "A Note on Grants," p. 419. The latter contention is dealt with in a more general theoretical context in the next chapter. For the present, it is the effect of public services (especially of increases in the level of services in poor municipalities) that is of interest.

a bearing on this study. The provincial government must decide what roads shall be built or maintained in one part of the province compared with another and its decisions will affect economic development. Furthermore, roads are in the nature of a general service, and localities in some other provinces do have some responsibility for them in rural areas, as they once did in Nova Scotia. Buchanan argues that highways have little directly to do with decisions of people to move but do make a region more attractive to industry, because of their importance for transportation, and so encourage an inward movement of capital. According to his premises, such a movement would have a corrective effect on the allocation of resources.[24]

In the Nova Scotian context the effect of provincial responsibility for roads is that the poorer areas tend to have better roads than they would have if they had to provide them themselves. Since it is almost certain that the province in any case would be responsible for the trunk roads, which link the main centres, it is the other roads serving the rural areas, including the numerous small villages, that are relevant here. It is not likely that manufacturing, since it is mostly located in towns and villages on the trunk roads, would be much affected by the secondary roads. These secondary roads are mainly, although certainly not entirely, of benefit to the people in the areas served by them. (They are also of benefit to those who sell and distribute goods to those living in the rural areas.) From the industrial point of view they serve mainly the primary industries of farming, fishing, and forestry with which the low-income groups are particularly associated.

The cost of roads is a relevant factor. The province cannot be expected to provide as good roads in a remote rural area with sparse population and small potential for economic development as in a densely populated area or one which has good prospects for economic development. While particularly important in the case of roads, the cost of providing a service to an area in relation to that area's population density and potential for economic development is also relevant in determining the level of some other services. While this factor will not be examined in detail here, it is assumed that the province would take it into account.

The effects of the province providing better roads than the rural localities could themselves provide probably on balance improve the use of resources in the case of farming and forestry, because they make markets more accessible to agricultural and forestry products and do not impede, but rather tend to encourage, the adjustments recom-

24Buchanan, "Federal Grants," p. 212.

mended in chapter v.[25] Still, there would likely be some instances of
these roads inducing farmers to stay who should leave. In the case of
fishing, too, the better the roads the more accessible the markets. The
effect in some cases is likely to be contrary to that desired, for good
roads facilitate the continuance of inefficient fishing and fish processing
in the many small fishing villages and so impede the rationalization of
the industry by its concentration in a smaller number of centres and
continue the unnecessary duplication of social capital.

The tourist industry is dependent to a considerable extent on good
roads, and as tourist attractions in Nova Scotia are to a large extent in
rural areas, including the poorer ones, better roads than could be
maintained by the poorer rural municipalities themselves permit the
tourist resources of the province to be put to better use; that is, they
enhance the productivity of both labour and capital used in the tourist
industry and so have a favourable effect. It is also appropriate to note
here that good roads make possible the operation of bigger, consolidated schools serving larger areas, which results in better, often
more economical, education. Better education, in turn, raises the productivity of the labour force and likely increases its mobility by making
its members more aware of the range of opportunities open to them.
This favourable educational effect of roads would tend in the long run
to offset the unfavourable effects where operative in the case of fishing
and farming.

While the effects of better roads are neither all corrective nor all
distortive with respect to the allocation of resources, it appears that
the net effect should be quite strongly corrective, although along
rather more complex lines than Buchanan suggests.

Education

The present educational programme of the province is designed to
make a good standard of educational facilities available to all sections

[25]It is not claimed that the roads are at present satisfactory to the farmers. The
fact that some rural roads are bogged down for several weeks in the year limits
the kinds of operations available to the farmers concerned. They cannot generally,
for example, specialize in dairy farming or egg production since such operations
require uninterrupted access to markets. In a recent study of Hants County, the
authors, in discussing this same point, conclude: "The improvement of roads may
be the most important single factor in the creation of conditions favourable to
economic change in the whole area." (N. H. Morse and R. E. L. Watson, "A
Report on a Preliminary Survey of Rural Conditions in Hants County Nova
Scotia" [With special reference to farmer organizations in the County; Acadia
University Institute, 1957], p. 29.) What is claimed here is that the rural areas are
generally better served with roads than if the rural municipalities, especially the
poorer ones, were responsible for them.

of the province. The provincial contributions to the financing of this programme vary directly with the poorness of the localities as measured by equalized assessments of property. The provincial proportions shown in Table XXXIII are used by the province as an inverse measure of the ability of the municipalities to pay for educational services. They

TABLE XXXIII

PROVINCIAL PROPORTIONS[a] FOR THE NOVA SCOTIAN MUNICIPALITIES
BASED ON THE 1958 EQUALIZED ASSESSMENTS AND ON THE
1957 COST OF THE FOUNDATION PROGRAM

Towns and Cities

	%[a]		%[a]
Amherst	27.44	Middleton	9.59
Annapolis Royal	nil	Mulgrave	71.49
Antigonish	47.12	New Glasgow	nil
Berwick	29.83	New Waterford	74.63
Bridgetown	9.83	North Sydney	55.87
Bridgewater	.87	Oxford	62.44
Canso	80.00	Parrsboro	63.88
Clark's Harbour	53.79	Pictou	53.32
Dartmouth	nil	Port Hawkesbury	70.05
Digby	18.19	Shelburne	49.70
Dominion	86.74	Springhill	61.46
Glace Bay	58.57	Stellarton	56.06
Halifax	nil	Stewiacke	56.31
Hantsport	16.60	Sydney	8.23
Inverness	79.95	Sydney Mines	63.01
Kentville	20.55	Trenton	nil
Liverpool	33.02	Truro	.65
Lockeport	66.30	Westville	75.95
Louisburg	41.20	Windsor	32.22
Lunenburg	nil	Wolfville	25.49
Mahone Bay	34.10	Yarmouth	34.93

Rural Municipalities

Annapolis	68.05	Hants, East	72.23
Antigonish	84.95	Hants, West	61.72
Argyle	84.02	Inverness	86.32
Barrington	81.60	Kings	61.46
Cape Breton	66.75	Lunenburg	62.81
Chester	45.37	Pictou	75.81
Clare	74.80	Queens	35.58
Colchester	69.32	Richmond	86.51
Cumberland	73.65	Shelburne	81.66
Digby	77.19	St. Mary's	78.58
Guysborough	83.81	Victoria	67.82
Halifax	33.00	Yarmouth	60.82

TOTAL, towns and cities	37.22
TOTAL, rural municipalities	63.79
TOTAL, all municipalities	52.84

SOURCE: "Summary: Foundation Program Percentage Proportions," based on Academic School Year, 1957–58 (supplied by Government of Nova Scotia, Department of Education).

[a]The "provincial proportion" is the province's share of the non-capital costs of the Foundation Program for education. See chapter IV, p. 72.

also serve as quite a good index of poverty of the municipalities, to the extent poverty can be measured in terms of value of real and personal property.[26] The table is given to indicate the great variation of wealth among the municipalities and between the rural and urban municipalities, and at the same time to show the extent to which the province pays for education in the poorer areas.[27] The full impact of the new programme will not be felt for a number of years. It takes time for standards of teaching to rise in response to higher salaries and for physical facilities to be improved. The consolidation of small (sometimes one-room) rural schools into larger, better-equipped, better-staffed regional schools has been greatly accelerated in the postwar period, but is still far from complete.

As already suggested in the brief reference to education in the previous section, it is expected that improvement in education in the poorer areas will work in favour of better allocation of resources. Buchanan states that evidence for the United States indicates a direct correlation between education and migration and that this correlation exists because the better-educated are both better informed about "the availability of alternative employment opportunities," and "more fully cognisant of the advantages to be secured from the higher real income which migration to other areas may make possible."[28] Mrs. Levitt's study does not show any clear correlation between migration and level of education in the Atlantic Provinces;[29] but this is likely explained by the greater migration from the rural, lower-income areas where the educational attainment was generally less than in the urban,

[26]There is strong negative correlation between the ranking of towns and of rural municipalities according to provincial proportions and according to the 1958 equalized assessments per capita.

[27]As stated in chapter IV, the province pays a minimum of 25 per cent of non-capital costs in all municipalities, but contributes to capital costs only according to the provincial proportions.

[28]Buchanan, "Federal Grants," pp. 212–13. Buchanan's analysis is not altogether clear. He seems to argue that increased education will increase the mobility of labour and so will be resource corrective. But he does not take into account the fact that with greater education the labour force will in the long run become more skilled. This latter effect, according to his premises, will be corrective, but at the same time will make the movement of labour less desirable. He is not explicit in the first part of his argument about the desirable direction of migration. He proceeds to argue that in the short run as well as in the long run the skilled, professional, and managerial groups, to whom education matters most, will be encouraged to stay by increased educational facilities, with desirable effects, and that furthermore, a better-educated labour force will make a province more attractive to outside capital. He appears not to be altogether consistent, although he seems to place greater emphasis upon the latter considerations, which are more in accord with his premises.

[29]Levitt, *Population Movements in the Atlantic Provinces*, pp. 30–8.

higher-income areas. The rate of migration from the rural areas may well have been much greater if there had been a higher level of educational attainment there.

There seems little doubt, in terms of *a priori* reasoning at least, that education has a favourable effect with respect to use of resources. The effect is twofold. It increases the quality of human resources and so makes them more productive and, as Buchanan suggests, it makes people more alert to the opportunities open to them and more able to take advantage of them; that is, it makes them more mobile and on that account more productive.[30]

Both effects have been operative in Nova Scotia, but the second is the central one here, since it relates to allocation of resources. The fact that a comparatively large proportion of the province's population attends university, combined with the comparatively small proportion of persons with university training in the labour force, suggests that there is a positive correlation between the amount of education and the degree of mobility of labour. The heavier weighting in Nova Scotia of activities closely related to primary production is conducive to outward migration of part of the better-educated population.

It is not only with respect to inducing movements of population to more productive pursuits outside of the province that education has a favourable allocative effect. It is also favourable in inducing internal movements into more productive pursuits. The extension of good educational opportunities into the poorer rural areas is conducive to just the types of adjustments deemed desirable. For example, in rural areas where agriculture and forestry are prevalent, good education induces some people to give up low-income operations and to move on to other pursuits (some of them in the province) where they are more productive. And it induces others to seize the opportunities for better farming and forestry practices by consolidating holdings and using better techniques and equipment. In fishing, effects will be similar; not only is the rationalization of the industry in both catching and processing speeded up, but a greater appreciation of social amenities stemming from better education is conducive to the forming of larger communities, which further favours rationalization.

There is another way in which improved education in the poorer areas favours better allocation of resources. It is related to Buchanan's suggestion that skilled, professional, and managerial groups, to whom

---

[30]Scott takes note of the first effect, but argues, correctly, in his debate with Buchanan that the real point at issue is not whether education will make the labour force more productive but whether, when educated, people are not more productive elsewhere.

education matters most, will be encouraged to stay in poor areas by improved educational facilities for their children. They are not likely to stay if their economic opportunities are better in wealthier areas, where educational facilities are also likely to be good. But the point is that if their economic opportunities are best in the poorer areas, they will be encouraged to stay there or go there if educational facilities are good, whereas otherwise they would not.

Although the above propositions are made with respect to rural areas, they are also valid for the poorer towns. Good schools also have favourable allocative effects in wealthier localities but it is the effect of improved services in poor localities made possible by provincial-municipal fiscal adjustment on which this study is focused.

Health and Social Services

The province now assumes most of the responsibility for public health, except in Halifax which is one of the wealthier localities, and with the new hospital plan, free ward care and diagnostic services are available to all of the citizens of the province. In effect, then, there are provincial transfers to the poorer localities. The localities are still responsible for capital costs, but even here the uniform provincial grants for hospital construction, also financed by the sales tax, provide for some transfers. The province takes responsibility for treating the curable, mentally ill who require institutional care and now contributes to the maintenance of municipal custodial hospitals for the mentally ill.

Buchanan argues that improvements in public health have effects similar to improvements in education by enhancing mobility and improving the quality of the part of the labour force which remains in the poor area, with the result that capital and natural resources are put to more effective use and incomes are raised. These favourable effects would seem to apply in Nova Scotia. Better health also enables children to get more benefit from their education and so accentuates the favourable effects of education already described.

The provincial provisions for public health services can be expected to have favourable effects on allocation of resources, although probably the effects are weaker than in the case of education. Improved hospital care increases the productivity of the labour force, but is not likely to have much influence on where people live and work.[31] To the extent

[31]Compare Buchanan, "Federal Grants," p. 214: "Few, if any, families are influenced in their occupational and locational choices by the availability of better hospitals, and those who are so influenced are either the better educated or the unproductive."

that it has, its effect will likely be favourable, in that, if hospital service in low-income localities is similar to that in high-income localities, workers will not be influenced in their decisions of where to live and work by the quality of hospital service, but will tend to live wherever they will be most productive, that is, wherever they can earn the highest incomes, which may be in a low- or high-income locality. The effect is weakened by the existence of the provincially-operated general hospital in Halifax whose facilities are available to all provincial residents. Provision for treatment of the mentally ill at the provincial institution at Dartmouth also increases the productivity of the labour force but has no allocative effects, except to the extent that families of the mentally ill may be drawn to the Halifax-Dartmouth area even though their working members may be more productive elsewhere.

The incurable insane in the municipal mental hospitals are not productive factors, so there are no direct allocative effects from improving these institutions. To the extent that members of families of the mentally ill in these institutions are productive, there will be some effect, for they will be less influenced in deciding where to locate by the quality of the mental hospitals if their standards are generally good, even in poor localities, and more influenced by economic factors. The allocative effect on them will be favourable.

In the field of social services, Buchanan considers Scott's argument—that higher levels of services in poor provinces made possible by federal grants are likely to impede mobility and so distort allocation of resources—to be sounder than in the case of the other services. He states that grants for the blind, aged, and otherwise infirm will encourage these groups to remain; but since they are usually not productive resources, he claims that there is no allocative effect except with regard to members of their families who are productive. He adds that it is to the advantage of the poorer provinces to have these groups move out, but probably to the advantage of the richer provinces to support transfers to prevent their migration. Although he feels that grants for unemployment relief probably distort the allocation of resources when unemployment is not general, he sees no particular reason why unemployment should be in low-income provinces.[32] But it so happens that, in the particular case of Nova Scotia, a low-income province, there has in recent years been persistently greater unemployment than in the country as a whole.

The situation of a province with respect to its localities is quite different from that of a federation with respect to the provinces. This

[32]*Ibid.*, pp. 213–14.

difference exists because the only flow of services into a province from other jurisdictions is from the federal government, while the localities receive services from both the provincial and federal governments. Some services which benefit people in the localities are provided directly by the federal government, as in the case of unemployment insurance, old age pensions for those over 70, and family allowances. Other services, such as old age pensions for those 65–69 years old who are in need, pensions for the blind and disabled, and social assistance, are administered by the province but partly financed by the Dominion. The social assistance is paid to the municipalities to assist them in meeting the costs of outdoor relief (municipal assistance) and of running their poor homes. The other payments are made by the provincial government directly to persons. Then there are services such as mothers' allowances and provisions for child welfare which are entirely provincial; the mothers' allowances are paid directly to individuals and the payments for child welfare are paid partly to local Children's Aid Societies, partly directly to foster parents, and partly to child-caring institutions.

It has already been suggested how unemployment insurance, family allowances, and old age pensions reduce the mobility of labour in Nova Scotia, especially in the poorer areas, and so distort the allocation of resources. But these services are all federal, except for old age pensions for those 65–69 years old, and so while of interest in considering the general question of the effects of public services on the allocation of resources in the province, they are not within the scope of this study since they are out of the control of the province.[33] It is worth pointing out, however, that contrary to Buchanan's contention that grants for the blind, aged, and otherwise infirm have no direct allocative effects since these groups are not productive resources, in the case of Nova Scotia such grants, especially old age pensions, do have some allocative effects to the extent that they enable the recipients to remain on farms without working them and so delay improvements in the use of some of the province's agricultural resources. Since the province administers the payments to the aged in the 65–69 year range, the payments to the

[33]It is not suggested that public services are undesirable simply because they adversely affect the allocation of resources. But it is of importance in framing policy to take into account their effects on the allocation of resources so that, if possible, distortion can be avoided. It is possible, for example, that farms not being actively farmed by old people living on them could be consolidated for farming purposes and worked by other farmers without interfering with the old people, and that loopholes in the law that permit chronic abuses of unemployment insurance could be plugged.

blind and disabled, and also pays part of the costs, it is partly responsible for the distortion, and this study is therefore concerned with it.

As already mentioned, there are two general types of unemployment
relief which are the direct responsibility of the municipalities but for
which unemployment assistance payments are now being made by the
province and the Dominion. One is institutional care in poor homes.
People cared for in these institutions are not capable of taking care of
themselves and are therefore not productive resources and, as
Buchanan points out, can have allocative effects only to the extent
that members of the inhabitants' families are productive. A raising of
standards of the municipal poor homes in the low-income municipalities will cause members of the labour force who have members of their
families in poor homes to be less influenced by the non-economic
factor of quality of poor homes in deciding where to work. They will
then work in a low- or high-income locality, according to where they
are most productive.

The other kind of unemployment relief relevant here is outdoor
relief for those unemployed who are not eligible for unemployment
insurance or whose benefits have run out. Some chronic periodic unemployment (seasonal unemployment) is relieved by federal unemployment insurance as noted earlier; but most relief required for the
chronically unemployed is provided by the municipalities. It is the
chronic unemployment of those who are employable that is particularly
serious from the point of view of allocation of resources.[34] It is difficult
to determine the distribution of chronic unemployment among the
municipalities, but one can say the higher are the payments to the
chronically unemployed who are employable, the less is the incentive
for them to seek employment elsewhere. The relief administered to
the chronically unemployed by the municipalities can reasonably be
assumed to impede desirable economic adjustments.

The above proposition probably has validity as a first approximation
but requires some modification. To the extent that amounts of relief in
the poorer municipalities are raised to meet standards required to
qualify for the federal and provincial grants administered by the
provincial government, the incentive of those chronically unemployed
who have malingering tendencies to seek jobs in other parts of the
province or outside of the province will be weakened. On the other

[34]Much relief given is for what is sometimes called "case poverty" arising from
such causes as the head of the family being alcoholic or mentally deficient and
therefore unemployable. Relief to such groups has no effect on allocation of
resources.

hand, for those earnestly desiring to take some initiative in alleviating their plight, more generous relief payments may not only give hope but help provide the means of moving to where jobs are available. Malingerers are a problem in all types of programmes for cushioning the distress resulting from unemployment. Their abuses, although they have important economic consequences, constitute in the first instance a sociological, psychological, and moral rather than an economic problem. When these modifications are taken into account, it seems questionable that the modest levels of relief in Nova Scotia have on balance a strongly distortive effect on allocation of resources.

The payment of mothers' allowances and provisions for child welfare by the province would not appear to have any appreciable effects on allocation of resources.

A CONCLUDING STATEMENT

The argument in this chapter shows that the kinds of economic adjustment which are desirable in Nova Scotia *vis-à-vis* the rest of the country are more in accord with Scott's contentions than with Buchanan's; that is, the marginal productivity of capital and of most types of labour is lower than in other provinces. The picture for internal adjustments is more complicated. In the case of towns suffering from loss of basic industry, with no sound alternative, outward movements of both capital and labour are called for—the type of adjustment Scott said might be desirable in some cases. The adjustments called for in the rural areas in farming, fishing, and forestry, requiring as they do greater ratios of capital to labour, are in line with Buchanan's prescription, with an important qualification. The marginal productivity of both labour and capital is low in much of the farming, fishing, and forestry operations, as they are presently carried on. If there were no alternatives to these types of operations, the desirable adjustment would be that suggested by Scott: move both labour and capital out. It is the opportunity for improved use of resources by rationalization of these primary operations, that is, for combining the factors of production in more productive ways, that leads to a prescription for adjustment similar to Buchanan's of using less labour and more capital.

The conclusions regarding the second question of the effect of public services for which the provincial and municipal governments are responsible on factor mobility within the province are more in line with Buchanan's treatment than with Scott's, in that it appears from the analysis that public services have some favourable and some unfavourable effects upon factor mobility. There are, however, some differences from Buchanan's conclusions, both in terms of the premises about the kinds of adjustments in the use of resources that are desirable and about the effects of some types of public services on factor mobility. These differences have been brought out in the course of the analysis and need not be repeated here. On balance, the effect of those public services discussed on allocation of resources would appear to be favourable, but the presence of some unfavourable effects and the difficulty in assigning precise weights to the favourable and unfavourable effects preclude the drawing of a completely unequivocal conclusion as to the over-all effects. Being able to make an unequivocal conclusion about the net effect of public services on allocation of resources, however, is less important than determining the effects of particular services so that these effects can be taken into account in framing policy in each case.

~~~ VII ~~~

Principles of Fiscal Adjustment

NOW THAT THE TYPES OF ADJUSTMENT conducive to better use of Nova
Scotia's resources have been sketched and the effects of public services
in question on factor mobility have been examined, the pattern of
provincial-municipal fiscal relations, most conducive to optimum use
of the province's resources, may be determined.[1]

THE PRINCIPLE OF FISCAL EQUITY[2] AND ITS APPLICABILITY
TO PROVINCIAL-MUNICIPAL FISCAL ADJUSTMENT

In his discussion of the pure theory of government finance, J. M.
Buchanan works with the "individualistic" theory of the state, which
regards the state as reflecting in its decisions the balancing of the
aggregate benefits from public services of the individuals who comprise the state against the aggregate costs to them of these services.
He rejects the alternative of what he calls the "organismic" theory,
which regards the state as an organic unit, as being of little use in

[1]There are many criteria according to which a fiscal system can be judged,
such as the traditional norms of equity, certainty, convenience, economy in collection, low cost of compliance, flexibility of revenue, and fiscal adequacy. The
validity of these norms is not denied here. But the focus of this study is on the
effect of provincial-municipal financial relations on economic development; and
even more particularly, on the way in which the principle of fiscal equity can be
applied by means of adjustments in provincial-municipal fiscal relations. To the
extent that the principle of fiscal equity has ethical virtues as well as economic
ones, the argument for implementing it is further strengthened.

[2]Buchanan's treatment of the principle of fiscal equity and of its application
to problems of federal finance is developed in two articles: "The Pure Theory of
Government Finance: A Suggested Approach," *Journal of Political Economy*,
XLVII (December, 1949); and "Federalism and Fiscal Equity," *American
Economic Review*, XL (September, 1950).

practical problems.³ While perhaps useful as an initial abstraction, as Professor Pigou uses it in his discussion of the theory of public expenditure,⁴ it is unacceptable on more fundamental grounds than on any concerning its practicability; for it implies the existence of collective wants in the sense of their being felt by the state as a collection of individuals which in itself is a "sentient organism"; whereas wants can only be felt by individuals as such, although, of course, they can arise from the fact that individuals live together in society and they may be capable of being satisfied only, or best, by collective action, as through governments.⁵ This line of reasoning leads back to the only approach that has ultimate validity in questions of public finance, that is, to considering the effect of public services and of the burdens of taxation on *individuals*.

In order to facilitate comparisons between the fiscal treatment of individuals for whom the level of benefits from public services might vary, Buchanan introduces the concept of the "fiscal residuum," which he defines as being equal to an individual's tax burdens minus his benefits from public services. "Only by a comparison of the residuums of individuals can the total effects of a fiscal system be analyzed and evaluated. Tax-burden comparisons alone are likely to yield quite different and perhaps misleading conclusions."⁶ The residuum defined the other way around, as being equal to benefits minus burdens, will be used here, so that an individual with a positive residuum would have an excess of benefits.

One of the advantages of taking benefits as well as burdens into account in this way is that it permits a more satisfactory approach to questions concerning the redistributive effects of a fiscal system. Buchanan notes that a progressive tax system does not necessarily redistribute income in an egalitarian way if, for example, those in the upper income brackets benefit more from public services financed by taxation than in proportion to their taxes, that is, have a positive residuum, and those in the lower income brackets benefit less than in proportion to their taxes, that is, have a negative residuum. This way of looking at a fiscal system is particularly useful in examining a new public service that is financed by a particular tax. An extension of a

³Buchanan, "The Pure Theory," pp. 496–8.
⁴A. C. Pigou, *A Study in Public Finance* (3rd edition, revised; London: Macmillan and Co., 1949), pp. 30–4.
⁵This point is carefully made in Antonio de Viti de Marco, *First Principles of Public Finance* (Translated by E. P. Marget; New York: Harcourt Brace and Co., 1936), p. 38.
⁶Buchanan, "The Pure Theory," pp. 501–02.

regressive tax, say a general retail sales tax, if accompanied by an increase in a service that especially benefits lower-income groups, such as "free" hospital care, may have egalitarian redistributive effects.

Another advantage, whether fiscal residua are used or not, and one of greater concern for this stndy, is that the rationale for grants or other types of transfer from rich provinces to poor provinces, or from rich localities to poor localities within a province, can be examined more clearly. There are two relevant points in considering the rationale for such transfers, which Buchanan develops. One has to do with equity in terms of equal treatment for similarly situated individuals;[7] the other with the effect of transfers on the allocation of resources. Buchanan argues that transfers[8] are desirable on both ethical and economic grounds: to permit similarly situated people in different provinces to be treated equally in terms of the net fiscal pressure on them as measured by their residua and, at the same time, to prevent distortion in allocation of resources which would result from unequal fiscal pressure on otherwise well-allocated resources, that is, from heavier pressure on an individual in a poor province or locality than he would bear in a rich province or locality.[9] Buchanan calls this concept of equal treatment of equals "fiscal equity." The principle of fiscal equity applies to both labour income and to income from capital. Thus, differential fiscal pressure in different provinces or localities may cause movements of capital or labour or both to where they are less productive. "If 'equals' are thus pressed more in one area than another, there will be provided an incentive for migration of both human and non-human resources into the areas of least fiscal pressure."[10]

Buchanan gives two cogent arguments to support his contention

[7]In many instances the "family" or "household" is a more relevant unit than the individual, but the term "individual" will be used here, for convenience.

[8]Buchanan presents some theoretical arguments in favour of effecting transfers by differential personal income taxation in the different provinces (Buchanan, "Federalism and Fiscal Equity," pp. 595–6). As long as the province was renting its right to levy personal income taxes, to the federal government, this method of effecting transfers with respect to the localities was not available, even if it were practicable otherwise. The use of differential provincial taxation as an adjustment device is discussed briefly in chapter IX.

[9]In considering questions of equity (justice), it is necessary to think in terms of similarly situated individuals in different provinces or localities. In considering questions of fiscal effects on allocation of resources, it is preferable to think in terms of the fiscal pressure on the same individual in different provinces or localities, although generally for convenience the term "similarly situated individuals" will be used even in the latter context.

[10]Buchanan, "Federalism and Fiscal Equity," p. 589.

that the appropriate political unit for the application of the principle
of fiscal equity is the whole country in spite of the heterogeneity of
the provinces or states which is inherent in a federation. (These arguments hold, if anything, more strongly for the application of the
principle within a province with respect to its localities, for each
province is more homogeneous than the federation of provinces of
which a nation consists.)

(1) Since the economy is national in scope, the diversified political
framework notwithstanding, the fiscal system should be designed to
interfere as little as possible with the optimum allocation of resources
on a national scale. Since the provinces vary as to average productivity,
as measured by income per capita, fiscal transfers are necessary to
make possible equal fiscal treatment of similarly situated persons in
different provinces. Otherwise, people in low-income provinces will be
subject to greater fiscal pressure than they would be in high-income
provinces, and will have an incentive to move themselves or their
capital, or both, to the higher-income provinces. In other words, a
province is poor because its average income is low; but it will likely
at the same time have many factors of production which are more
productive there than they would be elsewhere. In the absence of
equalizing fiscal transfers, the heavier fiscal pressures that will be
exerted on individuals of any given economic circumstances in a
low-income province will induce some uneconomic movements of
labour and capital from low-income to high-income provinces and
impede some economic movements of labour and capital from high-
income provinces to low-income provinces. As Buchanan puts it:

Requiring state areas to remain integrated in the national economy is
inconsistent with the forcing of the governmental units of these areas
to act as if the economies were fiscally separate and independent. This
inconsistency can only be removed by centralization of fiscal authority
or by the provision of some intergovernmental fiscal adjustment.[11]

(2) Income distribution is arrived at through the market forces
operating over the whole nation. If one of the functions of a fiscal
system is to alter this distribution according to some concept of social
justice, then "the fiscal system . . . should operate in a general manner
over the whole area of the economy determining the original distribution."[12] Otherwise, "the system necessarily operates in a geographically

[11]*Ibid.*, p. 590. This argument becomes all the stronger when applied in the
provincial context, where the localities are creatures of the provincial government.
[12]*Ibid.*, p. 590. Compare with the following statement relating to state grants-
in-aid, in State of New York, *Report of the New York State Commission on State*

discriminatory fashion."[13] In this same connection, it should be stressed that a prime virtue of the principle of fiscal equity is that it puts the emphasis on the effect of the fiscal system on the individual citizen rather than on political units. It makes sense to speak of equalization, where questions of economic welfare and justice are at issue, only with regard to individuals, not, in any ultimate sense, with regard to provinces and localities.

Buchanan's arguments are strengthened by the fact that even with perfect mobility of resources, that is, even when each factor is located where its marginal productivity is a maximum,[14] interprovincial or intermunicipal differences in per capita income will almost certainly persist. For only if all factors were homogeneous, or distributed, when all units of each factor were earning their maximum rewards, in the same proportions in all provinces (an extremely unlikely occurrence), or distributed in different proportions but in such a way that per capita incomes were the same (an even more unlikely occurrence), would per capita income be the same for all provinces. Without transfers and failing these unlikely conditions, the achievement of optimum allocation of resources is impeded because the fiscal pressure will be heavier on at least some factors in the poorer provinces than on otherwise similarly situated factors in the richer provinces, creating an incentive for them to move to the richer provinces.[15] The discussion in chapter v indicated that Nova Scotia, even if it were in economic equilibrium both with the rest of the country and internally, would have a lower per capita income than some of the other provinces and would also have discrepancies in per capita income among its municipalities.

Aid to Municipal Subdivisions (Legislative Document No. 58, memorandum submitted by the State Tax Commission; Albany, 1936), p. 356. "The term 'state aid' is perhaps a misnomer. Substantially all funds finding their way into the treasury of the state have been withdrawn from those of the citizens of all the municipal subdivisions. Government never created anything of considerable taxable value. Government garners from where the thrifty or skillful have already sown. The benefits of government should in turn be distributed according to the actual needs of the entire body politic. It is a long and devious journey from the 'horse and buggy' conditions of the past to the air-minded and high-flying attitude of the present generation. In many ways the necessities of a locality are neither wholly nor in the major part local. They carry with them a large element of the needs not only of their neighbours but also those of far distant localities."

[13]Buchanan, "Federalism and Fiscal Equity," p. 590.

[14]It is assumed here that non-monetary inducements are taken into account.

[15]The qualification "at least some" is necessary because with different distributions of the tax burden or of benefits, some taxpayers in a poor province or locality could be better off in terms of the fiscal pressure on them than similarly situated taxpayers in a rich province or locality.

As has already been pointed out in chapter ɪ, for the principle of fiscal equity to be fully applied in a federal country by means of grants, it *must* be followed through at the provincial and municipal levels to assure that similarly situated people within the province are accorded equal fiscal treatment. It was shown in chapter ɪɪɪ that the grants now being made by the federal government to the government of Nova Scotia, large though they may seem, are far from sufficient to permit as favourable fiscal treatment of Nova Scotians as similarly situated persons in the richest provinces. In any case, whether the principle of fiscal equity is applied at the federal-provincial level or not, it will still be appropriate to apply it at the provincial-municipal level. Buchanan himself considered that his analysis applied to fiscal adjustment among localities as well as among provinces although he did not pursue this application. Adjustment among localities is easier than adjustment among provinces. A province, holding the power over the localities it does, is free, to a degree the federal government in dealing with the provinces is not, to use conditional or unconditional grants or to alter the powers of the localities, without being concerned about poaching on the powers of another jurisdiction.[16] If, for example, a province considers it desirable on the one hand that the localities take some responsibility with regard to education and on the other that minimum standards be maintained throughout the province, it is free to charge the localities with this responsibility, even to specify the way their share of the necessary revenue is to be raised, to define the minimum standards it requires in as much detail as it chooses, and make grants, if it deems them necessary, to enable these standards to be maintained. Not only are there no constitutional barriers to provincial-municipal fiscal adjustment, but the greater uniformity of the local than of the provincial tax structures makes the application of the principle of fiscal equity a simpler, though perhaps still not an easy, task.

A CRITICISM OF THE USE OF THE FISCAL RESIDUUM IN

IMPLEMENTING THE PRINCIPLE OF FISCAL EQUITY

There is an important respect in which Buchanan's analysis must be called into question. He uses the fiscal residuum to measure the fiscal pressure on similarly situated individuals in different provinces

---

[16]As Buchanan puts it: "the scope for adjustment by non-fiscal means, through political or administrative devices (local government consolidation, state assumption of local functions, etc.), seems broader in state-local relations." ("Federalism and Fiscal Equity," p. 525.)

or localities and argues that if their residua are equal, their fiscal treatment will be equal.

The whole fiscal structure should be as neutral as possible in a geographic sense. An individual should have the assurance that wherever he should desire to reside in the nation, the *over-all fiscal treatment* which he receives will be approximately the same.[17]

Neither the tax burdens nor the standards of public service need be equal for "equals" in any of the states. Satisfaction of the equity criterion requires only that the residua be substantially the same.[18]

Buchanan, in working with residua in his discussion of fiscal adjustment among provinces, is trying to take account of the fact that even in provinces with the same fiscal capacity there would be differences in the levels of public services provided. But the question arises: does the equalizing of residua of similarly situated taxpayers necessarily make their "over-all fiscal treatment" the same? The answer is "no" because the *level* of services itself has a bearing on a person's welfare apart from the net fiscal pressure on him. Since the legislators or councillors have to determine the level of public services (as well as of taxes) for *all* of the residents of the province or locality, some residents will feel that their welfare would be enhanced by more public services and less private goods, and some the reverse.[19] For example, individual A may live in locality Y in which the people as a whole choose to maintain a lower level of educational services than in locality Z, and he may prefer to have available the higher level of services in Z even if his residuum would be the same in both places. And individual B living in Z may prefer the lower levels of services in Y even if his residuum would be the same in both places. The receipt of benefits costing the government $2,000 and the payment of taxes of $1,800 is not the same thing to an individual as the receipt of benefits costing $400 and the payment of taxes of $200, even though the residuum is the same ($200) in both cases. Transfers are still necessary

[17]*Ibid.*, p. 589, italics mine.
[18]*Ibid.*, p. 591.
[19]This situation arises from the fact that there are no close substitutes in the private economy for many public services. It is doubtful that any fiscal device could adjust for differential fiscal pressure in different provinces or localities arising in the way described here, since it arises from the fact that an individual is not free to choose the level of most of the public services made available to him. This element of coercion with regard to the level of services is generally recognized with respect to the taxes levied to pay for services. The coercion with respect to the level of services itself is the opposite side of the same coin, with the important difference that an individual may be coerced into having a *lower* level of public services than he wants and than he would be willing to pay for voluntarily.

to make it possible to equalize fiscal pressures of equals in rich and poor provinces and localities and can be justified on this ground; but the equalizing of residua is, in itself, insufficient to equalize "over-all fiscal treatment" of similarly situated individuals.

Nevertheless, where one objective is to enable all localities in a province to maintain a minimum level of services (especially general services), with equal burdens, the difficulties which would otherwise stem from the use of fiscal residua, because of the flaw in Buchanan's argument, do not arise.[20] The problem becomes one of equalizing burdens of similarly situated individuals.

In the case of Nova Scotia, the trend, as shown in chapter IV, is generally towards establishing the same minimum standards of the general public services throughout the province. It is true that to the extent some localities provide services above the minima, some differential fiscal pressures will be generated. In particular, as long as municipal fiscal capacities, as measured by the equalized value of property per capita, differ, the municipalities with the higher fiscal capacities will be more attractive to residents and to prospective residents, for any supplements to the minimum levels of services can be provided with a lower increase in the property tax rate than in municipalities with lower fiscal capacities and so are more likely to be provided, to the benefit of both the property owner and the resident who owns no property.[21] But if the minima are kept quite high, the effects of the differential pressure will not be very great. Moreover, the raising of standards in the richer localities will exert upward pressure on the minima which will tend to eliminate the differentials. The criticism of the use of the residuum is more serious in considering the

[20]Interestingly enough, although Buchanan did not in his earlier articles perceive this flaw in his argument, he did express the opinion that variations in the levels of particular services in different provinces stemmed mainly from variations in fiscal capacity and that if these variations were compensated by transfers, the levels of services would be brought into approximate equality ("Federalism and Fiscal Equity," p. 597). If he is correct, he no longer needs to rely on the faulty concept of equalizing fiscal treatment by equalizing residua.

[21]Buchanan makes a similar point in a recent paper. In this paper, while still upholding the general validity of the principle of fiscal equity, he points out a weakness in using residua in comparing the fiscal treatment of individuals similar to the one discussed above, although in a different context. In discussing the case of *quid pro quo* relationships between individuals and the state, where the residuum is zero, he argues: "The total fiscal situation in which the individual finds himself is determined . . . by the total tax pressure exerted on him by the fisc in comparison with the total benefits he received from having public services available to him." (A comment, kindly supplied directly by Professor Buchanan, which appears in the conference volume entitled *Public Finances: Needs, Sources, and Utilization* [New York: National Bureau of Economic Research, 1959].)

application of the principle of fiscal equity at the federal-provincial level than at the provincial-municipal level. In any case, it is not claimed that the principle of fiscal equity can be applied with great precision. At best, it can only be approximated.

The proposition that transfers should be made in order to make possible the equalization of residua of "equals" is still valid if the proviso is added that the level of services must also be the same. But if services are the same in the different localities, they can be ignored in examining differential fiscal treatment of similarly situated individuals. Moreover, the concept of the fiscal residuum is both valid and useful in examining the redistributive effects of a fiscal system with respect to income within any political unit.

Buchanan's central proposition, that in an economically integrated country or region the equalization of the fiscal treatment of similarly situated individuals should be made possible by transfers from the rich to the poor sections in order to prevent distortions in allocation of resources, is unaffected. What is called into question is his argument that the equalization of residua of similarly situated taxpayers will accomplish this end. Transfers are still necessary to permit equivalent benefits to be financed by equivalent burdens in rich and poor localities and are still justified by the fact that even in economic equilibrium per capita incomes of provinces and localities will differ. Given differences in natural resources and in locational factors of different areas, any programme designed to equalize per capita incomes of the areas would only result in gross distortion from the optimum use of resources, for there are bound to be, in equilibrium, considerable differences in per capita incomes resulting from the different mixtures of factors of production appropriate to each area. The equal fiscal treatment of similarly situated individuals throughout the country or throughout the province, to the extent it is practical, retains both its ethical and economic virtues and remains a better basis for transfers than the vaguer notion of fiscal need as between provinces or localities.

An important consequence of the acceptance of the principle of fiscal equity, as Buchanan points out, is that "the principle establishes a firm basis for the claim that the citizens of the low income states within a national economy possess the 'right' that their states receive sums sufficient to enable these citizens to be placed in positions of fiscal equality with their equals in other states."[22] Although the use of the term "right," even in quotation marks, may be subject to challenge, the strong economic and ethical arguments for equalizing transfers should

[22]Buchanan, "Federalism and Fiscal Equity," p. 596.

still remove from them the stigma, which has often been attached to them in the past, of being regarded as subsidies that smack of being handouts.

THE PRINCIPLE OF FISCAL EQUITY AND THE CONDITIONS
FOR ECONOMIC EQUILIBRIUM

It is worthwhile at this point to show more formally than has been done so far how provincial-municipal fiscal adjustment according to the modified principle of fiscal equity would be conducive to optimum allocation of resources.

The necessary condition for economic equilibrium (optimum allocation of resources) under conditions of perfect competition is that the marginal productivity of each factor of production must be the same in all of its uses throughout the region, with each unit of every factor earning its maximum possible reward, so that total production could not be increased by any sort of factor movement. This equilibrium is stable in that any departure from it will tend to be self-corrective, since a departure would result in the factor in question having a higher marginal productivity in one employment than in another and in its being enticed by the opportunity for greater remuneration to that employment in which its marginal productivity is higher.

What is required is a fiscal system which will not induce changes in factor allocation when the economic system is in equilibrium and which will not impede movements of factors towards their equilibrium allocation when the economic system is not in equilibrium. A fiscal system based on the principle of fiscal equity meets these requirements. If an individual, regardless of where he lived in the province, received the same level of public services and incurred the same tax burdens with respect to his given income, wealth, expenditure, and whatever other tax bases were used, he would have no differential fiscal pressure on him to move himself or his capital if both were employed where their marginal productivities were highest. If his marginal productivity or that of his capital, or both, were higher elsewhere, the inducement to move himself or his capital in the directions required for the restoration of economic equilibrium would remain.[23]

A policy of fiscal adjustment based upon the principal of fiscal equity may be called "neutral" in that it neither reinforces nor impedes geographical movements called for by the marginal productivity

[23]Provided, of course, that the fiscal system would not deprive him of all, or more than, his increased remuneration.

principle. Such a policy is in general advocated here. It should be noted, however, that desirable movements of labour and capital can be accelerated by withholding benefits or imposing particularly severe tax burdens for as long as these factors continue to be used where they are less productive than elsewhere. (Alternatively, the province could offer additional benefits or reduced burdens in the localities to which it wished to encourage them to move.) For example, if it is clear that a town has no economic future and that its inhabitants and their movable capital would be better employed elsewhere, the province could give notice that at the end of a given period of time sufficient for the factors to move, it would no longer give grants to support local services and would reduce the level of services it provided to the town's inhabitants. Or, to give another example, if it wished to discourage the continuation of low-income fishing operations in small villages, the province could refrain from improving the roads to these villages and build especially good roads into the fishing communities whose development it wished to encourage.

While governments may be reluctant to take such measures for humanitarian and political reasons, the possibility of their usefulness in some instances should not be overlooked. These measures could probably be applied only where it is considered desirable to move all of the labour and movable capital from a locality. Usually only some of the factors in a given locality are poorly allocated there. While there may be some instances where it would be possible to use differential fiscal pressure on individuals to accelerate economic adjustment where maladjustment is particularly intractable, it is unlikely that in general the application of unequal fiscal pressure as part of a scheme of fiscal adjustment can be made a sufficiently selective device for that purpose, quite apart from the probably overwhelming political and administrative difficulties that would be encountered.

Mention should be made of the fact that the condition for economic equilibrium, in terms of the marginal productivity principle described above, is met in a free enterprise economy only under conditions of perfect competition. What modifications need to be made to take account of the existence of imperfect competition?[24] Economic equilibrium from the social point of view requires the output of each firm to be that at which the marginal cost of the product equals its price, assuming that social costs and benefits are equal to private costs and benefits. From the point of view of allocation of factors of produc-

[24]"Imperfect competition" is used here to include monopoly, oligopoly, and monopolistic competition.

tion, the corresponding condition is that the value of the marginal product of each factor must be equal to its marginal cost and be the same in all of its uses. In the case of perfect competition, the meeting of these conditions is consistent with the aim of entrepreneurs to maximize their profits, but in the case of imperfect competition, it is not. The reason is that in a firm in a perfectly competitive industry, a factor tends to be used up to the point where the value of its marginal product is equal to its marginal cost; whereas in an imperfectly competitive industry, it tends to be used only up to the point where its marginal revenue productivity equals its marginal cost. In an economy in which there are varying degrees of competition, the value of total production could be enhanced by the movement of factors from the more competitive to the less competitive industries.

It is not necessary to go further into the intricacies of price theory here. It is sufficient to note that where there are varying degrees of competition, and Nova Scotia is no exception to this condition generally found in advanced capitalist countries, the allocation will tend to depart from the social optimum. Nor is it necessary to go into the arguments for and against a policy designed to induce each business firm to produce at the output where the marginal cost of its product equals its price, for it is the effect of provincial-municipal fiscal relations on allocation of resources which is of concern in this study.

Although fiscal adjustment according to the principle of fiscal equity would not likely eliminate departures from the optimum allocation of resources in an imperfectly competitive world, it may still be the best guide if more specific information is lacking as to the kinds of fiscal adjustments which are required to compensate for imperfections.[25] It also has the virtue of not impeding the implementation of other types of policy aimed at correcting the departures.

It appears that provincial-municipal fiscal adjustment based upon the principle of fiscal equity would be conducive to optimum allocation of the province's resources.

THE VARIATION OF INCOME AMONG LOCALITIES OF A PROVINCE AND AMONG PROVINCES

It might seem offhand that the localities of a province are more homogeneous with regard to per capita income than the provinces,

[25]For a discussion of the problem of determining the best position when one or more conditions for optimum equilibrium are lacking, see R. G. Lipsey and R. K. Lancaster, "The General Theory of Second Best," *Review of Economic Studies*, XXIV, 1 (1956–7), pp. 11–32. It appears that a geographically neutral

since the latter represent more diverse geographical regions, hence that the need for equalization is much less. But the reverse may very well be true; for the per capita income of each province is the outcome of averaging incomes of rich and poor throughout the province, while the per capita incomes of the localities of a province will be determined by less diverse economic conditions in much smaller areas and so will be subject to greater variation than those of the provinces. Thus there will likely be greater variation in the per capita incomes of localities for any province than in the per capita incomes of the ten provinces. For example, in 1958, the standard deviation of per capita incomes of those paying personal income tax was $235 for the Canadian provinces, and $289 for the eighteen counties of Nova Scotia. The coefficients of variation were 6.18 per cent and 8.71 per cent, respectively.[26] If the variation in income is greater for Nova Scotian localities than for the provinces of Canada, as the evidence just given indicates, then, if equalization of some sort is desirable, the need for it is even more urgent with respect to the localities of Nova Scotia than for the provinces of Canada. (Or, if equalization has resource-distorting effects, the distortion would be more severe for the localities.) Against this contention must be set the more limited functions assigned to the localities by the province compared with those assigned to the provinces by the British North America Act.

THE ADDITION OF THE EGALITARIAN POSTULATE

Although this study is more directly concerned with questions relating to the equal fiscal treatment of equals than with those relating to equitable treatment of unequals, sufficient comment will be made on the latter very important question relating to the redistribu-

---

system of fiscal adjustment, such as is proposed here, would be consistent with a "second best" solution for allocation of resources, since the burdens of taxation and the benefits from public services would be uniform with respect to all similarly situated factors of production.

[26]Calculated from Department of National Revenue, *Taxation Statistics, 1960* (Ottawa: Queen's Printer), Tables 1 and 5. Per capita personal income data would be preferable for this illustration, but they are not available for units below the provincial level. The taxable personal income data used are available only for the counties (including towns and cities) and for the cities and a few towns. Although the counties are not synonomous with municipalities in Nova Scotia, the variation in income for them gives a measure which is likely indicative of the variation for Nova Scotian municipalities and which is if anything on the low side because of the averaging out of incomes for the cities and towns and rural municipalities. The range was $3,402–$4,152 for the provinces and $2,697–$3,668 for the Nova Scotian counties.

tive effects of the fiscal system to show how it should be taken into account. Since both benefits and burdens must be considered, these redistributive effects can best be examined in terms of the behaviour of the fiscal residuum with changes in income (a use of the fiscal residuum which is valid). The problem of how the burden of taxation to pay for public services should be distributed among individuals with varying incomes is probably insoluble in absolute terms. Social justice with respect to this question is what society acting through its government deems it to be at any given time. Nevertheless, the vague notion that public services should be paid for according to ability to pay has wide acceptance. In the egalitarian spirit of the present time this criterion is generally, although not universally, believed to require a progressive tax system.[27]

Without discussing here the arguments in the literature of public finance related to this whole question, it will be assumed that it is at least desirable that the fiscal system have an egalitarian tendency in its redistributive effects. For a fiscal system to be egalitarian requires simply that the fiscal residuum of benefits minus burdens must decrease as income rises. This minimum requirement could be met even with a regressive tax system, providing the regressive tax burden increased more rapidly than benefit as income increased. Of course the more progressive the tax system is, and the greater the extent to which public services particularly benefit lower-income groups, the more egalitarian the fiscal system will be.

Figure 2 illustrates the egalitarian postulate that benefits minus burdens must decrease with income, both in terms of absolute benefit from public services and absolute tax burden, and in terms of rates of benefit and tax, with respect to income. Benefits are measured here in terms of the cost to the government of rendering them, and are assumed to be constant for all individuals regardless of income to simplify the illustration. Measuring benefit in this way is consistent with measuring tax burdens in terms of money income taken in taxes, and it avoids complications arising from the behaviour of marginal utility of income as income increases. In fact, the benefits from public services accruing to persons will vary with their circumstances, such as their tastes, or whether they have children of school age and whether they live in a town or in the country. These variations, which will occur at each income level no matter how benefits are measured, are

[27]For a critical view of the ability to pay principle and of associating it with progressive taxation, see M. Slade Kendrick, "The Ability to Pay Theory of Taxation," *American Economic Review,* XXIX (March, 1939), pp. 92–101.

A

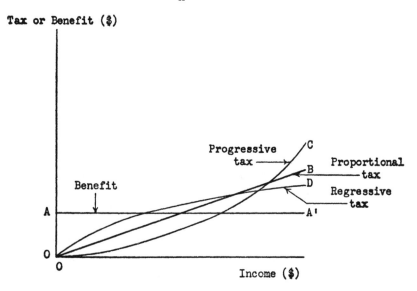

B

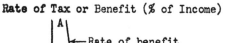

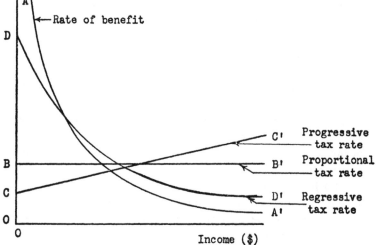

FIGURE 2. GRAPHICAL ILLUSTRATIONS OF THE EGALITARIAN POSTULATE

regarded as being averaged out here. The assumption that benefits from public services are constant for all individuals regardless of income permits a less rapidly falling regressive rate, for the egalitarian postulate to hold, than does the more likely situation that benefits will decrease with income. Of course, the money value of benefits *to the individual,* as opposed to their cost to the government considered above, would likely increase with income if the marginal utility of money declines quite rapidly with income.

Figure 2a illustrates the egalitarian postulate in terms of absolute benefit and burden, for all three kinds of tax system. It is necessary for all tax curves to cross the benefit curve if a balanced budget is at least approximated: the excess of benefits to those with low incomes must be offset by the excess of burdens of those with high incomes. The slope of the regressive tax curve is positive throughout the income range. If it became zero or negative, the egalitarian postulate would be violated.

Figure 2b illustrates the egalitarian postulate in terms of benefits and burdens expressed as percentages of income. The benefit curve is a rectangular hyperbola (the rate of benefit × income = the constant benefit). The postulate is clearly met by progressive and proportional tax rates. The progressive rate is represented in the chart by a positively-sloped straight line, but may be of any shape provided its slope is positive for all incomes. As already pointed out, for the egalitarian postulate to hold with a regressive tax system, the regressive tax burden must increase more rapidly than benefit as income increases. Expressed in terms of rates, this condition requires that the regressive tax rate must fall less rapidly than the rate of increase in income, where the benefit is constant for all incomes as is assumed here. The curve representing the regressive rate in the chart clearly satisfies the postulate, since past the point of intersection with the benefit curve it falls less rapidly than the benefit curve. It could even fall more rapidly than the benefit curve and still satisfy the postulate as long as the rate of benefit × income (= the amount of benefit) minus the rate of tax × income (= the amount of tax) decreases with income.

It is most likely that in practice the Canadian public finance system (and *a fortiori* that of Nova Scotia) will be egalitarian when benefits as well as burdens are taken into account. Many important public services benefit the poor more in absolute terms than the rich, even when they are of general benefit to society and cannot therefore be valued only in terms of the gains to the immediate recipients. This is especially true of the kinds of services with which the provinces are

concerned. Social welfare measures (including social security), public
health, education, and recreational and cultural facilities (including
parks) are probably all of this nature. Other services, such as defence,
are likely of equal benefit to all. Services relating to the protection and
enhancement of property may be of greater benefit to the rich, but are
provided to some vague degree on a benefit basis.

THE EFFECT OF INCOME TRANSFERS ON ALLOCATION OF RESOURCES

It is now possible to summarize the arguments that have been developed regarding an important contention of A. D. Scott. Scott argues
that transfers made in federal countries from rich to poor provinces,
providing as they do services for people in poor provinces, interfere
with the migration of labour according to the marginal productivity
rule. Since public services form a larger part of the real incomes of
low-income than of high-income groups, they will, he argues, especially
impede the mobility of low-income groups, which are likely to be
especially numerous in a low-income province.[28] Presumably, if these
arguments were valid, they would also apply to provincial transfers to
poor municipalities. In this regard, three lines of argument will be
considered briefly.

(1) In the Nova Scotian context it was shown that improved services
of the kind which the province and the municipalities provide would
probably on balance have corrective rather than distortive effects on
allocation of resources, although some kinds of services to some kinds
of localities, such as roads to some fishing villages, may have distortive
effects.

(2) Buchanan maintains that the generality of the argument that
distortion of allocation of resources results when levels of public services in poor provinces are raised is further reduced if it can be shown
that even perfect mobility of resources need not eliminate inter-area
differences in per capita income. The validity of his position has been
demonstrated both theoretically and, with respect to Nova Scotia,
empirically. Without transfers, under such conditions, the allocation of
resources cannot reach its optimum because the fiscal pressure will be
heavier on factors in the poor provinces or localities than on similarly
situated factors in the rich provinces or localities, creating an inducement for them to move to the richer ones. (It has already been pointed
out that the cost to the government of supplying a unit of a service to

[28]A. D. Scott, "A Note on Grants in Federal Countries," *Economica*, XVII
(November, 1950), p. 419.

an area, relative to its population density and economic potential, must
be taken into account.)

(3) Even if public services do form a large part of the real incomes
of people in low-income groups, and therefore make private rewards
relatively less important for them when they compare their position
with the possibly better positions they can obtain elsewhere in other
provinces or other municipalities, this situation is a result of the decision of society that the provision of public services on such a scale
is desirable.[29] It is no argument for providing inferior services or
imposing heavier tax burdens in poor provinces and localities. People,
especially poor people, in rich localities as well as in poor ones, have
their incentives to move blunted because the public services make
them better off than they would otherwise be and so diminish the
marginal utility of higher private incomes they could obtain by moving
in response to better opportunities elsewhere. This blunting effect
depends on there being some substitutability between private and
public goods.

Scott is actually arguing that an egalitarian fiscal system impedes
the movement of resources to their most productive uses. While it is
useful to point this out, it is important to recognize that such distortion
is attributable to a redistributive fiscal system that society deems best
serves its interests rather than to federal or provincial transfers as
such. In fact, federal and provincial transfers are necessary to equalize
the fiscal pressure on similarly situated individuals in rich and poor
provinces or localities. Consider, for example, two individuals, C and
D, with equal incomes in the form of wages, C in a low-income
province or locality P, and D in a high-income province or locality Q,
before any transfer, that is, when fiscal pressures on them are unequal.
Transfers are made from Q to P and are allocated so that the fiscal
pressure on C and D is the same. C and D need not have the same
occupation. If they have, and if they are equally competent, they are
in geographical equilibrium and neither of them should move. (Without transfers C would be pressed to move to Q, even if he were somewhat less productive there.) If they have not, C might be more
productive in Q and therefore be induced to move. Or D might be
more productive in P, even though the *average level* of incomes is
lower there, and so would have an incentive to move there. C and D
may have a relatively high or low income, compared with others in
the two provinces or localities.

[29]A similar point is made in J. E. Meade, *The Theory of International Economic
Policy*. II. *Trade and Welfare* (London: Oxford University Press, 1955), p. 419.

All three of these lines of argument point to conclusions that, in the Nova Scotian context at least, are opposed to Scott's arguments about the effects of transfers on allocation of resources. Transfers could be used in ways in which they would distort the allocation of resources, but they would not do so if they were used in accordance with the principle of fiscal equity.

CONDITIONAL AND UNCONDITIONAL GRANTS AND PUBLIC WELFARE:
THE CONFLICT OF LOCAL AND PROVINCIAL INTERESTS

If the principle of fiscal equity is to be implemented by means of federal equalization grants to provinces and provincial equalization grants to localities, should such grants be conditional or unconditional?

The Conflict of Federal and Provincial Interests in the Case of Federal Grants[30]

The answer depends in part upon the answers to two other questions: (1) How much importance is to be attached to the doctrine of financial responsibility and (2) is maximizing of provincial or of national welfare to have priority? Conditional grants, since they must be used for specified services, are more in accord with the doctrine of financial responsibility and with expenditures being made according to national interests, while unconditional grants violate the doctrine of financial responsibility but are conducive to expenditures being made according to provincial interests. If conditional grants require matching in whole or in part, there is the additional consideration (related to the second question above) that provincial expenditures may be distorted by the drain of funds from other provincial services to provide part or all of the matching expenditures. Whether matching is required or not, a conditional grant is less conducive to welfare as far as a province is concerned than an equivalent unconditional grant.

Scott ably compares the effects on provincial welfare of conditional and unconditional federal grants using the indifference curve technique.[31] His main conclusion is essentially that, whether the federal conditional grant requires matching or not, whether the matching is contingent upon a minimum expenditure by the province for the

[30]For an interesting, although not conclusive, discussion of this question with reference to the United States, see J. A. Maxwell, *The Fiscal Impact of Federalism in the United States* (Cambridge: Harvard University Press, 1946), chap. xvii. See also the same author's *Federal Subsidies to the Provincial Governments in Canada* (Cambridge: Harvard University Press, 1937), *passim*.

[31]A. D. Scott, "The Evaluation of Federal Grants," *Economica*, XIX (November, 1952), *passim*.

service in question or not, whether the federal share has a limit or not, the province would be better off if an unconditional grant were made equal to the conditional grant which the province would receive in equilibrium. Furthermore, if a grant does require a minimum outlay by the province and if the amounts of expenditure involved are quite large, "the outcome may be the extension of taxation and spending by the state well beyond the point which would have been chosen if the state had freedom of action."[32] This analysis takes into account only the discrepancy in welfare between a conditional and an equivalent unconditional grant for the province itself. It does not take into account the discrepancy in the opposite direction for the country as a whole which may outweigh the discrepancy for the province.[33] For a scheme of conditional grants requiring matching to be in accord with the principle of fiscal equity, it would be necessary either for the provinces' share to be scaled in such a way that no province would have to impose heavier tax burdens to pay its share than any other province, or for the burdens incurred in the matching of conditional grants to be equalized within the framework of a concomitant scheme of unconditional grants.

As already noted earlier in this chapter, Buchanan argues with respect to the United States that there is very little conflict between state and national interests in the way equalizing unconditional grants would likely be used by the states. He believes that states, if they had sufficient revenue, would of their own accord undertake at adequate levels the functions the federal government wishes to encourage.

It seems highly probable that, if an equalization policy of the sort proposed here were carried out, national interests would be adequately served without any national government direction of state expenditure. The low income states provide deficient educational standards largely because of their fiscal plight; remove this, and it seems likely that their service standards would approach those of other states without any restraints upon state budgetary freedom.[34]

Buchanan is inclined to regard the doctrine of financial responsibility as a traditional precept without much intrinsic merit, which should not be permitted to impede the implementation of sound principles of fiscal adjustment.

[32]*Ibid.*, p. 391.

[33]Scott recognizes this problem, but argues: "The resolution of the deadlock cannot be achieved by economics alone." (*Ibid.*, pp. 392–3.) He probably has in mind that there is no objective means of comparing the discrepancies, since it requires making interpersonal comparisons between the people in the whole country and the people in the province in question.

[34]Buchanan, "Federalism and Fiscal Equity," p. 597.

For services of national importance but best administered by the provinces, conditional grants would probably not lead to much conflict of interest. For services solely or very largely of provincial interest, conditional grants would not only constitute too blatant interference with provincial autonomy but would be impractical where the nature of such services varies from province to province. In any case, there would be little conflict between national and provincial interest in regard to such provincial services and hence less justification for conditions.

In so far as federal grants are made for the purpose of equalization, in accordance with the principle of fiscal equity, Buchanan argues cogently that they should be unconditional:

> The fact that the central government must enter the adjustment process and transfer funds to effectuate equity in the over-all fiscal system does not . . . imply that the central government should be allowed to direct the recipient states in the allocation of their expenditure. There seems no apparent reason why there should be more central interference or direction in the financial operation of the recipient states than in that of the non-recipient states. States are made claimant through no fault of their own or of their respective citizens. They are made claimant by the income distribution arising from a resource allocation and payment in a national economy. Once it is recognized that the transfers are adjustments which are necessary to coordinate the federal political structure with a national economy, and as such are ethically due the citizens of the low income state units, then the freedom of these citizens to choose the pattern of their states' expenditure follows.[35]

The choice of conditional or unconditional grants will in fact depend to a large extent upon the traditions of the country. The strong tradition of financial responsibility in the United States has resulted in the use solely of conditional federal grants there, whereas financial dependence of the provinces on the federal government from the time of Confederation combined with insistence on provincial autonomy in Canada, especially by Quebec, has favoured unconditional grants, although an extensive network of conditional grants has also evolved. In Australia, the emphasis on unconditional grants is also strong, for somewhat similar reasons.

The Applicability of Conditional and Unconditional Grants to Provincial-Municipal Fiscal Adjustment

To what extent do these arguments concerning federal conditional and unconditional grants apply to provincial grants to municipalities?

[35]*Ibid.*, p. 598.

Since a provincial government faces no constitutional barriers in dealing with its municipalities (as the federal government does in dealing with the provinces which have certain sovereign powers), its scope for using conditional grants is much greater than the federal government's, at least with regard to general services. Although there are no constitutional barriers to prevent the province from withdrawing or altering the delegated powers of the localities, or even dissolving the localities, there are very real political barriers to such action. In the course of time, the localities, with their functions, have become so cemented in the political fabric of the province, that major alterations in their powers are not likely to be taken lightly by the citizenry of the province. It would not be easy, for example, to merge two small rural municipalities, even if obvious gains in administrative efficiency would ensue.

Even so, the provincial government can require that standards, set provincially, be met by non-recipient as well as by recipient localities—something the federal government could not think of doing with respect to non-recipient provinces. Buchanan's argument for unconditional grants is therefore far less relevant to provincial-municipal than to federal-provincial relations. Furthermore, a provincial government having a smaller unit to administer than the federal government can, in administering conditional grants to localities, take local conditions into account more satisfactorily than can the federal government in dealing with the provinces.

There would still be some conflict between provincial and local interests if conditional grants were used by the provinces with respect to services primarily of local concern, such as services relating to property, community development, and recreational facilities. The municipalities owe their existence primarily to the general recognition of the fact that the nature and extent of these local services can best be determined by the people whom they directly concern. It is likely that if the municipalities were of equal fiscal capacity (or if their unequal fiscal capacities were compensated for by unconditional grants) and if they were free to determine the level of the general services, such as education (as well as of the local services), for which they were responsible, there would be considerable variation in the level of the general services.[86] Since the services are of a general nature and since the

[86]Otherwise there would be no need in the case of Nova Scotia, for example, for the elaborate definitions of educational services in the province's educational programme; or for requiring the municipalities to meet standards to qualify for

province's jurisdiction over them is complete, it is quite appropriate for the province to exert as much control over them as it deems in the general provincial interest even when one outcome is a distortion of municipal expenditures from those that would be made if they were entirely under municipal control. Moreover, as already pointed out earlier in this chapter, the principle of fiscal equity is easier to apply if minimum levels of general services are maintained throughout the province.

One effect of conditional grants to municipalities accompanied by the imposition of minimum standards of services and by the requirement that the municipalities make a minimum contribution to their support is that the municipalities tend to become tax-collecting and administrative units of the provincial government. As far as the fiscal impact on the persons in the municipalities is concerned, the effect may be much the same as if the provincial government took over both full fiscal and full administrative responsibility for the services.

It appears that the conflict of provincial and local interest arising from conditional grants is much less significant in provincial-municipal relations than is the conflict of federal and provincial interests in federal-provincial relations. To the extent it exists in the former case, it is with respect to local services with which a province would not likely wish to interfere in any case. Conditional grants are quite appropriate for general services, probably even superior to unconditional grants,[37] while unconditional grants are appropriate for local services. Such a combination of grants is quite consistent with the

---

unemployment assistance grants and grants for mental hospitals. It appears that Buchanan's contention that if the states have sufficient funds they will supply the nationally-desired level of services does not hold at the municipal level in Nova Scotia. (A number of people interviewed referred to the "penny-pinching" attitude of some Nova Scotian municipalities, not all of them poor.) The variation in the level of services would be in part a result of the small size of the municipalities (which is less conducive to an averaging out of attitudes than in larger units), and in part of the fact that some of them are rural and some urban, leading to different social conditions and therefore different attitudes.

[37]Whatever importance may be attached to the doctrine of financial responsibility, conditional grants are more consistent with the doctrine than unconditional grants. As in the case of federal grants to provinces, for provincial conditional grants requiring matching to be in accord with the principle of fiscal equity, it would be necessary for the municipalities' shares to be scaled in such a way that no municipality would have to impose heavier tax burdens to pay its share than any other municipality, or for the burdens incurred in the matching of conditional grants to be equalized within the framework of a concomitant scheme of unconditional grants.

application of the principle of fiscal equity in a province,[88] as is also the complete assumption of responsibility for general services by the provincial government. There is not only greater scope for adjustment at the provincial-municipal level than at the federal-provincial level by non-fiscal means, that is, by political and administrative devices, but also by fiscal means.

[88]Of course, equalization might not be the only aim of grants. Grants might also be made to effect a general adjustment in the relation between functions and revenues of municipalities. Both elements of equalization and of adjustment for a general deficiency of revenues might be present in a system of grants (as might stimulation of particular services). At present, as was shown in chapter IV, the provincial government in Nova Scotia is making conditional and unconditional grants, both of which have equalization and deficiency elements. Some of the conditional grants have strong stimulative elements.

VIII

The Present Fiscal System in Nova Scotia and the Criterion of Fiscal Equity

THE FISCAL EQUITY CRITERION calls for equal fiscal treatment of similarly situated individuals in the different municipalities of the province. It is not enough that the residua of similarly situated individuals be equal; their actual benefits from public services must be equal. The criterion would be met if, regardless of where he lived in the province, an individual would receive the same public services and would incur the same tax burdens with respect to his given income, wealth, expenditure, and whatever other tax bases were used.

It is unlikely that these rigid conditions could be met in practice; nor is it desirable that they be met. Even with complete centralization of all services, both general and local, in the hands of the provincial government there would be differences in the levels of some services which it would be practical to supply in rural areas compared with urban ones—street lighting and sewers, for example. Without centralization, there are bound to be variations in local services even among municipalities of the same type (urban or rural), as well as variations in the supplements to general services. There would be such variations even if the fiscal capacities of municipalities of each type were equal. To require a perfectly uniform level of services would result in considerable loss of satisfaction of wants, for a municipality would not be free to determine the level of local services or to supplement the general services according to the consensus of its own citizens. Nevertheless, the fiscal equity criterion, with these reservations, can be useful as a guide to an evaluation of any given provincial-municipal fiscal system and as a basis for adjustments to that system.

The purpose of this chapter is to show how the provincial-municipal fiscal system in Nova Scotia measures up to the fiscal equity criterion. There are also brief discussions of the fiscal flexibility of the provincial government, and of the redistributive elements in the provincial-municipal fiscal system. Means by which the fiscal system might be adjusted in accordance with the fiscal equity criterion, to the extent that it does not already measure up to it, will be discussed in the next chapter. The approach in this chapter will be based in part upon the distinction between general and local services developed in earlier chapters. The local services are deemed to be the particular concern of the localities, while some general services are the concern of both the province and the localities and some only of the province. With complete centralization in the hands of the provincial government of *all* public services presently provided by the province and the municipalities, and with uniform policies of taxation and expenditure throughout the province, the principle of fiscal equity would be most fully implemented. An individual with given income and wealth and expenditure would receive the same benefits from public services and incur the same burdens of taxation anywhere in the province. Violations of the criterion occur essentially because municipalities are responsible for local services and, in part, for some general services, and because they have unequal fiscal capacity.

Provincial Taxes

Since the provincial tax system operates uniformly throughout the province, there is no inter-municipal discrimination arising from it. An individual pays the same liquor monopoly prices for alcoholic beverages, the same percentage retail sales tax,[1] and the same taxes on his motor vehicle and on each gallon of gasoline he uses regardless of where he resides in the province.

Purely Provincial Services

These services are, in general, provided at a uniform level throughout the province although the differences in urban and rural conditions,

[1]The retail sales tax may have a higher incidence in rural areas, compared to towns and cities, to the extent that prices are higher in the country, but access to mail order facilities of department stores tends to eliminate such differences.

especially with respect to density of population, inevitably lead to some differences in services. In the case of roads, for example, some people in the rural areas have property abutting on paved highways, and some are provided with only gravel or dirt roads and are a long way from paved highways. The provincial government builds and maintains paved highways according to priorities. Trunk roads ringing the province and cutting across it in a number of places are designed to link up the larger centres of population and at the same time put the unpopulated rural areas within as easy reach of pavement as is practicable. It is inevitable that some people in the rural areas will be better served than others. Nearness to pavement will also influence the value of rural property. There will be varying levels of services with respect to highways in each of the rural municipalities but the services provided will not be related to their being rich or poor. The sort of road available to people in remote parts of poor municipalities will by and large be comparable to that available in remote parts of rich municipalities. It is in this sense true to say that similarly situated people in the different rural municipalities are treated similarly even with respect to roads.

Local Services, and General Services for Which the Municipalities Have Some Responsibility

The question of unequal fiscal treatment of similarly situated individuals does arise with respect to those general services for which the municipalities have some responsibility as well as for local services for which they are entirely responsible, that is, with regard to all services provided by the municipalities. Municipalities of unequal fiscal capacity cannot provide, on their own, the same levels of services without there being different burdens on their taxpayers. Significant differences in fiscal capacity do in fact exist among the Nova Scotian municipalities, whether fiscal capacity is measured in terms of per capita value of taxable property (Table XXXIV) or in terms of per capita income, using per capita incomes of payers of personal income tax, by counties (Table XXXV). The range of the index in the second column of Table XXXV is less than it would be if similar data for municipalities could be shown separately, since using the larger county unit results in considerable averaging out of the high and low values for the municipalities within each county.

Since at present nearly all local taxation revenue is obtained from the property tax[2] on real property and tangible personal property, per

2See Tables XIV and XVI.

TABLE XXXIV

UNIFORM ASSESSMENTS PER CAPITA OF NOVA SCOTIAN MUNICIPALITIES,[a] 1958

	Assess. per cap.	% of av. assess. per cap.[b]		Assess. per cap.	% of av. assess. per cap.[b]
		Towns and Cities			
Amherst	$1805	96	Middleton	$3011	159
Annapolis Royal	2933	155	Mulgrave	837	44
Antigonish	2061	109	New Glasgow	2669	141
Berwick	2788	148	New Waterford	985	52
Bridgetown	2653	140	North Sydney	1424	75
Bridgewater	2945	156	Oxford	1076	57
Canso	765	40	Parrsboro	1181	63
Clark's Harbour	1177	62	Pictou	1168	62
Dartmouth	3540	187	Pt. Hawkesbury	1168	62
Digby	2144	113	Shelburne	1550	82
Dominion	519	27	Springhill	749	40
Glace Bay	1431	76	Stellarton	966	51
Hantsport	3320	176	Stewiacke	1574	83
Inverness	634	34	Sydney Mines	1104	58
Kentville	3107	164	Trenton	3170	168
Liverpool	2507	133	Truro	3035	161
Lockeport	1350	71	Westville	659	35
Louisburg	1689	89	Windsor	2299	122
Lunenburg	3320	176	Wolfville	2727	144
Mahone Bay	1613	85	Yarmouth	1892	100
Halifax	3907	b	Sydney	3158	b
		Rural Municipalities			
Annapolis	1341	119	Hants, East	1260	112
Antigonish	773	69	Hants, West	1397	124
Argyle	558	49	Inverness	663	59
Barrington	618	55	Kings	1358	120
Cape Breton	1118	99	Lunenburg	1066	95
Chester	1380	122	Pictou	1040	92
Clare	867	77	Queens	2453	217
Colchester	1419	126	Richmond	496	44
Cumberland	1222	108	Shelburne	870	77
Digby	981	87	St. Mary's	1047	93
Guysborough	462	41	Victoria	1363	121
Halifax	2121	188	Yarmouth	1208	107

SOURCE: Calculated from Government of Nova Scotia, *Report of the Revaluation Commission for the Province of Nova Scotia, 1958*, using 1956 population figures from *Annual Report of Municipal Statistics, 1956*.

[a]These assessments include real property and tangible personal property. They are estimates of "full value" made on the basis of the municipal unit, rather than individual property, and include all taxable property and all property owned by the federal and provincial governments and their Crown Corporations for which grants in lieu of taxation are made.

[b]The average values of per capita assessments are $1889 for towns, and $1128 for rural municipalities. These are unweighted averages as they are more appropriate for comparing the values of the municipalities than weighted averages. (The weighted averages are $1990 for towns and $1351 for rural municipalities.) Since there are only two cities, there is not much point in computing the percentages of average assessment per capita for them.

TABLE XXXV

INCOME PER TAXPAYER OF PAYERS OF PERSONAL INCOME TAX
FOR THE COUNTIES OF NOVA SCOTIA,[a] 1958

	Income per taxpayer	Income per taxpayer as % of average	Number of taxpayers as % of population[b]
Annapolis	3279	99	9.4
Antigonish	3313	100	9.2
Cape Breton	3689	111	18.3
Colchester	3402	102	14.4
Cumberland	3335	100	11.9
Digby	2968	89	7.4
Guysborough	2697	81	5.4
Halifax	3678	111	24.4
Hants	3451	104	10.0
Inverness	2930	88	5.9
Kings	3271	98	11.8
Lunenburg	3652	110	11.7
Pictou	3464	104	12.4
Queens	3668	110	15.1
Richmond	3076	93	7.7
Shelburne	3566	107	5.4
Victoria	2953	89	7.3
Yarmouth	3338	101	9.5
AVERAGE	3318[c]	100	

SOURCE: Calculated from Department of National Revenue, *Taxation Statistics, 1960*, Table 5; using 1956 population figures from D.B.S., *Census of Canada, 1956*, Bulletin 3–1, Table 1.

[a]Includes all taxpayers in each county, regardless of whether they live in cities, towns, or rural municipalities.

[b]This column is given to show that the variation in taxable capacity, to the extent it can be measured with the data in this table, is even greater than is indicated by the second column.

[c]This is an unweighted average, as it is more appropriate for comparing the values of the different counties than a weighted average. The weighted average, that is the income per taxpayer for the province as a whole, is $3,839.

capita value of taxable property provides the best index of municipal fiscal capacity. That there is considerable variation in tax burdens is indicated by Table XXXVI. As would be expected, the burden of the property tax is greater, on the average, for cities and towns than for the rural municipalities, since the cities and towns provide a wider range of services. Table XXXVII shows the great variation in municipal assessments in 1958 in relation to the equalized assessments made by the Revaluation Commission. (One should bear in mind that the commission's assessments were made on the basis of the municipal unit not on the basis of each individual property.) There is also great variation in assessments *within* many municipalities which would

TABLE XXXVI

PROPERTY TAX REVENUES OF NOVA SCOTIAN MUNICIPALITIES IN 1959[a]
AS PERCENTAGES OF THE 1958 UNIFORM ASSESSMENTS

Towns and Cities

Amherst	2.6%	Kentville	2.4%	Pt. Hawkesbury	3.2%
Annapolis Royal	2.1	Liverpool	2.8	Shelburne	3.0
Antigonish	3.0	Lockeport	2.8	Springhill	4.3
Berwick	2.3	Louisburg	4.1	Stellarton	3.6
Bridgetown	2.5	Lunenburg	2.1	Stewiacke	2.0
Bridgewater	2.2	Mahone Bay	3.5	Sydney Mines	2.8
Canso	5.8	Middleton	2.1	Trenton	2.4
Clark's Harbour	3.0	Mulgrave	6.1	Truro	2.2
Dartmouth	1.8	New Glasgow	2.5	Westville	4.1
Digby	2.6	New Waterford	4.0	Windsor	2.9
Dominion	4.5	North Sydney	3.3	Wolfville	2.4
Glace Bay	2.9	Oxford	3.7	Yarmouth	3.9
Hantsport	2.6	Parrsboro	3.0	Average (towns)	3.1[b]
Inverness	3.2	Pictou	2.9		
Halifax City	2.9			Sydney	2.6

Rural Municipalities

Annapolis	1.7%	Cumberland	1.7%	Lunenburg	1.9%
Antigonish	3.1	Digby	2.3	Pictou	2.2
Argyle	2.6	Guysborough	4.9	Queens	1.5
Barrington	3.4	Halifax	1.7	Richmond	3.4
Cape Breton	2.3	Hants, East	1.8	Shelburne	2.7
Chester	1.8	Hants, West	1.9	St. Mary's	1.8
Clare	2.0	Inverness	3.0	Victoria	2.5
Colchester	2.0	Kings	1.6	Yarmouth	2.2

AVERAGE   2.3[b]

SOURCE: Calculated from *Report of the Revaluation Commission for the Province of Nova Scotia, 1958*; and *Annual Report of Municipal Statistics, 1959*.
[a]Includes real and personal property taxes and grants paid in lieu of property taxation by federal and provincial governments and enterprises of these governments.
[b]Unweighted average.

reduce the extent to which the principle of fiscal equity can be effectively implemented as long as the variation persists.

The policy of the province at present is to continue to charge the municipalities with responsibility for some of the services which are no longer regarded as being only local in character, that is, for general services, but to help them financially, in various ways, to perform them, and in addition to make some unconditional grants which may be applied either to local or general services.

Provincial Fiscal Practices and the Fiscal Equity Criterion

There are a number of kinds of equalization[3] with regard to municipal services in present provincial fiscal practices. The main ones are:

[3]The term "equalization," as used here, is not synonymous with equalization

TABLE XXXVII

ACTUAL MUNICIPAL ASSESSMENTS IN NOVA SCOTIA IN 1958
AS PERCENTAGES OF UNIFORM 1958 ASSESSMENTS MADE
BY REVALUATION COMMISSION

Towns and Cities

Amherst	29.4%	Kentville	57.1%	Pt. Hawkesbury	57.8%
Annapolis Royal	24.6	Liverpool	60.8	Shelburne	77.3
Antigonish	57.7	Lockeport	28.7	Springhill	52.8
Berwick	88.4	Louisburg	72.8	Stellarton	57.6
Bridgetown	72.4	Lunenburg	92.6	Stewiacke	23.5
Bridgewater	57.9	Mahone Bay	74.4	Sydney Mines	29.3
Canso	32.5	Middleton	74.8	Trenton	26.6
Clark's Harbour	95.9	Mulgrave	50.2	Truro	90.1
Dartmouth	40.1	New Glasgow	85.5	Westville	42.3
Digby	77.1	New Waterford	26.7	Windsor	91.0
Dominion	52.9	North Sydney	28.3	Wolfville	72.6
Glace Bay	26.1	Oxford	76.4	Yarmouth	71.8
Hantsport	25.0	Parrsboro	26.1	Halifax City	76.4
Inverness	45.6	Pictou	38.4	Sydney	23.9

Rural Municipalities

Annapolis	17.6%	Cumberland	14.9%	Lunenburg	53.6%
Antigonish	91.5	Digby	19.8	Pictou	24.6
Argyle	87.5	Guysborough	21.7	Queens	77.9
Barrington	59.4	Halifax	34.4	Richmond	50.8
Cape Breton	11.0	Hants, East	24.0	Shelburne	69.6
Chester	79.9	Hants, West	75.2	St. Mary's	78.6
Clare	78.9	Inverness	32.0	Victoria	96.6
Colchester	22.0	Kings	12.9	Yarmouth	88.8

SOURCE: Calculated from *Report of the Revaluation Commission for the Province of Nova Scotia, 1958.*

(1) Unconditional per capita grants, the size of the per capita grant varying with the type of municipality, being largest for the cities and smallest for the rural municipalities. (2) Conditional grants which cover a certain proportion of costs of municipal services, provided standards are met. The social assistance grants (for municipal poor homes and outdoor relief) covering two-thirds of the net costs, the grants to mental hospitals covering one-half of the net costs, the grants for administration of local welfare services covering half the costs, and the sharing of costs of highways passing through towns and cities are all of this type. The municipalities are not compelled to qualify for these grants. (3) Conditional grants for education which take into

according to the principle of fiscal equity. Equalization is a more general concept. It simply means any fiscal adjustment that tends to compensate for differences in municipal fiscal capacity. Note also that in neither case is the aim to equalize fiscal capacity itself. To achieve such an end would require that per capita tax bases themselves be made equal for all localities so that, for example, all localities would have equal per capita incomes, a result quite inconsistent with optimum allocation of resources.

TABLE XXXVIII

DIVISION OF MUNICIPAL EXPENDITURES IN NOVA SCOTIA INTO LOCAL AND GENERAL SERVICES,[a] 1959

	Cities		Towns		Rural municipalities		All municipalities	
	$'000	% of total	$'000	% of total	$'000	% of total	$'000	% of total
Local services								
General government[b]	1,121	7.2	788	6.5	970	8.4	2,879	7.4
Protection to persons and property[c]	3,024	19.6	1,856	15.4	615	5.3	5,495	14.0
Public works[d]	1,102	7.1	1,206	10.0	38	.3	2,346	6.0
Sanitation and waste removal	576	3.7	276	2.3	55	.5	907	2.3
Recreation and community services	529	3.4	192	1.6	58	.5	779	2.0
Other, including capital charges out of revenue	32	.2	434	3.6	48	.4	514	1.3
Debt charges[e]	3	—	4	—	101	.9	108	.3
TOTAL LOCAL SERVICES	6,387	41.2	4,756	39.4	1,885	16.3	13,028	33.3
General services								
Health								
Public Health	222	1.4	40	.3	20	.2	282	.7
General hospitals[f]	318	2.0	243	2.0	444	3.8	1,005	2.6
Mental hospitals	442	2.8	314	2.6	696	6.0	1,452	3.7
TOTAL HEALTH	982	6.2	597	4.9	1,160	10.0	2,739	7.0
Social welfare								
Municipal assistance	327	2.1	279	2.3	702	6.0	1,308	3.3
Child welfare	127	.8	143	1.2	257	2.2	527	1.3
Other, including grants	36	.2	17	.1	18	.2	71	.2
TOTAL SOCIAL WELFARE	490	3.1	439	3.6	977	8.4	1,906	4.8

TABLE XXXVIII (*Continued*)

	Cities		Towns		Rural municipalities		All municipalities	
	$'000	% of total	$'000	% of total	$'000	% of total	$'000	% of total
Debt charges[a]	7	—	10	.1	8	.1	25	.1
Education[a]								
Costs, except debt charges	4,505	29.1	4,215	34.9	6,251	53.9	14,971	38.3
Debt charges, schools	996	6.4	518	4.3	1,001	8.6	2,515	6.4
TOTAL EDUCATION	5,501	35.5	4,733	39.2	7,252	62.5	17,486	44.7
TOTAL GENERAL SERVICES	6,980	44.8	5,779	47.8	9,297	81.0	22,156	56.6
Unallocated debt charges and other costs (mostly local)	2,099[h]	13.6	1,535[i]	12.7	303[j]	2.6	3,937	10.1
TOTAL ALL SERVICES	15,466	100.0	12,070	100.0	11,585	100.0	39,121	100.0

SOURCE: Calculated from various data in *Annual Report of Municipal Statistics, 1959.*

[a]Only actual expenditures on services (including debt charges) are included. Adjustment items such as discounts, deficits, surpluses, and provision for reserves are excluded. Discount on debenture sales is included. As a result, the totals differ from those given in *Annual Report of Municipal Statistics.* Public utilities operated on a pricing basis are not included except for deficits paid on their account by municipalities. Joint expenditures, special district and area charges, and expenditures of village commissions and other similar commissions are included. The allocation of joint expenditures among the three types of municipality and between general and local services is quite rough.

[b]An undetermined part of the costs of general government, which includes legislative and administrative costs, should be allocated to general services.

[c]Includes fire protection, law enforcement and corrections, street lighting, civil defence, etc.

[d]Includes streets, sidewalks, sewers, etc.

[e]These debt charges are related to joint expenditures, special district and area charges, and village commissions and other similar commissions. The balance of the debt charges, except for education, are not allocated.

[f]Includes per capita hospital tax.

[g]Includes costs of ordinary public education, payments to schools for the blind and deaf, and payments for vocational schools. Provincial contributions to municipalities for education costs are not shown in the table. For costs other than debt charges, they were (in thousands of dollars): cities, 889; towns, 2,425; rural municipalities, 8,673; total, 11,987. For debt charges, they were: cities, 7; towns, 203; rural municipalities, 841; total, 1,041. Total provincial contributions were: cities, 896; towns, 2,628; rural municipalities, 9,514; total, 13,038.

[h]Of which $2,065,000 is debt charges, $34,000 unclassified expenditures.

[i]Of which $1,499,000 is debt charges, $36,000 unclassified expenditures.

[j]Of which $301,000 is debt charges, $2,000 unclassified expenditures.

account both the cost to the municipality of providing public education at the standards defined in the Foundation Program and municipal fiscal capacity measured by equalized valuation of property. Participation in this scheme is mandatory. These three types of grants are listed in order of the increasing degree of control exerted by the province. The third type is about as far as the province could go without completely taking over administrative and financial responsibility for a service.[4] This complete centralization is the fourth type of equalization found in Nova Scotia. The province has taken over full responsibility for public highways, hospitalization at the public ward level, and nearly all public health services except in Halifax. And it will probably not be long before the province assumes complete responsibility for the mentally ill.[5] It appears, too, that the responsibilities for maintaining jails will be reduced as a result of the federal government's, and perhaps also the provincial government's, assuming increased responsibility for prisoners.

In addition to the grants listed above, there are grants for general hospital construction, on a per bed basis, the grants to Children's Aid Societies, and the various shared grants for child care. The grants to Children's Aid Societies, however, are not grants to municipalities, although they do affect the child welfare services available to the municipalities. The provincial grants for hospital construction are similar in nature to the social assistance and mental hospital grants, as they are designed to cover a certain proportion of costs (about 25 per cent, or about 40 per cent if the federal grant is included). The grants for child care are also of this type.

In Table XXXVIII an attempt has been made to separate the local and general services for all three kinds of municipality. While, as indicated in some of the footnotes to the table, the allocation is only approximate, it serves to give some indication of the relative importance of local and general services and of particular categories of these services. This kind of information is very useful in assessing the importance of departures from the principle of fiscal equity with respect to the different services. A departure with respect to a service

[4]The province could go a bit further without completely centralizing a service; it could assume complete financial responsibility and leave some administrative responsibility in the hands of the municipalities.

[5]This opinion was expressed by a number of persons interviewed. The fact that Nova Scotia is the only province not completely responsible for the mentally ill strongly suggests that it is only a matter of time before Nova Scotia follows suit.

which is a minor item in municipal budgets is less serious than a similar relative departure with respect to a service which is a major item. The table will be referred to at times in the following discussion. One important observation from the table is that the general services are far more important, relatively, for the rural municipalities than for the towns or cities. This difference is to be expected, since most of the local services provided by towns and cities are not appropriate to rural areas. But it means that if the rural municipalities were deprived of their responsibilities for general services there would be little left to justify their continued existence.

Conditional grants of fixed proportions, with standards. The provincial grants for social assistance and for municipal mental hospitals have some equalizing effect, in that all municipalities meeting the standards have the same proportion of the costs of these services paid, but the balance of the costs remains a heavier burden for the poor municipalities (poor in terms of value of taxable property per capita) since no account is taken of their fiscal capacity.[6] Much the same can be said about the provincial sharing of costs of portions of highways passing through cities and towns. That is, in order to meet the standards and qualify for the provincial grants, a heavier burden must be imposed on the taxpayers in a municipality with a low per capita value of taxable property than in one with a high per capita value. These grants, therefore, do not meet the fiscal equity criterion, whatever their virtues in promoting minimum standards of the services concerned, although the larger the proportions of the services paid by the province, the closer the criterion comes to being met. For example, the criterion is closer to being met by the social assistance grants which cover two-thirds of costs than by the grants for mental hospitals which cover only one-half. Table XXXVIII shows that in 1959 mental hospitals accounted for 3.7 per cent and municipal assistance (including costs of operating poor homes and outdoor relief) 3.3 per cent of municipal expenditures. Costs of these services comprise a small part of total services, especially for towns and cities (they total 12 per cent for the rural municipalities). The provincial grants for hospital construction are similarly defective in meeting the criterion, as are the various grants made for child welfare.

[6]Value of taxable property per capita is a fairly good index of municipal fiscal capacity where most of the municipal revenue from taxation is obtained from the property tax; but for greater precision the costs of providing the services in question should also be taken into account, as they are in the programme of fiscal adjustment in chapter IX.

The conditional grants for education. The province's Foundation Program for education is to a considerable extent designed in accordance with the principle of fiscal equity in providing for a uniform minimum level of educational services and in aiming for a uniform burden for the municipal share, in all of the municipalities. There are, however, five elements which result in departures from the principle of fiscal equity: (1) the 25 per cent minimum provincial contribution for non-capital costs; (2) the choice of the 80-cent rate on equalized assessment to calculate each municipality's share of the costs; (3) variations in actual costs of the Foundation Program from the standard costs allowed by the provincial government in calculating grants, and variations in actual costs among municipalities; (4) variations in assessments within the municipalities; and (5) inaccuracies in the equalized valuation on the municipal unit basis. The first two, which are inherent in the formula, are of particular interest at this point. Departures due to the third could be eliminated only by the provincial government periodically revising the allowable costs in the Foundation Program and adjusting these costs to take account of variations between municipalities. The last two, although important, are difficult to measure. Departures stemming from them are dependent upon assessment practices and will be reduced as these practices are improved.

As already noted in chapter iv, the Pottier Commission recommended the 25 per cent minimum payment to the wealthier municipalities on grounds of political expediency, and the province implemented this recommendation. It was unfortunate that the commission and the province found it necessary to distort what is in many respects a sound formula by this compromise. The result is that the richer municipalities are favoured over the poorer ones.

Some recapitulation and examples are needed to show the effect of the 25 per cent minimum provincial payment clearly. The municipal share of the costs of instruction, maintenance, and transportation in the Foundation Program is determined by applying the rate of 80 cents per $100 (.8 per cent) to the municipality's equalized assessment. The municipal share expressed as a ratio of the non-capital part of the cost of the Foundation Program is called the "municipal proportion" and the provincial share (one minus this ratio) is called the "provincial proportion."

For example, in the case of the town of Amherst the three non-capital costs in the 1957–8 school year were $204,985.82. Amherst's share of these costs (using the 1958 valuation) would be .8 per cent of $18,593,603, or $148,748.82, the province paying the balance of

$56,237.00.[7] The municipal proportion would be 72.56 per cent (from $148,748.82/$204,985.82) and the provincial proportion 27.44 per cent. In addition the province would pay 27.44 per cent of the capital costs allowable in the Foundation Program.

With the 25 per cent minimum applying, the province pays 25 per cent of the three non-capital costs for all municipalities with provincial proportions in the range 0–25 per cent. However, it contributes to capital costs only according to the provincial proportions. As a result, the share of the non-capital costs for all municipalities with provincial proportions within the 0–25 per cent range is less than that determined by the 80-cent rate, and all other municipalities bear the full burden of the 80-cent rate. For example, the three non-capital costs for Bridgewater were $105,649.02 in the school year 1957–8. The 80-cent rate would yield $104,733.27 (.8 per cent of $13,091,659). The resulting provincial proportion would be .87 per cent (from 100.00–$104,733.27/ $105,649.02 × 100). But the province would pay a minimum of 25 per cent of $105,649.02, or $26,412.26, and the town would pay only $79,236.76, which it could raise with a burden of only 61 cents ($79,236.76/$104,733.27 × 80), that is, .61 per cent, on its equalized assessment. The province would, however, pay only .87 per cent of Bridgewater's allowable capital costs. For municipalities with provincial proportions within the range 0–25 per cent, which nevertheless receive the 25 per cent minimum payment, the burden of non-capital costs is least for a municipality with a provincial proportion of zero per cent and increases over the range until at 25 per cent it becomes equal to that of the municipalities beyond that range.

When a flat-rate grant is added onto an equalization scheme as was done here, the result is not in accord with the principle of fiscal equity. Even without the flat-rate grant, there would be some departure from the principle of fiscal equity in that a few municipalities could finance the Foundation Program with less than the 80-cent levy, and so impose a lighter burden on their taxpayers than the other municipalities. This latter departure carries over into the sharing of capital costs, which is not modified by a minimum payment.

The provision by some municipalities of educational services in excess of the Foundation Program may lead to some departure from the principle of fiscal equity, but such departures are not likely to lead

[7]The data used for this illustration and for the one relating to Bridgewater are from Government of Nova Scotia, *Report of the Revaluation Commission for the Province of Nova Scotia, 1958,* and from schedules supplied by the Department of Education.

to serious differences in fiscal pressure on similarly situated persons in different municipalities. Furthermore, the main point being argued here is that provincial transfers should as far as possible be made in accordance with the principle of fiscal equity. As long as the municipalities are left with the direct responsibility for a service they should be free, if their residents as a group so desire, to raise its level above the required minimum. To withhold this freedom would result in a reduction of the welfare of the residents of the province; and it would constitute repugnant and unwarranted interference with their activities.

Table XXXVIII shows that education is by far the most important item in municipal budgets, accounting for 44.7 per cent of the total for all municipalities and for 62.5 per cent of the total for the rural municipalities. The considerable extent to which the principle of fiscal equity is implemented with regard to public education is therefore all the more significant on this account.

Provincial assumption of general services: centralization. Centralization as has taken place in the cases of highways, the provision of hospital ward care and diagnostic services, and, to a lesser degree, public health is the most effective way of implementing the fiscal equity criterion. There are, of course, other points of view from which the means of adjustment should also be considered, such as administrative efficiency and the maintenance of local interest and participation.[8]

The per capita levy. A new element in provincial-municipal fiscal relations is the annual levy by the province on each municipality. The levy is a way of compelling municipalities that have inadequate hospital facilities to help pay the capital cost of hospitals where some of their residents are treated. However, it bears more heavily on the municipalities with relatively low values of taxable property (based on a uniform valuation) and so is inconsistent with the principle of fiscal equity. If the provincial government wished to make a levy consistent with that principle, it could determine the rate on the total equalized value of taxable property in the province necessary to raise the desired amount, and apply that rate to each municipality in order to determine the levy on it.[9]

Unconditional grants. Unconditional grants are being taken up last because discussion of them is relevant to the question of application of the principle of fiscal equity with respect to local services, which will be dealt with in the next section. The unconditional grants are paid by the province to the municipalities on a per capita basis, the per capita

[8]See chapter x for a discussion of these.
[9]An alternative to this method is given in chapter IX.

grants at present being $3.213 for cities, $2.10 for towns, and $.21 for rural municipalities. They are not closely related either to the differences in services performed by the three types of municipality or to the varying fiscal capacities of the municipalities. Unconditional per capita grants, by their nature, cannot be used to implement the principle of fiscal equity, except in the limiting case where they pay for all of the services in question performed by the municipalities. For whatever the balance of funds which must be raised by the municipalities to maintain some given level of service, the burden will be heavier in the poorer municipalities. To the extent it is appropriate that the different types of municipality should provide different levels of local services (especially the rural municipalities compared with the towns and cities), it is consistent with the principle of fiscal equity that smaller grants be given to the type of jurisdiction providing the smaller number of services, as long as the variation in grants between types of municipality is an accurate reflection of the level of local services they perform, and as long as the principle of fiscal equity is applied for each type of municipality. But this is anticipating the following chapter somewhat; the essential point to be made here is that the unconditional grants presently being made by the province to the municipalities (the only provincial grants available for local services), which in 1959 amounted to $987,000[10] and accounted for less than 8 per cent of the cost of local services,[11] are not in accord with the principle of fiscal equity; nor do they appear to have any other defendable basis.

The grants to towns and cities of $200 per mile of streets are also unconditional, in that they may be used for any purpose and do not have to be matched. They, too, are not in accord with the principle of fiscal equity, for reasons similar to those just given above. Nor do they take into account the likely substantial differences in costs of maintaining streets in different municipalities, for example, between gravel that is adequate for most streets in some municipalities and pavement that is required for most streets in other municipalities.

Local Services and the Fiscal Equity Criterion

It has already been assumed that the local services are the appropriate concern of the municipalities. If it could be established that property taxation, to the extent proceeds are used for local services, is taxation of property owners according to benefits received, then if assessments were uniform within each given municipality, all similarly

[10]See Table XXI.
[11]See Table XXXVIII.

situated taxpayers in the different municipalities would be treated equally and the principle of fiscal equity could be said to be applied. But although the element of benefit is greater with respect to local services, local services are still far from being provided on a *quid pro quo* basis to individual taxpayers.

Even for such services as the provision of fire and police protection, street lighting, sidewalks, and garbage removal, there is no close correspondence between cost or value of service and the value of property. It costs as much to remove a can of garbage from the door of a hovel as from the door of a mansion, and it is not possible to say that the owner of the hovel values the service less than the owner of the mansion.[12]

To the extent that special assessments are used, as in providing sewers and paving streets and sidewalks, the *quid pro quo* element is strong, but even here the benefits extend beyond the property owners who pay the special charges and the element of coercion characteristic of a tax is present. Moreover, as Table XIV shows, special assessments form a very small part of municipal revenues. The *quid pro quo* element is probably stronger with respect to licences and permits and the other similar revenue sources.

The element of benefit that connects local services and property taxes is one of general benefit to all the members of the community rather than one of measured benefit to particular individuals. The element of benefit derives from the direct and personal interest in the amenities of the locality of all those concerned and from the ability of members of the community to adjust the level of the services to their desires without those outside of the locality being very much affected.[13] The connection between local services and property taxation stems mainly from local services being of the type best performed by local governments, and from the property tax being the best source of local

[12]Professors Shultz and Harriss provide another illustration: "the owner of a 'firetrap' building with a low value and low tax might get more benefit from fire protection than the owner of a fireproof building on which the tax is much greater." (William J. Shultz and C. Lowell Harriss, *American Public Finance* (6th edition; Englewood Cliffs, N.J.: Prentice-Hall, Inc., 1954), p. 428.

[13]Compare Edward H. Spengler, "The Property Tax as a Benefit Tax," *Property Taxes* (New York: Tax Policy League, 1940), pp. 165–73. Spengler concludes that the property tax is a "benefit tax," because "at least part of the property tax revenue goes to pay for services and for capital investment which are of benefit, directly and indirectly to the property which is taxed" (p. 172); but he nevertheless opposes payment for these services by fees: "It is vital to recognize that the broad collective interest with respect to such services is paramount, even though in some instances there is present a clear element of individual benefit" (p. 172).

revenue, largely because it is the only major revenue source which can be administered efficiently by small municipal units.[14]

If the differences in per capita property values of different municipalities are taken into account, any given level of services will require a higher rate of tax in a municipality with a low per capita value than in a municipality with a high per capita value. And so the principle of fiscal equity will be violated because owners of properties of the same value in different municipalities will not be treated equally. The picture is further complicated by the fact that property values will tend to be depressed in municipalities with high tax rates to the extent capitalization takes place. Nevertheless, the fact is that there is a high degree of negative correlation between real and personal property taxes in 1956 as a percentage of the 1958 equalized valuation, and the per capita 1958 valuation; tax rates are in general low in the localities in which per capita assessments are high. The coefficients of linear correlation were −.842 for rural municipalities and −.587 for towns, and the coefficients of determination .709 and .344. The lower degree of correlation for the towns is to be expected, since the range of variation in the services they provide is greater than in the rural municipalities.

Since the unconditional per capita grants are not in accord with the principle of fiscal equity, and since local services cannot be regarded as being provided on a pricing basis, and since there is considerable variation in municipal fiscal capacity, the fiscal equity criterion is not met (in the sense of not being approximated) at present in Nova Scotia in regard to local services.

MUNICIPAL TAXES IN NOVA SCOTIA

Property Taxes

Since, to a considerable extent, the successful application of the principle of fiscal equity depends upon local assessment and taxation policies, it is of interest to examine them, at least briefly. As already noted, municipalities in Nova Scotia levy both real and personal tangible property taxes. Halifax also levies a business tax. In 1959 these taxes together accounted for 75.8 per cent of all municipal revenues and 91.4 per cent of revenues raised locally. They clearly dominate the local tax field. In the same year, the poll tax which all municipalities also levy yielded only 2.7 per cent of total municipal revenues

[14]See Shultz and Harriss, *American Public Finance*, pp. 427–9, for a good brief discussion of the distributional aspects of the property tax.

and 3.3 per cent of revenues raised locally. The usual miscellaneous assortment of licences, permits, rents, concessions, franchises, fines, and fees yielded about the same amount as the poll tax.[15]

Tables XIV and XVI show that the real property tax is by far the more important of the two property taxes. Real property is difficult enough to assess on a satisfactory basis but personal property is even more difficult.[16] Table XXXIX gives some indication of the wide variation in the assessment of personal property as between municipalities. No doubt the variations in assessment of real and personal property are also considerable within some municipalities.

Until recently the towns and rural municipalities were required by the Assessment Act to assess all items of personal property with some specified exceptions; but when the Pottier Commission made its equalized assessment, in 1954, of all taxable real and personal property on a municipal unit basis it observed:

> The assessment of personal property in the Province of Nova Scotia was so chaotic in many Municipal units that it was impossible to determine the ratio of assessment. In some of these units there was no assessment at all for a particular kind or type of personal property . . . , in others the assessment was more than full value.[17]

An amendment to the Assessment Act in 1956 now permits the assessment of household furnishings and personal effects at a percentage of the value of the real property. There has been a tendency for municipal units to adopt this procedure or to abolish assessment of household furnishings and personal effects and substitute a higher poll tax, although an effort is still made to assess personal property on business premises. The local taxes are levied, except for the City of Halifax, at a uniform rate on all taxable real and personal property on the assessment rolls.

[15]See Table XIV.

[16]For a discussion of some of the difficulties see, for example, Shultz and Harriss, *American Public Finance*, pp. 396–409. Reference has already been made to the particularly great difficulties of assessing timber land; these are discussed thoroughly in A. Milton Moore, *Forest Tenures and Taxes in Canada* (Tax Papers, No. 11; Toronto: Canadian Tax Foundation, 1957), *passim*. See also J. Harvey Perry, *Taxation in Canada* (2nd edition; Toronto: University of Toronto Press, 1953), pp. 273–84; K. Grant Crawford, *Canadian Municipal Government* (Toronto: University of Toronto Press, 1954), chaps. xiii, xiv, and xv; and especially the *Report of the Royal Commission on Public School Finance* (*The Pottier Report*; Halifax: Queen's Printer, 1954), pp. 20–7, and D. C. Rowat, *The Reorganization of Provincial-Municipal Relations in Nova Scotia* (A report prepared for the Government of Nova Scotia Municipal Bureau, Institute of Public Affairs, Dalhousie University; Halifax, 1949) pp. 85–9.

[17]*Pottier Report*, p. 25.

TABLE XXXIX

RATIO OF MUNICIPAL ASSESSMENTS OF PERSONAL PROPERTY
TO COMMISSION VALUATION, 1958

Towns and Cities

Amherst	.31	Middleton	.82
Annapolis Royal	.30	Mulgrave	.43
Antigonish	.63	New Glasgow	.91
Berwick	.88	New Waterford	.37
Bridgetown	.76	North Sydney	.38
Bridgewater	.77	Oxford	.68
Canso	.18	Parrsboro	.31
Clark's Harbour	1.10	Pictou	.61
Dartmouth	.30	Port Hawkesbury	.67
Digby	.84	Shelburne	.70
Dominion	.65	Springhill	.54
Glace Bay	.49	Stellarton	.94
Hantsport	.23	Stewiacke	.17
Inverness	.51	Sydney Mines	.32
Kentville	.74	Trenton	.35
Liverpool	.74	Truro	.95
Lockeport	.31	Westville	.43
Louisburg	.74	Windsor	1.01
Lunenburg	.83	Wolfville	.73
Mahone Bay	.80	Yarmouth	.99
City of Halifax	.66	City of Sydney	.16

Rural Municipalities

Annapolis	.11	Hants, East	.20
Antigonish	.84	Hants, West	.77
Argyle	.79	Inverness	.38
Barrington	.63	Kings	.44
Cape Breton	.16	Lunenburg	.59
Chester	.69	Pictou	.15
Clare	.58	Queens	.84
Colchester	.21	Richmond	.48
Cumberland	.86	Shelburne	.37
Digby	.21	St. Mary's	.73
Guysborough	.13	Victoria	.95
Halifax	.40	Yarmouth	.78

SOURCE: As for Table XXXIV.

When personal property is assessed at some fixed percentage of real property it becomes in effect a supplement to the real property tax levied as an occupancy tax directly on the occupant who may own or rent the property. When this stage of the evolution of the personal property tax is reached, it would seem that the tax might just as well be abolished and the tax on real property raised to make up for it. The tax would not then reach tenant-occupiers directly but would affect them indirectly, although less certainly,[18] in the rents they paid. And they would presumably pay the poll tax. When the abolition of

[18]This lack of certainty gives support to the case for an occupancy tax, although it must be borne in mind that the indirect effect of an occupancy tax on the owner of rented property is also uncertain.

the occupancy tax was suggested to a highly experienced assessor in Nova Scotia, he replied, in a letter:

> Many . . . feel that an occupancy tax should be imposed for two reasons. First, the poll tax is difficult to collect and the write-offs are much higher than [the] tax on personal property. Secondly, there is merit to the idea that as many persons as possible who enjoy the privileges of citizenship and services of the town should appear on the Assessment Roll and receive Asesssment Notices and Tax Bills like real property owners. Others argue that the elimination of personal property is restricting the tax base at a time when municipalities are seeking additional sources of revenue.

But, if the personal property tax levied as an occupancy tax is in effect a supplement to the real property tax, the tax base would not be restricted by consolidating the two taxes. Even so, the proposition that an occupancy tax is superior to the poll tax (if the poll tax is regarded as the alternative) may have some merit. In any case, the movement towards relating the personal property assessment to the real property assessment will improve the index of the fiscal capacity of municipalities based upon per capita assessment, because of the greater precision with which real property can be assessed. Such improvement will in turn increase the precision of this index as a guide in implementing the principle of fiscal equity.[19]

The City of Halifax[20]

The City of Halifax imposes higher rates of taxation on commercial property than on residential property. In 1961 the rates were $2.15 per $100 of assessment for residential property and $4.95 per $100 for commercial property.[21] Halifax also levied for many years a house-

[19]An improvement in local assessment practices is also important to this end. The appointment, in 1956, of a Director of Assessment to the Department of Municipal Affairs to advise the municipalities and of directors of assessment in most of the municipalities, and the holding of short courses for assessors by the department since 1952 have already resulted in big improvements.

[20]The best recent source of information on the taxation system of the City of Halifax is the City of Halifax, *Report of the Commission to Investigate the Taxation System in the City of Halifax* (Halifax, 1957). Justice V. J. Pottier, Q.C., was the sole commissioner.

[21]The residential rate is applied to rented residential property, although before 1955 the commercial rate was applied. Both rates include a fire prevention tax of $.09 per $100. The assessments of residential and commercial real estate were 82 per cent and 90 per cent, respectively, of sales values in 1957. (*Ibid.*, p. 99.) The commission found that residential tax burdens in Halifax were "at a reasonably high level" compared with other Canadian cities (p. 30) and that the commercial taxes were "slightly less than two and a quarter times the average of other cities in Canada" (p. 31). Market values have generally risen since 1957. Revisions of assessments in 1957 and 1960 have probably kept assessed values at about 80–90 per cent of market values.

hold tax on occupants at the residential rate on an assessment equal to 10 per cent of the residential real property assessment, and a business tax on occupants of commercial property, at the commercial rate, on 50 per cent of the assessed value of the real property. And it levies an occupancy tax at the residential rate on 25 per cent of the assessed value of property of certain clubs that are of a non-profit nature. This tax is in addition to the real property tax, which is levied at the residential rate. The household tax was abolished at the end of 1959. As payment of the household tax, or a share of it where there was more than one principal occupant, exempted persons from paying the poll tax, and as the household tax was often less than the poll tax, the city did not lose all of the revenue it previously obtained from the household tax. It did lose the revenue from those living in their own homes, who are thereby exempt from the poll tax. In 1959, the household tax yielded about $333,000 and the poll tax $272,000 in revenue, and in 1961, the poll tax yielded about $500,000, a net reduction over-all of about $105,000.[22] Both the household tax and the business tax are vestiges of the personal property tax.

The dual tax rate on residential and commercial property is unique to Halifax among Canadian municipalities, although in its report the Commission to Investigate the Taxation System in the City of Halifax supports the practice while advocating a fixed relation between the two rates which would at the same time reduce the very heavy burden on commercial property owners.[23] It argues that the traditional adherence to the belief that a single rate is desirable ignores the fact that payers of real property taxes on commercial property have their tax burden reduced by being allowed the tax as an exemption in paying federal income taxes, and the fact that they can pass on some of the balance of the tax in the prices of their goods and services (a good deal of it to outsiders who shop in Halifax), neither of these forms of relief being available to the home owner.[24]

[22]Office of the assessor, City of Halifax.

[23]From 1943 until some adjustments were made following a reassessment in 1955, the residential rate was fixed at $3.50 per $100 (at the old level of assessments) and the commercial rate allowed to rise to accommodate the need for increased revenues. The commercial rate was set at $4.25 per $100 for the year ending April 30, 1944, and rose to $9.95 per $100 in 1955. (*Report of the Commission to Investigate the Taxation System in the City of Halifax*, pp. 8–10.) The commission recommended rates of $2.00, $2.50, and $3.00 on residential, rented residential, and commercial real property, respectively, and urged that the ratios between the three rates be maintained if the rates were changed, to maintain the same relative burdens on the three types of property (p. 108).

[24]*Ibid.*, pp. 53–61.

Although the commission's argument has some merit, it carries less weight when one also notes a position it takes at an earlier point—that residential property does not and should not be expected to carry the municipal services its owners receive and that "the deficit on residential properties must be made up from commercial and industrial properties where more intensive utilization of the land justifies higher valuations and consequently a greater proportionate dollar return than the cost of services rendered demands."[25] If, even with a single tax rate, commercial property would be carrying more than its share of the services, the argument for a higher rate on commercial property becomes weaker. The contradiction illustrates one kind of difficulty that arises from attaching more significance than is warranted to the element of benefit in property taxation. Apart from this difficulty, a major objection to the dual rate as long as it is an uncommon feature is the heavy burden it imposes on business property compared with other municipalities, with the result that it discourages business from locating in the city.

It would probably be preferable to adopt a uniform rate and to devise a business tax more closely related to ability to pay than the present one to raise additional revenue. As the commission very clearly points out, the present business tax, which was first levied as a substitute for the personal property tax, bears little relation to the value of movable property on business premises.[26] Nor does it bear any relation to the ability to pay of a business as measured by its profitability. The commission urged consideration of a gross receipts tax similar to the type commonly used by local governments in the United States because it considered it more equitable than the present business tax. It is a moot point as to whether this has generally been a very satisfactory tax in the United States.

There are other interesting problems relating to taxation in Halifax,[27]

25*Ibid.*

26*Ibid.*, p. 61. Business taxes have become very common in Canadian cities. Other bases for the tax than the one described here are annual rental value of business premises and area of business premises. For a good critical examination of this kind of tax, see Robert M. Clark, *The Municipal Business Tax in Canada* (Canadian Tax Papers, No. 5; Toronto: Canadian Tax Foundation, 1952).

27As the commission points out, the problems arise chiefly from the city's low ratio of commercial to total assessment and "the large ratio of low valued residential and commercial units" compared to other Canadian cities (p. 45). The unusually large tax exempt institutional base of the city is partly responsible for the city's financial difficulties, although not to the extent it was formerly. The federal government now makes grants in lieu of taxation on its properties in the city on the same basis as if they were taxable. The National Harbours Board and the Canadian National Railways, which are federal Crown corporations, also

but it is not appropriate to explore them further for the purpose of this study. The purpose of this section has been to show that the taxation practices peculiar to Halifax are inclined to result in heavier burdens upon business property than in the other urban units in the province, even allowing for the higher level of services in Halifax, in spite of that city's greater fiscal capacity as measured by per capita taxable assessment. Even so the over-all property tax burden for Halifax, as measured in Table XXXVI, appears less than in a number of towns.[28]

The Poll Tax

The poll tax in Nova Scotia has generally been a token tax levied especially on those income earners who do not pay other municipal taxes, but it is also levied at lower amounts on ratepayers in some municipalities. As Table XIV shows, it is not a very important source of revenue although it is more important in rural municipalities than in towns and cities. There is great variation in its rate, the maximum allowable in towns and rural municipalities being $20.[29] In 1959 the tax ranged from .7 to 5.9 per cent of total taxation revenue for towns and .7 to 7 per cent for rural municipalities, and was 1.5 per cent for Halifax and 2.6 per cent for Sydney.[30] With some tendency towards levying a higher poll tax in place of the personal property tax on household furnishings and personal effects, its importance is increasing somewhat, but it is not likely to become a very significant source of

---

make grants in lieu of taxation, but these fall far short of the amounts they would pay if their properties were taxable. The provincial government makes no grants of this type to any of the municipalities, except for its liquor stores on which it makes relatively smaller payments to Halifax than to other municipalities. Since there is a large concentration of provincial property in Halifax, the failure of the provincial government to make grants in lieu of taxation on its property is of greater consequence to Halifax than to other municipalities.

[28]The commission found, however, that residential property in Halifax in 1957 had a market value 10–30 per cent greater than comparable property in the several other Canadian cities it visited. This circumstance would increase the tax burden on Halifax property. The commission attributed the high property values in Halifax to the shortage of housing accommodation, the higher price of land, and the greater cost of construction. (*Report of the Commission to Investigate the Taxation System in the City of Halifax*, pp. 25–6.)

[29]Assessment Act, R.S.N.S., 1954, c. 15, ss. 5–6.

[30]D.B.S., *Annual Report of Municipal Statistics, 1959* (Ottawa: Queen's Printer), pp. 5, 14. The low ratio for Halifax is due to its use of the household tax, which exempted the payers of it from paying the poll tax. The abolition of its household tax after 1959 has caused Halifax's revenue from the poll tax to increase in relative importance. The poll tax in Halifax is presently $20, and in Sydney ranges from $4 to $15.

revenue.[31] The slight differences in fiscal pressure on taxpayers which might be generated by differences in the poll tax are not important enough to take into account.

Other Possible Sources of Revenue

Besides the property tax, there are no other major sources of taxation revenue presently being tapped. The commission on the Halifax taxation system did recommend the use of taxes on motor vehicles, retail sales, and deed transfers by the city, but only the last has yet been adopted;[32] although in view of its peculiar financial problems, some additional bases will likely have to be used, unless it gets sufficient relief from the province. A good case can be made, in terms of the benefit principle, for a local tax on motor vehicles in cities and towns, or for some sharing of the provincial gasoline or motor vehicle revenues, since the cities and towns are responsible for most of their own streets.[33] The provincial grant to towns and cities of $200 per mile of streets, begun in fiscal year 1960–1, though not formally related to these revenues, is akin to a sharing of them. Nova Scotian municipalities have not shown much interest in adopting new tax bases, and indeed, in the case of a sales tax, most of them are too small for a locally-administered tax to be practical.

PROVINCIAL REVENUES AND FISCAL FLEXIBILITY

Taxes on gasoline and motor vehicles, the retail sales tax, and the liquor profits of the provincial sales monopoly accounted, in the fiscal year 1960–1, for almost 90 per cent of provincial revenues exclusive of contributions from the federal government.[34] As the gasoline and motor vehicle revenues fail even to cover direct expenditure on highways, and as the retail sales tax no more than pays for the hospital benefits for which it is levied, the liquor profits are the only one of the three revenues sources available for general purposes. Since these

[31]Although practically the only virtues of the poll tax are that it compels citizens who pay no property tax to make a direct contribution to the cost of providing services and widens the local franchise, it is probably not inferior in terms of equity and administrative efficiency to a badly administered personal property tax on household furnishings and personal effects.

[32]*Report of the Commission to Investigate the Taxation System in the City of Halifax*, pp. 104–5. The deed transfer tax is ½ per cent of sale value. The sales tax was recommended before the provincial government introduced its retail sales tax.

[33]See Roger Carswell, *Taxes and Traffic: A Study of Highway Financing* (Canadian Tax Papers, No. 8; Toronto: Canadian Tax Foundation, 1955), *passim*; Roger Carswell, "Municipal Motor Vehicle User Taxes," *Canadian Tax Journal*, VI (November-December, 1958), pp. 427–30; and L. F. Hashey, "Municipal Motor Vehicle User Taxes," *Canadian Tax Journal*, VII (January-February, 1959), pp. 62–7.   [34]See Table XI.

profits and contributions from the federal government are also practically all committed, it is evident that an extension of provincial grants to the municipalities or the assumption of services now being performed by the municipalities, to implement more fully the principle of fiscal equity, will require additional provincial revenues.

Provincial tax burdens are already heavier in Nova Scotia than in some of the other provinces[35] and although contributions from the federal government will likely increase in amount as the Canadian economy grows, the province has little control over them. The provincial government is therefore not in a very flexible financial position with respect to its revenues. The best solution to the need of the province for more revenue, from both the national and provincial points of view, would be for the federal government to apply the principle of fiscal equity with respect to the provinces. The larger federal transfers that would then ensue would likely supply most, if not all, of the revenue the province would require to implement the principle of fiscal equity with respect to its municipalities. The provincial government could of course raise additional revenue by taxing its residents more heavily than those of other provinces are taxed. If it chose to do this, a further increase in its sales tax and increases in its personal and corporate income taxes would seem to be the most promising sources of extra revenue. Such increases might not be popular, but a declared intention to use the funds to ease municipal tax burdens and improve services provided by municipalities would make them more palatable. The over-all increase in tax burdens would be much less than the increases in sales and income taxes, for these increases would be offset in large degree by reductions in property taxes.

It may well be that fiscal adjustment of the kind envisaged in this study will come gradually, in the long run, as the provincial government acquires funds it feels it can use for the purpose. But whether adjustment can be made quickly or gradually, it is highly desirable that it be made on a sound basis.

THE REDISTRIBUTIVE EFFECTS OF THE NOVA SCOTIAN FISCAL SYSTEM

It would be very difficult to determine empirically with much precision how closely the combined provincial-municipal fiscal system satisfies the egalitarian postulate. Nevertheless, it is of interest, and perhaps some indication can be obtained if some of the major revenues and expenditures of the province and the municipalities are examined.

The benefits from highways are not confined to those who make

[35]This is shown in chapter III.

direct use of them and, even if they were, highway expenditures are not quite offset by gasoline and motor vehicle revenues. The element of benefit connecting the revenues and expenditures is, however, strong enough for both to be deemed to have no redistributive effects.

The sales tax combined with the hospital benefits to which it is related can be assumed to have quite strong egalitarian effects, for the benefits are uniform regardless of income and the tax collected increases quite rapidly with income.[36]

Although the profits from liquor sales are not called "taxes" by the government, they are in fact taxes similar in nature to retail sales taxes, the main differences being that they are not calculated on the basis of a given percentage of value of purchase and that the expenses of administration are incurred mainly in the operation of the stores rather than in tax collection in the ordinary way. Since the revenues are not allocated to any particular purpose, it is not possible to associate specific benefits with them. Nor can anything conclusive be said about the distribution of the tax burden without careful budget studies. It is interesting to note, however, that when liquor sales per capita, by counties, are plotted against income of payers of personal income tax per capita, there is no discernible correlation in the resulting scatter diagram.[37] This lack of correlation suggests that there is a very low income elasticity of demand for alcoholic beverages, that is, that the liquor "tax" is highly regressive with respect to income.

[36]Premier Stanfield in defending the sales tax argued that "The man who spends $6,000 a year will pay over twice the tax of the man who spends $3,000—because a substantial proportion of the $3,000 will be on tax exempt commodities." But he does not take into account the larger amount of saving (which may not be touched by the sales tax) which is likely to take place out of the higher income of the man who spends $6,000. The tax may be progressive with respect to expenditure, but regressive with respect to income. He also argued "those with modest incomes will pay far less in this proposed tax than they now pay for hospitalization—indeed, only a small fraction. Furthermore, those with modest incomes will pay far less toward the cost of the plan than those with larger incomes. And that is as it should be." (*Speech on Second Reading: Hospital Tax Act* [Halifax: 1958].)

[37]The liquor sales data used were for the year ended March 31, 1957, from Government of Nova Scotia, *Twenty-Seventh Report of the Nova Scotia Liquor Commission* (Halifax: Queen's Printer, 1957), p. 17. No attempt was made to allocate the sales of the mail order store in the City of Halifax, since there seemed no satisfactory principle for doing this. Simply pro-rating these sales among the counties on the basis of volume in the stores there would not have altered the results. Mail order sales were about 11 per cent of total sales. The income data used were for the year ended March 31, 1955, from the Department of National Revenue, *Taxation Statistics, 1957* (Ottawa: Queen's Printer), Table 5. The population data were for 1956, from D.B.S., *Census of Canada, 1956* (Ottawa: Queen's Printer, 1958), Bulletin 3-1, Table 1.

The evidence is too sketchy, and the liquor consumption pattern of individuals likely too varied, to give much weight to this finding. There is likely, on the average, some degree of positive correlation between income and liquor sales.

While the property taxes are almost certainly regressive with respect to income,[38] the degree of regression is not known. Nevertheless, property taxes and income would on the average be positively correlated, so that the tax paid rises with income. While the benefits from local services probably increase at least slightly with income, the benefits from the general services paid for with property tax revenues if anything are probably greater for those in the lower-income groups. There is, therefore, some evening out.

Prior to the alteration in federal-provincial arrangements beginning in the fiscal year 1962–3, 40 to 50 per cent of the revenues of the provincial government were obtained from the federal government.[39] Some of these were tax rental payments, which revenues are now raised directly by the new taxes levied by the province on personal and corporate income. To the extent that the payments from the federal government could be regarded as shares of direct taxes paid by Nova Scotian individuals and corporations to the federal government, they were progressive; so also are the new taxes levied by the province, tied as they are to the federal rate structure. To the extent that the payments from the federal government are equalization payments, they constitute no burden on Nova Scotian taxpayers.

The expenditures financed by these grants and taxes, along with revenues from other provincial sources not at least informally earmarked, relate mainly to education, social welfare, public health, debt servicing (which includes all provincial services, but especially highways), conservation and improvement of resources, industrial development, general government, protection to persons and property, and highway costs not covered by gasoline and motor vehicle taxes; and they include the unconditional grants to the municipalities.[40]

[38]See, for example, Clarence Heer, "The Property Tax as a Measure of Ability," *Property Taxes* (New York: Tax Policy League, 1940), pp. 155–64.

[39]For the fiscal year ended nearest to December 31, 1960, the federal payments to the Government of Nova Scotia are estimated to be as follows: tax rental agreement $11,981,000; share of income tax on power utilities $450,000; statutory subsidies $2,057,000; tax equalization payment $20,273,000; Atlantic Provinces Adjustment Grant $7,500,000; total $42,261,000; and total net general revenue $92,150,000. D.B.S., *Comparative Statistics of Public Finance 1956 to 1960. Part 1. Revenue and Expenditure* (Ottawa: Queen's Printer, 1960), Table 13; and special compilation by Dominion Bureau of Statistics.

[40]See Table XIII.

These services, according to the argument of the previous chapter, probably on balance benefit the lower-income groups more than the high-income groups.

Since no quantities have been attached to the benefits and burdens for different incomes, and since most of the propositions made above relating to the distribution of benefits and burdens are speculative, no very precise conclusions can be drawn about the redistributive effects of the fiscal system. But since the egalitarian postulate can be met even by a regressive tax system, providing taxes increase with income while benefits fall or at least increase less rapidly, it does appear from the above discussion that the postulate is quite comfortably met by the present provincial-municipal fiscal system in Nova Scotia. In any case, the adoption of the fiscal adjustments contemplated in the following chapter will tend to make the fiscal system still more egalitarian, since the burden of the property and poll taxes, probably the most regressive of the taxes now being used, would be eased by the substitution of less regressive revenue sources.

CONCLUSIONS

This chapter has shown that there are significant departures from the principle of fiscal equity in provincial-municipal relations in Nova Scotia arising from differences in municipal fiscal capacity, and that none of the adjustment devices used by the provincial government, except the complete assumption of services once performed by the municipalities, is fully in accord with the principle of fiscal equity. Although the provincial government is not in a very flexible position with respect to its revenues, it could raise additional revenue by further increasing the sales tax and by raising its rate of personal and corporate income taxes above those at which tax credits are given by the federal government. The provincial government can expect a gradual increase in its liquor revenues and its equalization payments from the federal government, at least some of which it could devote to provincial-municipal fiscal adjustment. The egalitarian postulate appears to be met in Nova Scotia at present; and it is likely that the fiscal system will become more egalitarian if adjustments are made in provincial-municipal fiscal relations according to the principle of fiscal equity.

IX

A Programme for
Fiscal Adjustment in Nova Scotia

THE PURPOSE OF THIS CHAPTER is to outline a programme for fiscal
adjustment according to the principle of fiscal equity in the province
of Nova Scotia. The formula presently used for the grants for education (often referred to as the "Pottier formula" after Justice V. J.
Pottier who proposed it in his report)[1] and certain proposals made by
D. C. Rowat[2] will be examined to see if they are, or can be adapted to
be, in accordance with the principle of fiscal equity. It is intended to
give not a completely detailed blueprint for fiscal adjustment, but a
sufficiently comprehensive outline for it that the details could readily
be filled in if the necessary data were made available. The suggested
programme will include some proposals in addition to those necessary
to implement the principle of fiscal equity.

FISCAL ADJUSTMENT BY MEANS OF GRANTS

*An Evaluation of the Extension of the Pottier Formula as a Basis for
Adjustment*

It was argued in chapter VIII that the Pottier formula was not consistent with the principle of fiscal equity because of the 25 per cent
minimum contribution, the choice of the uniform burden of 80 cents

[1]Government of Nova Scotia, *Report of the Royal Commission on Public School
Finance in Nova Scotia* (*Pottier Report*; Halifax: Queen's Printer, 1954).
[2]In Donald C. Rowat, *The Reorganization of Provincial-Municipal Relations in
Nova Scotia* (A report prepared for the Government of Nova Scotia by the Nova
Scotia Municipal Bureau, Institute of Public Affairs, Dalhousie University; Halifax,
1949).

which is used to calculate each municipality's share of the cost of the Foundation Program, variations among municipalities in actual costs of providing the Foundation Program, departures of actual costs from those used in calculating grants, and imperfections in assessments. The formula, without the minimum provincial contribution as it is applied in this case and with a change in the way the uniform burden is determined (as will be shown), is an excellent one to use for any service for which it is deemed desirable that the maintenance of given standards be required of the municipalities and that the burden be uniform for municipalities of varying fiscal capacity. In fact the formula, so adjusted, is "tailor-made" for implementing the principle of fiscal equity in such a case. (It is assumed that the departures from the principle relating to costs of the Foundation Program and imperfections in assessments would also be taken into account.) The method could appropriately be applied to all of the general services, in addition to education, for which the municipalities have some responsibility— indoor and outdoor relief, maintenance of mental hospitals, child care, and the portions of highways passing through towns and cities. But it is not appropriate for local services, if the position taken in this study that the localities should be free to determine their own level of these services is accepted. The implementation of the principle of fiscal equity with respect to local services can appropriately be accomplished only by unconditional grants.

With respect to each of the general services listed it would be easier than in the case of education to determine the cost for each municipality of maintaining a required "foundation" standard and just as easy to establish the uniform rate for the determination of each municipality's share of the burden. The method is in accord with the doctrine of administrative efficiency in that services which are best administered locally, even if they are of general interest, can continue to be so administered. It is also about as much in accord with the doctrine of financial responsibility as a system of grants could be. The municipalities would have to apply the grants to specific purposes and to maintain the standards required by the province. They would all have to impose the same burden on their taxpayers to raise their share, unless they administered the services wastefully, in which case their own taxpayers would bear the brunt of a heavier burden.

The plan is especially well-adapted to relief, for which the need varies greatly with fluctuations in unemployment. The municipal contributions could be limited to a share, varying with fiscal capacity, determined by the expected need under buoyant economic conditions, with the province paying the balance. The municipalities with their relatively inflexible revenue base would then be relieved of the worrisome situation, disastrous to many Canadian municipalities during the depression of the 1930's, of being faced with inordinate financial demands for local relief in time of a serious depression, imposed on a rather inflexible revenue structure. Federal unemployment insurance and the present federal and provincial social assistance grants have, of course, already much reduced this worry for the municipalities.

But what about the case where the province wishes to give some assistance to all municipalities in the performance of a given service and, at the same time, to give grants to equalize the burden for the remaining costs of the service? This question is of particular interest in view of the fact that the province is already making flat-rate grants[3] for all of the general services mentioned. Implementation of the principle of fiscal equity will likely have to be erected on this existing structure of grants. It is possible to do this. The reason the 25 per cent minimum grant under the Pottier formula resulted in some distortion from the principle of fiscal equity was that the equalization formula was worked out for all of the non-capital costs of the Foundation Program and then modified by the minimum grant of 25 per cent. If the flat-rate grant were first determined and the Pottier type of equalization formula then applied so that the same burden was imposed on all municipalities for the balance of the foundation costs, the result would be consistent with the principle of fiscal equity. It would mean lowering the uniform burden to the lowest rate necessary to raise the balance of the costs in any of the municipalities.[4] The provincial proportion for the balance of the costs would range from zero for the municipality which could just raise all of the balance of its costs with this burden up to whatever proportion was necessary to enable the "poorest" municipality to provide the foundation programme while bearing the uniform burden. It is true that in the case of education

---

[3]A flat-rate grant is one made to all municipalities at the same given percentage of the costs of the foundation programme in each municipality.

[4]Perhaps some compromise could be made in determining this rate by taking the average rate on the equalized valuation necessary to raise the balance of the costs for, say, the five municipalities with the lowest rates. In the case of the education grants the lowest rate would be 40 cents (Dartmouth) and the average of the five lowest rates about 48 cents, assuming a 25 per cent flat-rate grant. The five municipalities with the lowest rates besides Dartmouth are the town of Lunenburg, New Glasgow, the City of Halifax, and Trenton. The use of such an average has the virtue of eliminating undue influence of a single municipality with peculiar characteristics, without seriously impairing the implementation of the principle of fiscal equity.

the burden borne by the poorer municipalities would be lighter than the one resulting from the Pottier proposal which is in effect. But this lighter burden is an outcome of removing the elements of unequal treatment of municipalities from the Pottier compromise. The burden would now be the same on all of the municipalities. The lower share borne by the municipalities would mean a higher provincial share of the cost. But the total provincial share could be adjusted downward somewhat by lowering the flat-rate part of the grant. This downward adjustment would have the effect of reducing the funds distributed by the flat-rate grant and at the same time of raising the uniform burden on the municipalities and therefore raising their share.

TABLE XL

A PROVINCIAL GRANT SCHEME TO ENABLE THE MUNICIPALITIES TO MAINTAIN
A FOUNDATION PROGRAMME FOR A SERVICE WITH A UNIFORM TAX BURDEN,
WITH NO FLAT-RATE GRANT

Municipality	Cost of foundation programme[a]	Equalized assessment	Municipal share of foundation programme[b]	Provincial share of foundation programme
A	$1,000	$125,000	$1,000	$ 0
B	1,000	112,500	900	100
C	1,000	100,000	800	200
D	1,000	87,500	700	300
E	1,000	75,000	600	400
F	1,000	62,050	500	500
G	1,000	50,000	400	600
H	1,000	37,500	300	700
I	1,000	25,000	200	800
J	1,000	12,500	100	900
TOTAL	$10,000		$5,500	$4,500

[a]Taken as equal for all municipalities to simplify the illustration. The application of the principle is unaltered by this simplification.
[b]Determined by applying to the equalized assessments a rate equal to that which must be imposed on equalized assessment of A to cover the cost of the foundation programme for A, that is, $1,000/$125,000 \times 100 = .80$ per cent. The share of each municipality in the cost of the programme is thus determined by multiplying its equalized assessment by .008.

Tables XL–XLII illustrate with hypothetical examples the operation of a scheme of grants for a service where standards are determined in terms of a foundation programme. The tables show schemes of grants for supporting the same foundation programme (*a*) with no flat-rate grant (Table XL), (*b*) with a flat-rate grant of 10 per cent (Table XLI), and (*c*) with a flat-rate grant of 20 per cent (Table XLII). In each case the burden as measured by the rate applied to determine the municipalities' share of the costs of the programme is the same in all municipalities. The uniform burden on the municipalities is lighter

TABLE XLI

A PROVINCIAL GRANT SCHEME TO ENABLE THE MUNICIPALITIES TO MAINTAIN
A FOUNDATION PROGRAMME FOR A SERVICE WITH A UNIFORM TAX BURDEN,
WITH A FLAT-RATE GRANT OF 10 PER CENT

Muni-cipality	Cost of foundation pro-gramme[a]	Equalized assess-ment	Flat-rate grant of 10%	Balance of foundation pro-gramme	Municipal share of balance[b]	Pro-vincial share of balance	Total pro-vincial share
A	$1,000	$125,000	$100	$900	$900	$ 0	$100
B	1,000	112,500	100	900	810	90	190
C	1,000	100,000	100	900	720	180	280
D	1,000	87,500	100	900	630	270	370
E	1,000	75,000	100	900	540	360	460
F	1,000	62,500	100	900	450	450	550
G	1,000	50,000	100	900	360	540	640
H	1,000	37,500	100	900	270	630	730
I	1,000	25,000	100	900	180	720	820
J	1,000	12,500	100	900	90	810	910
TOTAL	$10,000		$1,000	$9,000	$4,950	$4,050	$5,050

[a]Taken as equal for all municipalities to simplify the illustration. The application of the principle is unaltered by this simplification.

[b]Determined by applying to the equalized assessments a rate equal to that which must be imposed on the equalized assessment of A to yield the balance of A's cost of the foundation programme, that is, $900/$125,000 \times 100 = .72$ per cent. The share of each municipality in the cost of the programme is thus determined by multiplying its equalized assessment by .0072.

TABLE XLII

A PROVINCIAL GRANT SCHEME TO ENABLE THE MUNICIPALITIES TO MAINTAIN
A FOUNDATION PROGRAMME FOR A SERVICE WITH A UNIFORM TAX BURDEN,
WITH A FLAT-RATE GRANT OF 20 PER CENT

Muni-cipality	Cost of foundation pro-gramme[a]	Equalized assess-ment	Flat-rate grant of 10%	Balance of foundation pro-gramme	Municipal share of balance[b]	Pro-vincial share of balance	Total pro-vincial share
A	$1,000	$125,000	$200	$800	$800	$ 0	$200
B	1,000	112,500	200	800	720	80	280
C	1,000	100,000	200	800	640	160	360
D	1,000	87,500	200	800	560	240	440
E	1,000	75,000	200	800	480	320	520
F	1,000	62,500	200	800	400	400	600
G	1,000	50,000	200	800	320	480	680
H	1,000	37,500	200	800	240	560	760
I	1,000	25,000	200	800	160	640	840
J	1,000	12,500	200	800	80	720	920
TOTAL	$10,000		$2,000	$8,000	$4,400	$3,600	$5,600

[a]Taken as equal for all municipalities to simplify the illustration. The application of the principle is unaltered by this simplification.

[b]Determined by applying to the equalized assessments a rate equal to that which must be imposed on the equalized assessment of A to yield the balance of A's cost of the foundation programme, that is, $800/$125,000 \times 100 = .64$ per cent. The share of each municipality in the cost of the programme is determined by multiplying its equalized assessment by .0064.

and the provincial share of the costs of the programme greater, the larger the rate of the flat-rate grant. This hypothetical illustration has been given to make it easier to understand the more complicated illustration of the province's financial aid to the municipalities for education and the effects of modifications of the scheme to make it conform to the principle of fiscal equity.

Table XLIII shows how the present Foundation Program and provincial grants for education affect all of the Nova Scotian municipalities. Without the 25 per cent minimum grant the provincial share would have been $1.054 million less ($9.067 million compared with $10.121 million). If the 25 per cent grant were made and the burden on the

TABLE XLIII

PROVINCIAL GRANTS TO SUPPORT NON-CAPITAL COSTS OF FOUNDATION PROGRAM FOR EDUCATION IN NOVA SCOTIA WITH AND WITHOUT 25 PER CENT MINIMUM[a]

Town, city or rural municipality	Equalized valuation ($'000)	Cost of Foundation Program ($'000)	80-cent rate on equal. val. ($'000)	Provincial proportion %	Provincial payment with 25 % min. ($'000)	Provincial payment without min. cont. ($'000)
Towns						
Amherst	18,594	205	149	27.44	56	56
Annapolis Royal	2,244	17	18	nil	4	nil
Antigonish	7,403	112	59	47.12	53	53
Berwick	3,162	36	25	29.83	11	11
Bridgetown	2,762	25	22	9.83	6	2
Bridgewater	13,092	106	105	.87	26	1
Canso	965	39	8	90.00	31	31
Clark's Harbour	1,112	19	9	53.79	10	10
Dartmouth	74,659	398	597	nil	100	nil
Digby	4,599	45	37	18.19	11	8
Dominion	1,538	93	12	86.74	81	81
Glace Bay	34,951	675	280	58.57	395	395
Hantsport	4,309	41	34	16.60	10	7
Inverness	1,285	51	10	79.95	41	41
Kentville	15,341	154	123	20.55	38	32
Liverpool	8,774	105	70	33.02	35	35
Lockeport	1,630	39	13	66.30	26	26
Louisburg	2,219	30	18	41.20	12	12
Lunenburg	9,491	56	76	nil	14	nil
Mahone Bay	1,789	22	14	34.10	8	8
Middleton	5,326	47	43	9.59	12	4
Mulgrave	1,027	29	8	71.49	21	21
New Glasgow	26,682	168	213	nil	42	nil
New Waterford	10,226	322	82	74.63	240	240
North Sydney	11,570	210	93	55.87	117	117
Oxford	1,662	35	13	62.44	22	22
Parrsboro	2,183	48	17	63.88	31	31
Pictou	5,332	91	43	53.32	48	48
Pt. Hawkesbury	1,259	34	10	70.05	24	24
Shelburne	3,623	58	29	49.70	29	29
Springhill	5,505	114	44	61.46	70	70
Stellarton	5,257	96	42	56.06	54	54

TABLE XLIII (*Continued*)

Town, city or rural municipality	Equalized valuation ($'000)	Cost of Foundation Program ($'000)	80-cent rate on equal. val. ($'000)	Provincial proportion %	Provincial payment with 25 % min. ($'000)	Provincial payment without min. cont. ($'000)
Stewiacke	1,612	30	13	56.31	17	17
Sydney Mines	9,643	209	77	63.01	132	132
Trenton	10,270	79	82	nil	20	nil
Truro	37,180	299	297	.65	75	2
Westville	2,799	93	22	75.95	71	71
Windsor	8,393	99	67	32.22	32	32
Wolfville	6,808	73	54	25.49	19	19
Yarmouth	15,312	188	122	34.93	66	66
Cities						
Halifax	364,509	2,412	2,916	nil	603	nil
Sydney	101,582	886	813	8.23	222	73
Rural Municipalities						
Annapolis	24,277	608	194	68.05	414	414
Antigonish	7,329	390	59	84.95	331	331
Argyle	4,250	213	34	84.02	179	179
Barrington	3,487	152	28	81.60	124	124
Cape Breton	41,789	1,005	334	66.75	671	671
Chester	10,461	153	84	45.37	69	69
Clare	7,192	228	58	74.80	170	170
Colchester	30,320	791	243	69.32	548	548
Cumberland	22,675	688	181	73.65	507	507
Digby	9,249	324	74	77.19	250	250
Guysborough	3,738	185	30	83.81	155	155
Halifax	177,212	2,116	1,418	33.00	698	698
Hants, East	12,958	373	104	72.23	269	269
Hants, West	13,482	282	108	61.72	174	174
Inverness	10,031	587	80	86.32	507	507
Kings	39,705	824	318	61.46	506	506
Lunenburg	19,418	418	155	62.81	263	263
Pictou	17,759	587	142	75.81	445	445
Queens	22,752	283	182	35.58	101	101
Richmond	5,437	322	43	86.51	279	279
Shelburne	3,890	126	27	78.58	99	99
St. Mary's	3,366	170	31	81.66	139	139
Victoria	11,159	277	89	67.82	188	188
Yarmouth	8,066	165	65	60.82	100	100
Totals						
Towns	381,590	4,591	3,052	45.96[b]	2,110	1,808
Cities	466,091	3,298	3,729	22.12[b]	825	73
Rural muns.	510,004	11,266	4,080	63.79	7,186	7,186
ALL	1,357,684	19,155	10,861	52.31	10,121	9,067[c]

SOURCE: Calculated from *Report of the Revaluation Commission for the Province of Nova Scotia, 1958*; and schedules supplied by the Department of Education.

[a]Based upon the 1958 equalized valuations and upon the costs of the Foundation Program for the school year 1957–58.

[b]The 25 per cent minimum payment is included in calculating these proportions. The 25 per cent minimum does not apply to any of the rural municipalities.

[c]This payment would be 44.73 per cent of the total cost of the Foundation Program.

municipalities for the balance of the costs were made equal to that
required on the average for the five municipalities with the highest
equalized valuation in relation to the cost of the Foundation Program,
the burden would be 47.8 cents per $100 of valuation and the total
provincial share would be $12.666 million, or 66.12 per cent of the
cost of the Foundation Program. If the flat-rate grant were 10 per cent,
the required uniform burden would be 57.4 cents and the total provincial share would be $11.361 million or 59.31 per cent. If no flat-rate
grant were made and the uniform burden calculated in the way suggested here, the required uniform burden would be 63.8 cents and
the provincial share $10.492 million, or 54.77 per cent. The provincial
share would have to be still larger if the municipal share were calculated from the minimum rate required by any one of the municipalities
to pay for all of the non-capital costs of the Foundation Program
(53.3 cents, for Dartmouth),[5] instead of the average for the five municipalities which would incur the lowest burdens.

It may be that the cost of maintaining the Foundation Program is
greater in some of the urban units, especially in the cities, than in the
other municipalities. If this is the case, as it likely is for the cost and
maintenance of buildings if not for other costs, the allowable costs
for these units should be raised to prevent them from being discriminated against. Possibly, some systematic provision should be made
throughout the province to take account of variations in costs.

If the province feels it cannot afford to go all of the way with
equalization to the extent required by the principle of fiscal equity, it
can still determine the amounts required for complete equalization
and make grants of some fraction of these amounts, depending upon
the amount of money it can devote to the purpose. Then if at some
future date it feels it can increase its contribution, it can easily do so
by increasing all grants by the same percentage amount.[6] It should be
emphasized that reducing the grants in this way is simply a convenient
way of accommodating the scheme to the province's financial resources.
This method of scaling down the grants, like any other method, results
in a departure from the goal of fiscal equity.

[5]The 80-cent rate actually used as the basis of the present scheme was
chosen mainly because it was the rate which would result in the province paying
about 50 per cent of both capital and non-capital costs of the Foundation Program, having some regard for the burdens borne for education before the Program
was implemented. (See *Pottier Report*, pp. 70–2.)

[6]A political objection to this suggestion from the point of view of the provincial government is that it would make the extent of equalization yet unaccom-
plished glaringly apparent.

Equalization grants according to the principle of fiscal equity should have priority over the making of general deficiency grants to all municipalities. With respect to equity and to the effect on allocation of resources, it is desirable that the burden of maintaining a foundation standard of services in the municipalities with low fiscal capacities be made equal to that in the municipalities with high fiscal capacities. It will always require a larger total amount of money to establish a structure of grants consistent with the principle of fiscal equity when there is a flat-rate grant than when there is not. If the province cannot devote sufficient funds for a service to achieve fiscal equity with the inclusion of a flat-rate grant it should sacrifice this component. It should adopt the scaling-down procedure suggested above only when it is financially unable to achieve fiscal equity even without the flat-rate element. When some of the funds are provided by the federal government for allocation in a specified way, as in the case of the social assistance grants, the province may have no choice.[7] And where the province is already making flat-rate grants, as in the case of all of the services considered here, it may not be considered feasible to withdraw them for use in the way proposed, since it would mean substantial reductions of grants to the wealthier municipalities. Perhaps the best that can be done is to use in the way recommended any additional funds which are directed to these services.

If a flat-rate grant must be made on grounds of political expediency, even where to do so reduces the extent to which the principle of fiscal equity is implemented, the rate of this part of the grant should be made as small as it can be while still achieving the political purpose of making it. Determining what such a rate should be falls within the realm of the "art" of politics rather than within the realm of the "science" of economics.

An Evaluation of Rowat's Recommendations as a Basis for Adjustment

In his report prepared for the Government of Nova Scotia in 1949, D. C. Rowat made two major recommendations[8] which are of interest here.

Regional units of local government. Rowat recommended that an

----

[7]Perhaps the federal government could be prevailed upon to make the grant on the basis of a given percentage of total costs of the service in all municipalities and leave it up to the province to make the actual allocation, so that it would be free to make it according to the principle of fiscal equity.

[8]Not all of the proposals in this excellent report will be discussed here. Some of them are not directly relevant to this study and others fall more in the realm of public administration than in that of public finance.

additional tier of local government be established, consisting of nine regions encompassing all of the present municipalities. The new regions would administer municipal services that cannot be efficiently administered by small municipal units, and provincial services where decentralized administration is desirable. The existing municipalities would continue to be responsible for some services, but would surrender

. . . *certain* of the municipal services, such as public health, welfare and possibly education, and certain *regional* services such as regional planning, the administration of justice, and public institutional care, for which inadequate provision is at present being made. The main effect upon the municipalities would be the raising of responsibility for social services to a higher level of locally elected regional government. Taxes to pay the local share of the cost of these services would then be levied at a uniform rate over a whole Region, and the Province would contribute a substantial share of the cost on an equalized basis.

The Province has already found it necessary to decentralize the administration of many of its health, welfare and education services into regions. It would therefore seem logical for the sake of coordination and efficiency to tie in the boundaries of the proposed municipal Regions with these administrative divisions, and to integrate the activities of both.[9]

Rowat gave a number of arguments in favour of the larger units: they would be more appropriate for performing services of greater than local concern; they could administer the major social services more effectively than the municipalities and at the same time maintain a closer contact with the citizens than the province could; they would iron out some of the inequalities in fiscal capacity of the municipalities; they would simplify provincial supervision; and they would make it easier to bring about uniform assessments.[10]

He suggested that the new regions be governed by councils made up of elected representatives from the municipalities comprising the regions. And he was in favour of the entry of the municipalities into the new regional units being voluntary, but of making the financial inducement of provincial assistance great enough to lure them in.

It is unnecessary for the purpose of this study to examine these proposals in detail. Probably larger units could administer some of the general services more efficiently than the smaller municipal units. And it is likely that an equalization scheme would be simplified by the reduction of inequalities of fiscal capacity which would result from amalgamation. But it is doubtful that the rural municipalities would

[9]Rowat, *Reorganization of Provincial-Municipal Relations,* p. 67.
[10]*Ibid.,* pp. 68–72.

continue to function, as Rowat envisaged they would, since there would probably be too little left for them to do to justify their continued existence. Furthermore, it can be argued that the problems of administering services in urban and rural areas are sufficiently different to warrant keeping the two separate. (Rowat proposed that rural and urban units be brought together in the new regions.)

The facts are that no move has been made to implement Rowat's recommendation of the additional tier of local government and that it has met with little favour. There are a number of reasons for this. One is the feeling that there is already too much government for a province the size of Nova Scotia and that an extra layer of government would complicate rather than simplify administration. Another important barrier to amalgamation stems from racial and religious differences among neighbouring municipalities. The scheme was not attractive to the wealthier municipalities which would have to bear part of the costs of services of the poorer municipalities with which they were amalgamated. One of the officials interviewed agreed that amalgamation of some of the municipalities into larger units was desirable but felt that the case for it would have to be built up over a long period and that when there was sufficient opinion in favour of it, it should be accomplished *in toto* by provincial statute, rather than on a voluntary basis.[11]

While the question of amalgamation does not have much bearing on the types of grant-in-aid formulas by which the principle of fiscal equity can be implemented, it does have a bearing on the application of the principle by means of the provincial assumption of responsibility for services. The gains in efficiency from provincial assumption of services might be less, or even nil, if the municipal units were larger.

Provincial grants to municipalities. Rowat proposed a system of block grants to the municipalities for social and educational services to replace the then existing educational and unconditional grants. He devised a formula for such grants which would take account of the fiscal capacity and the expenditure requirements of each municipality.

---

[11]Compare J. A. Maxwell, "Reports on Local Government," *Canadian Journal of Economics and Political Science*, XVII (August, 1951). While he is sympathetic with Rowat's objective, Maxwell is sceptical about leaving the initiative for amalgamation to the municipalities. "I believe . . . that provincial governments in Canada, and state governments in the United States, should assume responsibility for redefinition of the areas of local government. Localities cannot be expected to do this job themselves, and yet the job must be done if we are to secure efficient performance of governmental functions and effective democracy. Without it extension of provincial grants may entrench local units which are structurally unsound" (p. 382).

Fiscal capacity was to be measured by "taxable assessment relative to population,"[12] and expenditure requirements by present municipal expenditures and provincial grants, adjusted by a population index to be weighted by the percentages of population under 15 years of age and over 59 years of age and by density of population.[13] His proposal required an equalized assessment for all municipalities, for which he made provision in another section in his report.[14] At that time there was no equalized valuation even at the municipal unit level and assessment practices were much more chaotic than today.[15]

Before settling on the type of grant briefly described above, Rowat investigated the possibility of an equalization scheme "for specific services in which the Province would require a uniform minimum tax rate in all municipalities as the local share of the cost of a specified service, and then would provide enough provincial aid to bring the service up to a specified minimum standard in all municipalities."[16] He rejected this scheme, mainly because "a complex system of provincial grants for specific services grows up, requiring detailed supervision of municipal services and expenditures by provincial departments, and leaving unaided services to languish at the municipal level."[17] It has already been argued here that it is quite appropriate for the province to assume as much control over services provided by the municipalities as it deems to be in the general provincial interest.[18]

---

[12]Rowat, *Reorganization of Provincial-Municipal Relations*, p. 61.

[13]*Ibid.*, pp. 61–2. These adjustments were intended to take account of the facts that educational expenditures are determined by the number of young people and social welfare expenditures largely by the number of old people, and that it is more costly to supply social and educational services, especially the latter, in a municipality with a low population density than in one with a high population density. However, it is likely that when density of population increases past some point costs will rise with density. Rowat in fact proposed to use a density factor only for the rural municipalities.

[14]*Ibid.*, pp. 83–98.

[15]See Rowat, *ibid.*, pp. 85–9.

[16]*Ibid.*, p. 59.

[17]*Ibid.*, p. 60. This rejected suggestion is similar to the one defended here, Rowat's objections having largely been met.

[18]See chapter VII. A little later, in defence of unconditional grants, Rowat maintains "if this aid were granted on a general basis to municipalities according to generalized indicators of revenue raising ability and expenditure requirements, detailed supervision would not be necessary, and the municipalities would be left free to decide the details with regard to how the money should be spent. This would place municipal bodies in a more autonomous position and would save the Province a good deal of administrative work. The argument that municipalities could not be trusted to maintain proper social and educational services has been overworked, and has arisen mainly because municipalities have not been in a financial or administrative position to do so. Nevertheless, the Province could

And while it is true that services which are unaided might languish at the local level if grants are made only for general services, if unconditional grants for local services are also made according to the principle of fiscal equity, there will be no unaided services and therefore no such distortion in municipal expenditures. Rowat himself proposed additional grants to urban municipalities for local services that are not provided in the rural municipalities. He suggested a special grant to urban municipalities to help cover the costs of streets and argued that, since most local services are related to streets, the grants should be made inversely to total assessments to provide equalization with respect to these services.[19]

Rowat correctly argued that "a straight general purpose per capita grant, such as that used in New Brunswick, or a general percentage-of-expenditure grant, as a substitute for specific conditional grants would not take account of the variations in financial circumstances from one municipality to another, and in some municipalities the tax burden for the support of municipal services still would remain greater than the average."[20]

He continued: "In order to equalize the financial position of municipalities, then, the ideal solution would be to equalize the *existing* educational and general purpose grants according to the burden of municipal taxation upon the citizens in each municipality."[21] It is not clear precisely what this proposal means. Why should the "ideal solution" be to equalize an existing set of grants? And it is not quite clear what it means to equalize them "according to the burden of municipal taxation upon the citizens in each municipality." What his proposal would actually accomplish can be determined from examining the mechanics of it.

The amount Y each municipality was to be expected to raise was to be equal to $D/F \times E$, where D = "total expenditures of all municipalities from their own resources on social and educational services," F = "the total taxable assessment of all municipalities," and E = "the

justifiably expect to require a generalized approval of aided municipal expenditures in return for the provincial grant." (Rowat, *Reorganization of Provincial-Municipal Relations*, p. 60.) Compare with Buchanan's statement quoted above in chapter VII, p. 190. It has already been argued above (chapter VII) that the municipalities cannot be relied upon to provide adequate levels of services even if they have the financial resources to do so with equivalent burdens. Rowat's argument would likely have greater validity if the local units were enlarged as he proposes.

[19]Rowat, *Reorganization of Provincial-Municipal Relations*, p. 62.
[20]*Ibid.*, p. 60.
[21]*Ibid.*, italics mine.

municipality's taxable assessment."[22] As Rowat points out, the rate of this burden in relation to equalized assessment would be the same in all municipalities.[23]

The amount X which each municipality required was to be equal to $L \times P'/M$, where L = "the total need for expenditures by all municipalities (municipal expenditures plus present provincial grants for municipally administered social and educational services)," M = "the total population of the province," and P' = the weighted population of the municipality.[24]

The weighted population was to be the actual population adjusted for variations of the percentages of population under 15 and over 59 years of age, and of miles of road per 100 persons from the provincial averages, the density factor to apply only to rural municipalities.[25]

The provincial grant G was to be equal to $X - Y$. Rowat added: "Since the second index [X] would include provincial aid, it would be higher than the first [Y]."[26] But it is not necessarily true that X would exceed Y for each municipality, even though it would for all municipalities taken together, that is, $\Sigma X > \Sigma Y$.

The formula was proposed by Rowat as a means of making the burden for the services in question the same in all municipalities, with the province making up the difference between the revenues calculated on the basis of this uniform burden, and the "required expenditures." But there is nothing in the formula that ensures that the municipalities would be able to provide a satisfactory level of educa-

---

[22]*Ibid.*, p. 123. The symbols, D, E, and F were not used by Rowat. They are used here to simplify the explanation of the formula. Rowat proposed using only taxable assessment of real property, because of the great variations in the bases for assessment of personal property (p. 125).

[23]*Ibid.*, p. 123.

[24]*Ibid.* The symbols, L, M, and P' were not used by Rowat.

[25] $$P' = P + P \frac{(C - C')}{C'} + \frac{1}{3}P \frac{(A - A')}{A'} + \frac{1}{20}P \frac{(R - R')}{R'} ,$$

where P' = the weighted population of the municipality, P = the actual population of the municipality, C = the number of children under the age of 15 per 100 of population in the municipality, C' = provincial average corresponding to C, A = the number of people over the age of 59 per 100 of population in the municipality, A' = provincial average corresponding to A, R = number of miles of road per 100 persons in municipality, and R' = provincial average corresponding to R. The use of the weighting factor of one for children under 15 and of one-third for old people over 59 was based upon the fact that of the municipal expenditures for education and social services about three times as much was spent on children as on old people. The choice of the factor of one-twentieth for population density was based on a rough guess in the absence of information as to the relative fiscal capacity of urban and rural areas and in view of "the tremendous variations in the densities of the rural populations." (*Ibid.*, p. 127.)

[26]*Ibid.*, p. 123.

tional and social services with the provincial grant plus the revenues raised at the uniform rate, since the total "required expenditures" would be equal roughly to "present" expenditures plus "present" grants. If the "required expenditures" were only sufficient for sub-standard services, then a wealthy municipality would be able to raise the level of its services to a satisfactory standard with a smaller burden on its taxpayers than in a poor municipality. A further deviation of the formula from the principle of fiscal equity arises from using D/F as the uniform rate of burden, for D/F is really a weighted average of the ratios of present expenditures to equalized assessments for all munici-palities. Therefore, raising the municipalities' shares of their "expendi-ture requirement" would result in a heavier burden in the municipalities with low per capita assessment than in those with high per capita assessment. Nevertheless, under the conditions prevailing when Rowat was writing, the formula would have increased the extent of equaliza-tion and it would have taken some account of the variation in local costs of services. The method suggested was crude but it would have operated in the right direction.

If L were raised until expenditures were sufficient to maintain a satisfactory level of services, and if D/F were adjusted so that the municipal share was just enough on the average to equal the amount required in the five municipalities with the least need for aid,[27] the results would be similar to those of the modified Pottier formula suggested in the first section. Determining the desirable level of L, however, would require a careful calculation of the costs of maintain-ing the services in question, so careful that the costs for each munici-pality could be determined directly in the process of calculation. The results would be more precise than those obtained by the use of Rowat's rather crudely weighted population index.

It would still be possible to make block grants for the services to be aided, without stipulating how the grants were to be spent; but there would be greater inter-municipal variation of services than with mandatory foundation programmes. Requiring the municipalities to provide foundation programmes would be more in accord with the principle of fiscal equity as well as being a legitimate use of the power of the provincial government to promote what it deems to be the general provincial interest.

Rowat made his recommendations in 1949. Since then the Founda-tion Program for education and an equalized assessment on a municipal unit basis have been established as a result of the *Pottier Report* of 1954.

[27]If this were done, "D/F" would have a different meaning. It would cease to be the weighted average just described above.

The problems of defining a foundation programme and setting up the administration for it have now been largely overcome for the most important of the general services for which the municipalities are responsible and the one for which the problems are most complicated. The setting up of foundation programmes for the other general services would be a relatively easy if not a simple matter. Whether the grants are earmarked for particular services or not, the use of foundation programmes as the basis for the grants is superior to the cruder indices which Rowat proposed. The position taken and already argued in this study is that it is desirable, or at least appropriate, that the provision of the foundation programme be mandatory for each general service.

In addition to his recommendation for block grants, Rowat recommended "that the Province pay the cost of urban streets forming parts of provincial highways" and that "the Province make a special grant to cities and towns for the general support of streets, the amount to a particular unit being determined on an equalized basis."[28] His proposed grant for streets has already been referred to above. He suggested a total grant for this purpose of $200,000,[29] which was about 20 per cent of the expenditures of towns and cities on streets at that time. He also recommended that if the towns and cities were permitted to levy an amusement tax, the grant should be reduced accordingly. His only reference to the method of distributing the grant was that it "should be made on an equalized basis varying inversely with total assessments."[30] It is not clear what he means by "equalized basis" and there is no reason why such grants should vary inversely with total assessments. Why should municipality A with $3 million in assessment necessarily get more than B with $4 million? Municipality B might have twice the population of A or twice as many miles of streets.

The suggestion that some of the costs of maintaining urban streets should be borne by the users of vehicles that ride on them has merit, especially in Nova Scotia where the provincial government assumes responsibility for all roads in the rural municipalities. The recently instituted annual grant of $200 per mile of city streets is a concession to this view, although a provincial grant-in-aid to urban municipalities

[28]*Ibid.*, p. 63. Rowat also made recommendations relating to the reform of the real and personal property taxes, the poll tax, and exemption from property taxes, which will not be discussed here.

[29]This figure happens to be identical with the amount budgeted for the purpose by the province for fiscal year 1961–2. The method of allocation is, of course, quite different from the one Rowat proposed.

[30]Rowat, *Reorganization of Provincial-Municipal Relations*, p. 62.

equal to a given percentage of the costs of streets, taking local requirements into account in terms of types of street as well as miles of street,
might be a more appropriate way of helping these localities.[31] Such a
grant would be in the nature of a shared revenue and should be extended to all towns and cities without regard to equalization. Equalization grants according to the principle of fiscal equity could be given
for the balance of the costs as part of unconditional equalization grants
for local purposes. An alternative would be for the urban municipalities
themselves to levy a motor vehicle user tax as was suggested in the
report of the commission on taxation in Halifax.[32] One difficulty with
this alternative is that, especially in the larger urban areas, many of
the regular users of streets are from outside of the limits of the city or
town and are therefore difficult to tax.

Grants for Local Services

Many writers on the subject of provincial-municipal or state-local
fiscal relations favour grants-in-aid to municipalities to help pay for
general services. There is less support for grants for local services. A
typical view is that expressed in a memorandum of a New York State
Tax Commission in 1936. Strongly in favour of grants for general
services, the Commission asserts: "It seems axiomatic that local governments should bear the expense of purely local governmental functions,
and that the state should contribute only to those governmental services
in which the state has an immediate interest."[33]

It has already been shown that the full implementation of the principle of fiscal equity calls for equalization grants for local as well as
for general services. It has also been argued that smaller grants should
be given to rural than to urban municipalities because the range of
local services appropriate to rural areas is smaller and their level
lower. As Table XXXVIII shows, local services are far more important
in the towns and cities than in the rural municipalities. Finally, it has
been argued that grants for local services should be unconditional.

Finding a satisfactory formula for unconditional grants for local
services is more difficult than finding one for conditional grants for
general services. Per capita equalized valuation is a reasonably satis-

[31]Compare Roger Carswell, *Taxes and Traffic: A Study of Highway Financing*
(Canadian Tax Papers, No. 8; Toronto: Canadian Tax Foundation, 1955), especially pp. 123–6.
[32]City of Halifax, *Report of the Commission to Investigate the Taxation System
in the City of Halifax* (Halifax, 1957), p. 75.
[33]State of New York, *Report of the New York State Commission on State Aid
to Municipal Subdivisions* (Legislative Document No. 58, memorandum submitted by the State Tax Commission; Albany, 1936), p. 352.

factory index of relative fiscal capacity, but the problems remain of (1) determining how much larger grants should be for urban than for rural municipalities and (2) determining the expenditure requirements of the different municipalities within each of the two main groupings. An additional problem is that of how to treat the village commissions and other similar commissions which provide one or two local services. The present system of unconditional grants has already been criticized on two grounds: that the distribution between the types of municipalities is not soundly based and that per capita grants, by their nature, do not provide the degree of equalization required by the principle of fiscal equity.

A possible approach is to base the grants on foundation programmes for local services but to leave the municipalities free to use the grants as they wish. But to determine the grants in this way would add greatly to the cost of administering the programme of grants and would be more difficult than in the case of the general services because of legitimately wider variations in the levels and types of services among the municipalities.

Perhaps the best solution would be to determine the average per capita costs of providing local services for all municipalities of each type, for the latest year for which statistics are available, and to multiply this figure by the population of each municipality. The result could be called the "standard expenditure."[34] From there the grants could be determined on the same basis as that proposed for the conditional grants. The uniform burden would then be the average rate necessary to raise the standard expenditures in the three[35] municipalities of each type for which the ratios of these expenditures to their equalized valuations would be lowest. The grants to the rest of the municipalities would be equal to their standard expenditures minus the average rate of burden multiplied by their equalized assessments. The village commissions and other commissions could be treated as a separate class of municipality. Population figures are not available for these localities, but the number of properties on the assessment rolls

[34]The use of an average to determine the "standard expenditure" was objected to in the case of Rowat's proposed grant for social and educational services, because it was regarded as an inadequate measure of the desirable level of general services. However, such an average is quite appropriate for local services, since the municipalities themselves are the best judges of the desirable level of these services.

[35]Three are suggested instead of five, as in the case of the conditional grants, because of the division of the municipalities into smaller groups. It would not, however, be necessary to use the same number for all groups in calculating the uniform burden.

could perhaps be used instead. An alternative would be to lump their expenditures in with those of the rural municipalities, make grants only to the rural municipalities and leave it up to them to decide whether and on what basis to pass some of the grants on to the commissions.

It might be advisable to make a division among the towns, since the larger towns generally provide a wider range of services than the smaller ones. Perhaps they should be divided into three groups: small towns of under 3,000 population, medium towns of 3,000 to 9,999, and large towns of 10,000 and over. The large towns could then be grouped with the three cities in calculating the grants. Using these classifications and the 1956 populations there would be 21 small towns, 14 medium towns, and 4 large towns (grouped with the 3 cities).

This scheme of grants would at one and the same time take care of the two problems raised earlier in this section, and the grants would be reasonably simple to calculate and would be easily understood by municipal officials and the general public. The scheme would be in as close conformity with the principle of fiscal equity as any practicable scheme could be expected to be. If the province wished to give flat-rate unconditional grants to all municipalities, it could do so and at the same time erect the proposed equalization structure on top of it. If, on the other hand, it felt that it could not even afford to put the equalization scheme fully into operation, it could implement some given percentage of the full equalization formula. The lower the percentage it chose, however, the greater the departure from fiscal equity would be. The grants would be very similar in all these respects, as well as in the mode of calculation, to the proposed conditional grants.

If no flat-rate grant were made, it would mean that a few of the municipalities would get no grants. However, if the towns and cities were given special grants as a share of the motor vehicle and gasoline taxes to help cover the costs of streets in the way suggested in the previous section, all of the urban municipalities would receive some aid on a fair basis. Such grants for streets should be subtracted from the expenditures for local services in calculating the unconditional grants.

A Suggested System of Grants to Implement the Principle of Fiscal Equity

A system of grants which would implement the principle of fiscal equity with respect to both general and local services is implicit in the discussion in the preceding sections. There are three elements to it.

(1) Conditional grants for general services, determined by the following formula: $G_c = F - rA$, where G_c = the grant for a given service paid to a given municipality, F = the cost of the foundation programme for the service in the municipality, A = equalized valuation of taxable property in the municipality, and r = uniform rate (burden) determined by taking the average of the ratios of F/A in the five municipalities for which the ratios are lowest.

(2) Unconditional grants for local services, determined by the following formula: $G_u = L - rA$, where G_u = the unconditional grant paid to a given municipality of a given type, L = population of the municipality $\times$ average per capita cost of local services in all municipalities of its type, A = equalized valuation of the municipality, and r = uniform rate (burden) determined by taking the average of the ratios of L/A in the three municipalities of the given type for which the ratios are lowest, except for the rural municipalities for which an average for five municipalities is suggested.

(3) Grants in lieu of motor vehicle revenues to towns and cities towards the cost of their streets. These should be based on mileage and on the types of streets. Perhaps the simplest basis would be to pay some given percentage, say 50 per cent, of the costs of the streets, based upon standard costs for different types of surfaces and any other relevant characteristics, such standard costs to be determined by the Department of Highways. These grants would be deducted from the cost of local services in calculating the unconditional grants. Such a grant is favoured over municipal taxes on motor vehicles or gasoline, because of the greater administrative efficiency of having provincial collection of these revenues and because of the difficulty of taxing out-of-town users of a municipality's streets. Such grants would give some property tax relief to all urban municipalities; the other grants would not do this unless they included flat-rate payments. The principle of fiscal equity would not be violated by these special grants for streets, for it would be applied with regard to the balance of local expenditures for streets along with the other expenditures for local purposes.

Since a foundation programme has already been drawn up for education, the implementation of the scheme of grants suggested here would not be difficult administratively. The standards already drawn up for mental hospitals and for indoor and outdoor relief could serve as the basis for foundation programmes for these services. There is already, in effect, a foundation programme for child welfare in the form of minimum payments per child for the various types of child care provided.

Instead of applying the formula for conditional grants to the portion of highways passing through towns and cities for which these municipalities are responsible, it would be simpler, and appropriate, to consider the towns' and cities' shares of these roads as part of their local expenditures in calculating the unconditional grants.

The unconditional grants would be quite simple to calculate. Even the allocation of debt charges between local and general services should not pose very difficult problems. If the provincial government wished to discourage municipal borrowing, it could scale down its grants by deducting a certain portion of each municipality's debt charges from its grant, in order to encourage the local governments to finance their expenditures as far as possible out of current revenues. To do this would mean some departure from the principle of fiscal equity. But the departure need not be great and if the "penalty" resulted in faster debt retirement and therefore lower debt charges, there would gradually be a movement towards full implementation of the principle of fiscal equity.

If the municipalities continue to be charged with the responsibility for building and maintaining local general hospitals, the costs incurred by municipalities for these purposes could be included in calculating the unconditional grants.

FISCAL ADJUSTMENT BY MEANS OF A REDISTRIBUTION OF FUNCTIONS OR REVENUES

It would not be feasible to effect adjustment according to the principle of fiscal equity by a redistribution of functions or revenues. The inequalities in fiscal capacity of the municipalities are considerable whether measured by per capita equalized valuation or by per capita net income of payers of personal income tax. Making additional taxation bases available to the municipalities would increase their general revenue-raising capacity, but would not eliminate these inequalities. The burden of raising a given amount of revenue would still be heavier in some localities than in others. Furthermore, such taxes as might be made available—the retail sales tax and motor vehicle user taxes are examples—can be much more effectively administered by the province than by the municipalities, especially the small municipalities. The use of shared taxes is also unsatisfactory from the point of view of equalization and little better with respect to administrative efficiency, or for that matter with respect to financial responsibility, and in addition poses difficult problems with respect to determining satisfactory principles of allocation.[36]

Even a redistribution of functions, with the province assuming the responsibility for some municipal services, would leave the municipalities with unequal burdens in paying for the balance of their services. Nevertheless, the greater the assumption of functions by the provincial government the greater the extent to which equalization according to the principle of fiscal equity is implemented. The province could conceivably take complete financial responsibility for all of the general services and make unconditional grants for local services as well as grants for streets; and the municipalities could be left with prime responsibility for local services. If the province did so, the municipalities could continue to be charged with the administration of the general services they presently provide. It is unlikely that such an arrangement would be satisfactory. The complete divorce of financial responsibility and administrative responsibility would likely either seriously reduce local incentive for efficient administration or require such close provincial supervision of local administration that the advantages that ideally stem from it would be lost. Though preferable to local administration with no financial responsibility, it is also questionable whether the complete administration by the province of the general services, even accompanied by some decentralization into regions and by the setting up of locally elected advisory boards, is a good substitute, in the cases of education and relief at least, for local administration along with some local financial responsibility.

Moreover, the assumption of complete financial and administrative responsibility for general services by the province would spell the end of local government in rural Nova Scotia. There would then be no point in merging the rural and urban municipalities, since the people in the rural municipalities would have no interest in such an amalgamated unit. Whether these consequences are deemed to matter or not depends upon how much importance is attached to local government in these areas, where in any case nearly all of the services performed are mandatory.

A more promising approach would be to consider complete assumption of responsibility for certain general services by the province. Two

[36]Compare *Report of the New York State Commission on State Aid to Municipal Subdivisions*, p. 10. "The objections to shared taxes in general are that (1) they are difficult to adapt to local needs because of the uniform rate, (2) they fluctuate so greatly in yield that they are not dependable sources of income, and (3) their use is not readily controlled."

in particular which it would seem appropriate for the province to take over are mental hospitals and child care. As already suggested, the eventual provincial assumption of care for the mentally ill appears to be inevitable in view of the fact that all other provinces have taken on this responsibility and in view of the province's commitments with respect to hospital care. In the case of child care, the municipalities themselves take no active part in the administration of child-caring facilities; they simply pay a share of the costs as laid down by statute. Nothing substantial would be lost in terms of local autonomy if the province assumed the municipalities' share of the payments.[37] It is not suggested that the Children's Aid Societies, which are private welfare agencies, should be abolished, for they are a good way of maintaining local interest in child welfare. To the contrary, it is urged that the municipalities should give them more financial support than they do and that the province should continue its support of them.

It appears that the municipalities will soon be relieved of the responsibility for prisoners serving sentences of three months or more, but they will still bear the costs for the larger number serving shorter sentences and for those awaiting trial or sentence. The province could assume the costs for the prisoners in this latter group who are serving sentences for provincial offences and it could also well assume the costs of the administration of justice at present borne by the municipalities, without any significant loss of decision-making at the local level, since here again, in both cases, the municipalities have little administrative discretion.[38]

Relieving the municipalities of the responsibility for these four

[37]Compare Crawford, *Canadian Municipal Government* (Toronto: University of Toronto Press, 1954), p. 360. "In considering which of the present municipal functions might be transferred to the provinces, there are some respecting which there would appear to be little argument. Such would be those in which discretion on the part of local authorities is not a factor, but in which the local authority is merely a bill-paying agency. . . . The . . . situation applies where children are taken into care by a Children's Aid Society. Where the Society is a voluntary statutory agency the municipality merely pays a bill for maintenance of wards which under the legislation are its responsibility." Crawford was talking about Canadian municipalities in general, but his remarks are applicable to Nova Scotia.

[38]Compare Crawford: "Considering the extent to which the officials involved are appointed by the provinces and the extent to which the administration is controlled by detailed provincial rules and regulations, about the only local discretion involved is the decision as to who shall supply the fuel to heat the buildings involved, or who shall get the manual labour jobs. . . . So slight is the local discretion and so obviously is the administration of justice a service to our society as a whole, that it would seem to be a logical service to transfer entirely to provincial administration and financing." (*Ibid.*, p. 361.)

services (mental hospitals, child care, most of the jails, and the administration of justice) would give considerable financial relief to them, thus easing the burden on property or freeing funds to improve other services, or, more likely, resulting in a combination of both. Such a shift in responsibility would be wholly in accord with the principle of fiscal equity and would mean little real loss in local administrative responsibility, except possibly in the case of the mental hospitals for which a shift in responsibility seems to be likely in any case.

DIFFERENTIAL PROVINCIAL TAXATION AS AN ADJUSTMENT DEVICE

Buchanan argued that theoretically the most effective means of implementing a federal policy of fiscal equity would be by discriminatory federal taxation of personal income from province to province.[39] His argument need not be examined in detail here. The use of this device was precluded as long as the province surrendered its right to levy personal income taxes to the federal government in return for tax rental payments. While its use at the federal-provincial level is no longer precluded by the new federal-provincial fiscal arrangements, it is probably precluded on political and administrative grounds. Furthermore, the use of differential personal income taxation as an adjustment device at the provincial-municipal level would require that the municipalities get a large share of their revenues from a local income tax. Such a tax can be ruled out on grounds of administrative efficiency.

Differential provincial taxation of property in the municipalities could be used as an equalization device, combined perhaps with a redistribution of the revenues to the municipalities. But such a measure would meet with strong resistance from the municipalities (especially the wealthier ones) which would resent direct provincial encroachment on what has become traditionally an exclusively municipal tax base. It is also the only major municipal tax base. The position taken here is that the property tax base should continue to be left entirely to the municipalities.

There is one "tax" which might appropriately be applied discriminatively in Nova Scotia. In making its per capita levy on the municipalities to help pay for the capital costs of local general hospitals, the

[39]J. M. Buchanan, "Federalism and Fiscal Equity," *American Economic Review,* XL (September, 1950), pp. 595–6. He argued in terms of equalizing fiscal residua. The criticism of using fiscal residua suggests that the precision with which differential personal income taxation could equalize fiscal pressure on similarly situated individuals is less than Buchanan thought.

provincial government could take the unequal fiscal capacity of the municipalities into account by making the levy proportional to per capita equalized assessment. The burden would then be uniform in all municipalities and the levy would be consistent with the principle of fiscal equity. For example, the per capita levy on a municipality with a per capita equalized valuation of $2,000 would be twice as great as on a municipality with a per capita equalized valuation of $1,000. This method of imposition is an alternative to the simpler suggestion made earlier that the provincial levy be made at a uniform rate on the equalized assessment of all of the municipalities.

THE RECOMMENDED PROGRAMME OF FISCAL ADJUSTMENT

The recommended programme of fiscal adjustment is a combination of provincial assumption of some municipal functions, provincial grants, and a differential per capita levy. Specifically, it is recommended:

(1) That the province assume full financial and administrative responsibility for mental hospitals, child care, the administration of justice, and prisoners jailed for other than local offences;

(2) That the systems of conditional and unconditional grants suggested earlier in this chapter be implemented for the other services not covered in (1), above;

(3) That the per capita levy to help cover the capital costs of local hospitals be made proportional to per capita equalized valuation or be imposed at a uniform rate on equalized valuation. This should not be included among expenditures for local purposes in making the unconditional grants, because the levy itself would be made according to the principle of fiscal equity;

(4) That the province adopt a policy of giving grants in lieu of taxation on its property, and on the property of its Crown corporations, equal to what would be paid if such property were taxed at the same rates as other property in the municipalities in which it is located. The implementation of this recommendation would be of particular value to the City of Halifax in helping to overcome its peculiar financial difficulties, and it would be in accord with the practice now followed by the federal government with respect to its property.[40]

---

[40]As already pointed out the policy is not followed fully by federal Crown corporations. It is strange that it is not, in view of their commercial nature. The grounds for it being followed by them are even stronger than for it being followed by the federal government itself.

Since full adjustment according to the principle of fiscal equity could be accomplished at a lower cost to the provincial government by implementing recommendations (2) and (3), it may be that these should have priority over (1).[41] Then the province could gradually assume a larger and larger share of the cost of the services in (1) until eventually it took them over entirely.

If the proposed programme of fiscal adjustment were fully implemented, not only would all municipalities be able to finance approximately equivalent services with approximately equivalent burdens, but in addition all municipalities would get considerable financial relief from the province undertaking responsibility for the general services in recommendation (1). One result would be to transfer much of the tax burden from the highly regressive property taxes to the less regressive revenue sources of the provincial government and, at the same time, make the economic conditions under which business firms operate in the province more favourable by reducing fixed costs. Since the programme has been designed to put all of the municipalities in the position of providing equivalent benefits with equivalent burdens, it is very much in accord with the doctrine of financial responsibility. The taxpayers in any given municipality would suffer from any wasteful administration in that municipality and would react in much the same way as if waste occurred when a lower level of services was financed to a greater extent by the municipality.

To a very great extent, the success of the programme of adjustment in achieving the objectives relating to the principle of fiscal equity both within and between municipalities depends upon the equalized valuations of property being accurate and upon uniform assessment practices being followed within and between municipalities. The importance of thorough and accurate assessment and frequent revisions of assessment cannot be over-emphasized. There is much to be said, in the interest of achieving a soundly based programme of adjustment, for having all assessment under provincial control. If such control is considered too great interference in the affairs of the municipalities, the province could at least establish procedures of assessment which all municipalities would be required to follow. This requirement would help to establish uniformity within municipalities and to increase the accuracy of equalized valuations made on a unit basis.

[41]The proposed grant for streets included in (2) is not in itself connected with the principle of fiscal equity, but is recommended rather as an additional source of revenue for towns and cities in lieu of municipal motor user taxes. The fact that the balance of the cost of streets is taken care of by the unconditional grant assures that the principle of fiscal equity is implemented with respect to streets.

Special consideration should be given to the assessment and taxation of industrial and commercial property. Accurate and equitable assessment of such property is difficult to achieve even in large urban units where it is generally easier to estimate market values than it is in small towns and rural areas. Not only is the accurate assessment of such properties in small towns and rural municipalities a task often beyond the abilities of local assessors, but there is a strong temptation to assess such property, especially that of firms in one-firm municipalities, at relatively higher values than other property and so to impose a disproportionately great burden of taxation on such property. Such a burden adds to the fixed costs of a business and may retard its growth, force it to close down or move elsewhere, and discourage new industries from moving in. This practice is likely to have particularly serious effects in a province like Nova Scotia that lacks the general economic buoyancy of the central and western provinces. If assessment of such property is to remain in the hands of local assessors, there should be provision for appeal by a company that considers its property to be assessed inequitably to a provincially constituted board of well-qualified assessors.

An alternative, one that has been considered in Alberta, would be to have all or certain types of industrial property in the province assessed and taxed at a uniform rate by the provincial government. The proceeds could be distributed among the municipalities in the form of unconditional or conditional grants in accordance with the principle of fiscal equity. Such a method would make it easier to assure that the burden of taxation was the same on a given type of industrial property throughout the province and that the burden was not heavier than that generally prevailing in other provinces.

The possibility of abandoning the taxation of personal property should be thoroughly investigated, as personal property is even more difficult to assess accurately than real property. The transfer of the personal property burden to real property would likely have small effect on the total burden on particular taxpayers and would result in a more equitable and a more efficiently administered tax. Moreover, with the easing of the burden on property that would result from the implementation of the adjustment programme, the personal property tax could be eliminated with very little addition, and perhaps in some cases no addition, to the taxes on real property.

Another important way in which assessment could be improved is by making sure that all taxable property is in fact assessed. This is especially important when adjustment is based upon equalized valuation, for unassessed property escapes inclusion in the equalized valuation.[42] It is also important of course from the point of view of equality of treatment of individuals within each municipality. The discovery of unassessed property is so important that if the municipalities retain the responsibility for assessment the province would be justified in levying a penalty, deductable from the municipality's grants, on any municipality for unassessed property which is discovered after, say, a two-year period. A suitable penalty would be one equal to twice the amount of tax revenue lost after the two-year warning period.

It might also be advisable, for the purpose of promoting improved administration, to introduce a penalty for municipalities that fail to collect all of the taxes which are due to them, possibly a deduction of such taxes or at least a large portion of them from the grants.[43]

There would no doubt be some effect on real property values from the programme of fiscal adjustment proposed here, as there would be from any programme of equalization. Grants to a municipality would in themselves tend to raise real property values there because of the higher level of services made possible by them, with a resulting second order effect of increasing local property tax revenues and so reducing the amount of grants required to implement the principle of fiscal equity. But the over-all effect of the programme on real property values is more complex where a municipality in meeting the requirement of imposing a uniform burden is forced to increase its property tax rate, for such an increase would in itself tend to depress real property values. It is important at least to take cognizance of the possible effect of the programme on real property values and to observe that the programme itself would automatically adjust to such changes, in that provincial grants would change inversely with changes in these values in each municipality.

A reader of a preliminary draft of this study criticized the basing of the proposed scheme in part on equal burdens on property, on the ground that ownership of property is not a very good measure of an individual's ability to pay. Admittedly, it is quite possible, even likely, that people in some low-income locality will in general own more valuable homes than those in some other high-income locality. In such

[42]See *Pottier Report*, p. 26.
[43]In 1959 total collections as a percentage of the current tax roll varied from 77.1 to 108.4 for towns and cities, and 72.3 to 104.3 for rural municipalities; and arrears as a percentage of the current tax roll varied from .1 to 225.4 for towns and cities and 10.8 to 196.3 for rural municipalities. (D.B.S., *Annual Report of Municipal Statistics, 1959* (Ottawa: Queen's Printer), pp. 5, 14.)

a case, the low-income locality will get smaller grants than the high-income locality, even though the people with high incomes can afford to pay higher taxes on property than people with low incomes. This criticism misses the point. The proposed programme is designed to provide approximately the same level of services and impose approximately the same tax burdens on an individual wherever he may live in the province. To achieve this end, an individual who owns a home of given value in either locality must pay about the same amount of tax on it as he would if he owned it in the other locality. There is therefore no injustice in this scheme, whatever injustice there may be in property taxation itself, for similarly situated property owners will be treated similarly. Furthermore, while the two localities may differ in a general way in the practices of their citizens regarding home ownership, there will in fact be a wide range of such practices, perhaps even approximately the same range in both localities, just as there will be wide ranges in other tax bases, such as other forms of wealth, income, and expenditure. It is the treatment of individuals which is relevant, not the treatment of localities as such.

There are alternative ways of implementing the principle of fiscal equity. The one proposed is conservative in character, and therefore politically attractive, in that it is designed to accord with existing institutions and to disturb present practices as little as possible. A neater and perhaps ultimately more satisfactory way of providing conditional grants in accordance with the principle of fiscal equity is that recently adopted in Alberta for primary and secondary education. In that province, the government imposes a tax for school purposes on all municipalities at a uniform rate on equalized assessments and pays to each school board the amount necessary to provide a foundation programme measured at standard costs, the additional revenues required for this purpose being provided from general provincial revenues. A school board may supplement the foundation programme by obtaining the money directly from its municipal collecting body.[44]

THE COST OF THE PROPOSED PROGRAMME TO THE PROVINCE

No attempt is made here to obtain detailed or precise estimates of the cost to the provincial government of the proposed programme of fiscal adjustment. The government could make such estimates any

[44]Speech by A. O. Alberg, Minister of Education, Province of Alberta, "Foundation Program of Public School Finance," March 24, 1961.

time it chose. This study is more concerned with formulating the principles for provincial-municipal fiscal adjustment in Nova Scotia than with producing a detailed blueprint for it. Moreover, the cost would depend on when the scheme was implemented, on whether flat-rate grants were given, and on the level of the foundation programmes drawn up for indoor and outdoor relief and such other general services besides education not wholly assumed by the province. It was roughly estimated on the basis of 1956 data that the total additional cost of fully implementing the programme would be about $10 million. The cost has no doubt risen somewhat in subsequent years.

It should be borne in mind that to the extent the maladjustments in the use of the province's resources are corrected, the fiscal capacity of the province will be increased. Provincial tax revenues will increase without any increases in tax rates. The proposed fiscal programme should not only stimulate improved use of resources (in addition to its other virtues, particularly the ethical one of giving equal fiscal treatment to equals) but should also generate at least some of the increased provincial expenditures required to finance it.

Although the immediate implementation of the complete programme of adjustment may not be feasible without further transfers from the federal government, the provincial government could implement part of it by increases in income, sales, gasoline, and motor vehicle taxes. Such increases would be objectionable in that the rates of these taxes are already as high as or higher than the rates in other provinces; but they could be justified in part by the concomitant reduction in the tax burden on property and by the improved services, as well as by the ethical and economic advantages stressed in this study. The reduction of the property tax burden may be of particular importance to industry since property taxes constitute a fixed charge on industry and may have a particularly discouraging effect in a region lagging in economic growth. In such a region, retail sales taxes (including the general retail sales tax, the gasoline tax, and liquor revenues) probably have the least discouraging effects on industrial development, with personal and corporate income taxes coming somewhere in between them and property taxes.

It is not recommended that new types of tax be levied. The major revenue raisers at the disposal of the province are already in use. One of the virtues of Nova Scotia's fiscal system at present is the simplicity of its tax structure. Up to a point, diversity in the tax structure is desirable in that it prevents the escape of persons with taxpaying ability from paying their share of taxes. But refining the mesh in the taxgatherer's net soon ceases to be worthwhile.

Even if no large part of the programme is implemented in the near future, the programme can still serve as a guide for provincial policy whenever the provincial government feels that it can take some step in the direction of fiscal adjustment. The government could implement the programme in stages and could name a target date by which the programme would be fully implemented.

It should be emphasized that the proposals made in this study, along with the argument developed in support of them, are not intended as mere "academic" exercises. They are made with the view to their becoming the basis for public policy in the area of provincial-municipal fiscal relations. Fiscal adjustment in Nova Scotia according to the principle of fiscal equity has the paramount virtues of being both fiscally just to the residents of the province, and of being conducive to the optimum allocation of the province's resources. At the same time it provides a rational basis for easing the fiscal burden associated with the painful economic adjustments which must inevitably be made in some of the municipalities from time to time.

It is worth repeating that the proposed programme is not intended to preclude improvements in administration which may result from amalgamation of municipal units. Nor is it intended to preclude the use of other instruments of public policy to improve the use of the province's resources.

A Brief Summary of
Results, and Conclusions

FIVE MAIN QUESTIONS HAVE BEEN DISCUSSED IN THIS STUDY.

(1) Why is Nova Scotia a low-income province?

(2) What types of economic adjustment are necessary to bring about best use of the province's resources?

(3) What pattern of provincial-municipal fiscal relations is most conducive to the best use of the province's resources?

(4) What fiscal adjustments should be made to take account of increases in the scope and cost of services traditionally performed by municipalities in view of the heavy pressure on the limited municipal tax base—property—and in view of the fact that some of the services are of far broader than local interest?

(5) Can answers be found to (3) and (4) which are compatible?

In brief, the answers arrived at are the following.

(1) Nova Scotia is a low-income province mainly because of its relative paucity of resources and its unfavourable location with respect to markets and because there is considerable maladjustment in the use of the resources it does have, particularly with regard to the primary industries and the tourist industry. Even with considerable emigration, there will likely continue to be a substantial chronic surplus of labour unless primary processing and secondary manufacturing industries expand.

(2) Suggestions have been made about how the province's resources could be used more effectively. In particular, the types of adjustments required in the primary industries and the tourist industry have been indicated. Development of secondary manufacturing industry will

probably have to be based primarily on markets in the Atlantic region, although in some cases markets in other parts of Canada and in foreign countries will no doubt also be developed.

Refractory sociological factors will likely continue to impede economic improvement as they have in the past. As a result, the prescribed adjustments are not likely to be made quickly. It may even be necessary to think in terms of accomplishing them fully only over the next generation. Certainly, one way of accelerating adjustment would be by direct attempts to overcome these sociological impediments.

Economic improvement depends in very large part upon the knowledge, skill, and adaptability of the people, particularly since the resource base is narrow. A particularly high priority should therefore be given by the provincial government to achieving excellence in education at all levels and in technical and vocational training. The results would be three-fold. The people would be more productive. They would be more aware of economic opportunities elsewhere and of opportunities to make better use of the resources within the province, and would be better prepared to move about to take advantage of them. The province would be more attractive to new firms that might consider locating in it especially if the programme of technical training was geared very closely to the needs of industries locating or expanding there.

(3) It has been argued that the application of a modified version of the principle of fiscal equity developed by Buchanan has great virtue from the point of view of effecting provincial-municipal fiscal adjustment that is conductive to optimum allocation of resources. This principle is also attractive from the ethical point of view, requiring as it does equal treatment of "equals." It was argued that, in Nova Scotia at least, raising the levels of services in the poor municipalities would itself on balance have favourable effects on allocation of resources, contrary to the general contentions made by Scott. Not the least favourable of the effects would be the tendency, especially in the case of education, to overcome some of the sociological impediments to economic adjustment, already referred to above.

On the other hand Scott's theory appears applicable and Buchanan's inapplicable, with respect to the types of economic adjustment that are appropriate to Nova Scotia *vis-à-vis* the rest of the country. It is likely that there is a tendency for both labour and capital to have higher marginal productivities in other parts of the country and therefore likely that there will be a continued emigration of both factors from the province. The internal adjustments required in the province are more complicated. In the case of towns suffering from the loss of basic industry, with no sound alternatives, outward movements of both labour and capital are required. These movements are the type Scott said might be desirable in some cases. For the rural areas, rationalization of primary operations in farming, fishing, and forestry is called for, a prescription for adjustment similar to but not identical with Buchanan's.

(4) With regard to questions (4) and (5), it was found that many adjustments in municipal functions and revenues, in the latter by means of provincial grants, can be made in ways which are consistent with the principle of fiscal equity. The adjustment programme actually proposed would implement the principle with respect to both general and local services and would give some financial relief to all municipalities, but greater relief to the municipalities with low fiscal capacities relative to foundation or standard levels of expenditure. At the same time the municipalities would be left with considerable flexibility in determining the actual levels of their services in that they would be free to supplement any of them they wished, by taxing themselves more heavily, by applying their unconditional grants for the purpose, or by doing both.

Within the framework of the analysis and proposals in chapter ix there is considerable choice open to the province as to how fiscal adjustment according to the principle of fiscal equity could be accomplished. At one extreme, the province could take over the administration and financing of general services entirely. At the other extreme, it would be possible to implement the principle quite fully by the province making unconditional grants for both local and general services. It would be possible, for example, to increase the power presently in local hands by the provincial government ceasing to make the Foundation Program for education mandatory, but continuing to make unconditional grants based upon the Foundation Program. No doubt those who would condemn any reduction in local powers, because they believe a wide area of local government is essential in order to sustain a democratic form of government throughout a country, would favour the latter alternative.

One does not have to look far to find strong expressions of the view that a wide range of local government is the cornerstone of democracy.

The following are some examples.

Democratic process is an invention of local bodies. It has been extended upward and may be extended gradually toward world organization. In any case, modern democracy rests upon free, responsible local government and will never be stronger than this foundation. Free, responsible local bodies correspond, in the political system, to free, responsible individuals or families and voluntary associations in the good society. A people wisely conserving its liberties will seek ever to enlarge the range and degree of local freedom and responsibility. In doing so, it may sacrifice possible proximate achievements. Doing specific good things by centralization will always be alluring. It may always seem easier to impose "progress" on localities than to wait for them to effect it for themselves—provided one is not solicitous about the basis or sources of progress.[1]

The municipal level of government offers the best opportunity for the ordinary citizen to participate directly in public affairs, and to develop an insight into the processes of provincial and federal government as well. The latter, being carried on at a great distance from the direct observation of the average citizen, tend to be obscured. But the services rendered by his local authorities, whom he elects and whom he often knows personally, touch him at a thousand points. They are almost as pervasive as the air he breathes. The citizen who keeps his eyes and his mind open can observe the operation of these services from day to day, and has thus the material and the opportunity to think about public affairs, to form judgments and to act thereon. . . . In this sense local institutions are the laboratories of democracy.[2]

To have services performed at the municipal level is an essential feature of a democracy. Such an arrangement makes government more responsive to local needs and allows the citizen an active participation in the affairs of the community. It develops leadership and prepares local talent for work in a wider field. If, therefore, the main social functions of government should for the sake of efficiency be transferred to a higher level, a valuable training ground for democratic government would be lost.[3]

It is not difficult to visualize an impairment of democracy by adminstrative decisions which would enhance economic welfare in a highly centralized superior jurisdiction, like a province or nation. It may be that in such a political unit some sacrifice of administrative efficiency is a price which must be paid to maintain democracy.

The fact that the programme of adjustment favoured here would

[1]Henry C. Simons, "Introduction: A Political Credo," *Economic Policy for a Free Society* (Chicago: University of Chicago Press: 1948), p. 13.

[2]Horace L. Brittain, *Local Government in Canada* (Toronto: Ryerson Press, 1951), pp. v–vi.

[3]D. C. Rowat, *The Reorganization of Provincial-Municipal Relations in Nova Scotia* (A report prepared for the Government of Nova Scotia by the Nova Scotia Municipal Bureau, Institute of Public Affairs, Dalhousie University; Hailfax, 1949), p. ix.

mean increased provincial influence over the localities in their provision of general services, and even the complete provincial assumption
of some of these services, indicates a measure of disagreement with
the views quoted. It is certainly agreed, providing the quality of local
government is high, that considerable responsibilities should be left
with the municipalities, but not on the ground of safeguarding democracy at the expense of administrative efficiency; rather, on the opposite
ground that there will be greater administrative efficiency if the
responsibility for certain of the general services and for the local
services rests with the municipalities. The localities are best able both
to determine the level of local services and to administer them. And
where the localities are responsible for general services for which
minimum standards are prescribed by the province, there is the added
advantage that they are then free to supplement these services if they
wish.

If it were found that in fact the quality of local government administration was generally poor, the provincial government should consider
taking over the responsibility for administering all general services.
If it were to do this, it would mean the elimination of the rural
municipalities as units of local government, and therefore of municipal
councils, unless these councils were reconstituted as simply advisory
bodies. Villages and commissions could continue to provide local services in built-up areas. The province would then have to assess such
property as was to be taxed to support the general services and levy
its own taxes upon it. Such a move would be entirely in accordance
with the principle of fiscal equity.

The generalization that a large amount of local government is necessary for a healthy democracy is frequently repeated without being
convincingly demonstrated.[4] It is often regarded, without sufficient
justification, as being a maxim and when so regarded it stultifies
thought. The truth or falsity of the contention is not a matter of
unvarying law but is an empirical matter. Even if it were proven to be
valid for any particular place and time, it does not follow that it would
also be valid for other places or times. It would still have to be
demonstrated that it was valid for Nova Scotia. The relevant question,
therefore, is: what actually is the case in Nova Scotia?

Eighty years ago, people in the scattered localities of Nova Scotia
were more isolated than today from the main streams of events at the

[4]For a thoughtful discussion bearing on some of the questions raised here see
Hugh Whalen, "Democracy and Local Government," *Canadian Public Administration*, III (March, 1960), pp. 1–13.

higher levels of government, and public administration could not be as effectively decentralized as today, although government at these levels was then simpler and less extensive than now. Even at that time, interest in questions of local government was not particularly great. Since then, improvements in transportation and communication have made people less remote from provincial political life with respect to time and space. Another kind of remoteness, more serious in nature than remoteness of time and space, is that stemming from a greater range and complexity of governmental activities and their greater interdependence, with the growth of the welfare state, which makes understanding of the governmental processes more difficult. In Nova Scotia at least, this kind of remoteness has not in fact become very great. Most provincial governmental activities are still simple enough to be quite well understood, at least in broad outline, by the ordinary citizen, although there are certainly exceptions, such as programmes for economic development and some aspects of urban planning.

Some services, like education, health, and social welfare, once mainly of local concern, are now of general provincial or even national concern. It is therefore desirable that citizens should transfer some of their interest in these matters from the local to the provincial sphere. At the same time, provincial administration can be decentralized in a small province like Nova Scotia to permit local participation in decision-making. It is not a bad thing for democracy if people come to consider what were once regarded as local matters in a broader context and become less parochial in the process; and not a good thing if their attention is focused unduly on local matters that are often relatively trivial in nature.

As was pointed out in chapter IV, local government developed in Nova Scotia, especially in the rural areas, not because of popular demand for it, but because it was imposed by the provincial government. In these areas at least, and perhaps in the towns and cities as well, it is doubtful that Nova Scotia has ever had the vigorous kind of local government visualized by those who regard it as the corner-stone of democracy. A democratic edifice dependent on it would have crumbled long ago. The very opportunity for intimate contact of the citizens with provincial politics has probably made local government a less vital force in Nova Scotia than it might otherwise have become.

It appears that there is wide latitude in Nova Scotia for adjustments in local functions on grounds of administrative efficiency or of being conducive to the more general interests of the citizens of the province, without any essential impairment of democracy. In any case, the recommended adjustments would leave the municipalities with enough responsibility to foster local interest in their affairs. Far from impairing local autonomy, fiscal transfers made according to the principle of fiscal equity give positive content to this autonomy, for autonomy in carrying out their responsibilities is of little importance to the poorer localities unless they are provided with sufficient financial resources to provide services at levels comparable to those in the wealthier localities without imposing inordinate burdens of taxation on their residents.

Selected Bibliography

WORKS CITED

1. Books and Pamphlets

Beck, J. Murray. *The Government of Nova Scotia.* Toronto: University of Toronto Press, 1957.

Birch, A. H. *Federalism, Finance and Social Legislation in Canada, Australia and the United States.* Oxford: At the Clarendon Press, 1955.

Brittain, Horace L. *Local Government in Canada.* Toronto: Ryerson Press, 1951.

Brown, George W., ed. *Canada.* (United Nations Series, edited by Robert J. Kerner.) Berkeley and Los Angeles: University of California Press, 1950.

Cairncross, A. K. *Economic Development and the Atlantic Provinces.* Fredericton: Atlantic Provinces Research Board, 1961.

Carswell, Roger. *Taxes and Traffic: A Study of Highway Financing.* (Canadian Tax Papers, No. 8.) Toronto: Canadian Tax Foundation, 1955.

Clark, R. M. *The Municipal Business Tax in Canada.* (Canadian Tax Papers, No. 5.) Toronto: Canadian Tax Foundation, 1952.

Crawford, Kenneth Grant. *Canadian Municipal Government.* Toronto: University of Toronto Press, 1954.

Currie, A. W. *Economic Geography of Canada.* Toronto: The Macmillan Company of Canada Limited, 1945.

Dawson, R. MacGregor. *The Government of Canada.* 3rd edition, revised. Toronto: University of Toronto Press, 1957.

Due, John F. *Provincial Sales Taxes.* (Canadian Tax Papers, No. 7.) Toronto: Canadian Tax Foundation, 1953.

Easterbrook, W. T., and Aitken, Hugh G. J. *Canadian Economic History.* Toronto: The Macmillan Company of Canada Limited, 1956.

Innis, H. A. *The Cod Fisheries: The History of an International Economy.* Revised edition. Toronto: University of Toronto Press, 1954.

Keirstead, B. S. *The Theory of Economic Change.* Toronto: The Macmillan Company of Canada Limited, 1948.

Levitt, Kari. *Population Movements in the Atlantic Provinces.* Halifax and Fredericton: Commissioned by Atlantic Provinces Research Board and prepared by Atlantic Provinces Economic Council, 1960. (Mimeographed.)

Lounsbury, F. E. *Financing Industrial Development in the Atlantic Provinces.* Halifax and Fredericton: Commissioned by Atlantic Provinces Research Board and prepared by Atlantic Provinces Economic Council, 1960. (Mimeographed.)

de Marco, Antonio de Viti. *First Principles of Public Finance.* (Translated by E. P. Marget.) New York: Harcourt Brace and Co., 1936.

Maxwell, J. A. *Federal Subsidies to the Provincial Governments in Canada.* Cambridge: Harvard University Press, 1937.

—— *The Fiscal Impact of Federalism in the United States.* Cambridge: Harvard University Press, 1946.

Meade, J. E. *The Theory of International Economic Policy. II. Trade and Welfare.* London: Oxford University Press, 1955.

Mill, J. S. *Principles of Political Economy.*

Moffatt, H. P. *Educational Finance in Canada.* (The Quance Lectures in Canadian Education, 1957.) Toronto: W. J. Gage Limited, 1957.

Moore, A. Milton. *Forestry Tenures and Taxes in Canada.* (Tax Papers, No. 11.) Toronto: Canadian Tax Foundation, 1957.

Moore, A. Milton, and Perry, J. Harvey. *Financing Canadian Federation.* (Tax Papers, No. 6.) Toronto: Canadian Tax Foundation, 1953.

Parks, Arthur C. *Beef and Beef Possibilities in the Atlantic Provinces.* Halifax: Atlantic Provinces Economic Council, 1957. (Mimeographed.)

—— *The Economy of the Atlantic Provinces, 1940–1958.* Halifax: Atlantic Provinces Economic Council, 1960. (Mimeographed.)

Perry, J. Harvey. *Taxation in Canada.* 2nd edition. Toronto: University of Toronto Press, 1953.

—— *Taxes, Tariffs, and Subsidies.* 2 vols. Toronto: University of Toronto Press, 1955.

Pigou, A. C. *A Study in Public Finance.* 3rd edition, revised. London: Macmillan and Company Limited, 1949.

Reid, E. P., and Fitzpatrick, J. M. *Atlantic Provinces Agriculture.* Ottawa: Department of Agriculture, 1957. (Mimeographed.)

Rowat, Donald C. *The Reorganization of Provincial-Municipal Relations in Nova Scotia.* (A report prepared for the Government of Nova Scotia by the Nova Scotia Municipal Bureau, Institute of Public Affairs, Dalhousie University.) Halifax, 1949.

Saunders, S. A. *Studies in the Economy of the Maritime Provinces.* Toronto: The Macmillan Company of Canada Limited, 1939.

—— *Economic History of the Maritime Provinces.* (A research study prepared for the Royal Commission on Dominion-Provincial Relations.) Ottawa: King's Printer, 1940.

Shultz, William J., and Harriss, C. Lowell. *American Public Finance.* 6th edition. Englewood Cliffs, N.J.: Prentice-Hall, Inc., 1954.

Wheare, K. C. *Federal Government.* 2nd edition. London: Oxford University Press, 1951.

2. Articles and Periodicals

Beck, J. M. "New Look in Finance," *Queen's Quarterly*, LXIII, 2 (summer, 1956).

Buchanan, J. M. "The Pure Theory of Government Finance: A Suggested Approach," *Journal of Political Economy*, XLVII (December, 1949).

—— "Federalism and Fiscal Equity," *American Economic Review*, XL (September, 1950).

—— "Federal Grants and Resource Allocation," *Journal of Political Economy*, LX (June, 1952).

—— "A Reply," *Journal of Political Economy*, LX (December, 1952).

—— "Comment on Musgrave's and Tiebout's Papers," *Public Finances: Needs, Sources, and Utilization.* Papers: April 10 and 11, 1959. New York: National Bureau of Economic Research, 1959.

Burt, A. L. "The British North American Colonies," *Canada*, edited by George W. Brown. Berkeley and Los Angeles: University of California Press, 1950.

Canadian Fiscal Facts. (Principal Statistics of Canadian Public Finance, 1957.) Toronto: Canadian Tax Foundation, 1957.

Canadian Fiscal Facts: 1958 Supplement. Toronto: Canadian Tax Foundation, 1958.

Carswell, Roger. "Municipal Motor Vehicle User Taxes," *Canadian Tax Journal*, VI (November-December, 1958).

Gordon, H. Scott. "The Economic Theory of a Common Property Resource: The Fishery," *Journal of Political Economy*, LXII (April, 1954).

Graham, John F. "The Special Atlantic Provinces Adjustment Grants: A Critique," *Canadian Tax Journal*, VIII (January-February, 1960).

Hashey, L. F. "Municipal Motor Vehicle User Taxes," *Canadian Tax Journal*, VII (January-February, 1959).

Heer, C. "The Property Tax as a Measure of Ability," *Property Taxes.* New York: Tax Policy League, 1940.

Kendrick, M. Slade. "The Ability to Pay Theory of Taxation," *American Economic Review*, XXIX (March, 1939).

Lipsey, R. G., and Lancaster, R. K. "The General Theory of Second Best," *Review of Economic Studies*, XXIV, No. 1 (1956–7).

Maxwell, J. A. "Reports on Local Government," *Canadian Journal of Economics and Political Science*, XVII (August, 1951).

The National Finances. Various issues 1956–57 to 1961–62. Toronto: Canadian Tax Foundation.

Pottier, V. J. "Background of School Finance in Nova Scotia," *Proceedings of the Golden Anniversary Convention of the Nova Scotia Union of Municipalities* (1955).

Proceedings of the Annual Conventions of the Union of Nova Scotia Municipalities.

Proskie, John. "Operations of Modern Longliners and Draggers Atlantic Seaboard 1952–1957," *Primary Industry Studies*, no. 1, vol. 7, part 1. Economics Service, Department of Fisheries of Canada; Ottawa: Queen's Printer, 1959.

—— "An Appraisal of the Atlantic Fishing Craft Modernization Programme and the Otter Trawling Fleet," Ottawa, 1960. (Mimeographed.)

Scott, A. D. "A Note on Grants in Federal Countries," *Economica*, XVII (November, 1950).

—— "The Evaluation of Federal Grants," *Economica*, XIX (November, 1952).

—— "Federal Grants and Resource Allocation," *Journal of Political Economy*, LX (December, 1952).

Simons, Henry C. "Introduction: A Political Credo," *Economic Policy for a Free Society.* Chicago: University of Chicago Press, 1948.

Spengler, Edward H. "The Property Tax as a Benefit Tax," *Property Taxes.* New York: Tax Policy League, 1940.

Watson, James Wreford. "The Geography," *Canada,* edited by George W. Brown. Berkeley and Los Angeles: University of California Press, 1950.

Whalen, Hugh. "Democracy and Local Government," *Canadian Public Administration,* III (March, 1960).

3. *Publications of the Government of Canada*

Davis, John. *Mining and Mineral Processing in Canada.* (A study for the Royal Commission on Canada's Economic Prospects.) Ottawa: Queen's Printer, 1957.

Davis, John, *et al. The Outlook for the Canadian Forest Industries.* (A study for the Royal Commission on Canada's Economic Prospects.) Ottawa: Queen's Printer, 1957.

Department of Agriculture, Feed Grains Administration. *Statistical Information Relating to the Freight Assistance Policy for Eastern Canada and British Columbia,* compiled on basis of figures available up to November 30, 1958. Ottawa, 1958. (Mimeographed.)

Department of Fisheries of Canada and the Fisheries Research Board. *The Commercial Fisheries of Canada.* (A study for the Royal Commission on Canada's Economic Prospects.) Ottawa: Queen's Printer, 1958.

Department of National Revenue. *Taxation Statistics, 1957* and *Taxation Statistics, 1960.* Ottawa: Queen's Printer.

Department of Trade and Commerce, Dominion Bureau of Statistics. *Canada Year Book,* various issues. Ottawa: Queen's Printer.

—— *Census of Canada 1956.* Ottawa: Queen's Printer, 1958.

—— *Comparative Statistics of Public Finance 1956 to 1960.* Ottawa: Queen's Printer, 1960.

—— *The Control and Sale of Alcoholic Beverages in Canada,* fiscal year ended March 31, 1959. Ottawa: Queen's Printer, 1960.

—— *Financial Statistics of Provincial Governments, 1957,* Funded Debt— Direct and Indirect, Interim. Ottawa: Queen's Printer, 1958.

—— *Financial Statistics of Provincial Governments, 1955,* Revenue and Expenditure, Actual. Ottawa: Queen's Printer, 1957.

—— *Financial Statistics of Provincial Governments, 1958,* Summary of Estimates, Revenue and Expenditures, First Analysis. Ottawa: Queen's Printer, 1958.

—— *Fisheries Statistics of Canada, 1955.* Ottawa: Queen's Printer, 1958.

—— *Fisheries Statistics of Canada, 1958.* Ottawa: Queen's Printer, 1960.

—— *Fisheries Statistics of Canada, 1956, Nova Scotia.* Ottawa: Queen's Printer, 1958.

—— *General Review of the Manufacturing Industries of Canada, 1958.* Ottawa: Queen's Printer, 1961.

—— *Handbook of Agricultural Statistics.* Part II. *Farm Income—1926–57.* Revised edition. Ottawa: Queen's Printer, 1958.

—— *Highway Statistics, 1956.* Ottawa: Queen's Printer, 1958.

—— *Hospital Statistics.* Vols. 1 and 2. Ottawa: Queen's Printer, 1958.

—— *List of Canadian Hospitals, 1959.* Memorandum. Ottawa: Queen's Printer, 1958.

—— *The Labour Force, November 1945–July 1958.* Reference Paper No. 58. 1958 revision. Ottawa: Queen's Printer, 1958.

—— *The Lumber Industry, 1959.* Ottawa: Queen's Printer, 1961.

—— *The Manufacturing Industries of Canada, 1958.* Section B. *Atlantic Provinces.* Ottawa: Queen's Printer, 1960.

—— *The Motor Vehicle, 1959.* Ottawa: Queen's Printer, 1960.

—— *National Accounts, Income and Expenditure, 1926–1956.* Ottawa: Queen's Printer, 1958.

—— *National Accounts, Income and Expenditure, 1955–57.* Ottawa: Queen's Printer, 1958.

—— *National Accounts, Income and Expenditure, 1959.* Ottawa: Queen's Printer, 1960.

—— *National Accounts, Income and Expenditure, 1960.* Ottawa: Queen's Printer, 1961.

—— *Ninth Census of Canada, 1951.* Ottawa: Queen's Printer, 1956.

—— *Preliminary Report on Mineral Production, 1960.* Ottawa: Queen's Printer, 1961.

—— *Prices and Price Indexes,* May 1958. Ottawa: Queen's Printer, 1958.

—— *Review of Employment and Payrolls, 1959.* Ottawa: Queen's Printer, 1960.

—— *Survey of Production, 1951–1955; 1954–8.* Ottawa: Queen's Printer, 1958.

Dominion-Provincial Conference 1945. (Dominion and provincial submissions and plenary conference discussions.) Ottawa: King's Printer, 1946.

Dominion-Provincial Conference 1957. Ottawa: Queen's Printer, 1958.

Drummond, W. M., Mackenzie, W., *et al. Progress and Prospects of Canadian Agriculture.* (A study for the Royal Commission on Canada's Economic Prospects.) Ottawa: Queen's Printer, 1957.

Fullerton, D. H., and Hampson, H. A. *Canadian Secondary Manufacturing Industry.* (A study for the Royal Commission on Canada's Economic Prospects.) Ottawa: Queen's Printer, 1957.

House of Commons, *Debates.* 1947, 1958. Ottawa: Queen's Printer.

Howland, R. D. *Some Regional Aspects of Canada's Economic Development.* (A study for the Royal Commission on Canada's Economic Prospects.) Ottawa: Queen's Printer, 1958.

Report of the Committee to Inquire into the Principles and Procedures Followed in the Remission Service of the Department of Justice of Canada. Ottawa: Queen's Printer, 1956.

Report of the Royal Commission on Canada's Economic Prospects. (Final.) Ottawa: Queen's Printer, 1958.

Report of the Royal Commission on Coal. Ottawa: Queen's Printer, 1960.

Report of the Royal Commission on Dominion-Provincial Relations. 3 vols. Ottawa: King's Printer, 1940.

Report of the Royal Commission on Financial Arrangements between the Dominion and the Maritime Provinces. Ottawa: King's Printer, 1935.

Report of the Royal Commission on Maritime Claims. Ottawa: King's Printer, 1926.

Report of the Royal Commission on Transportation. Vols. I and II. Ottawa: Queen's Printer, 1961.

Statutes of Canada. Various years.

Urwick, Currie Limited. *The Nova Scotia Coal Industry.* (A study for the Royal Commission on Canada's Economic Prospects.) Ottawa: Queen's Printer, 1957.

4. *Publications of the Government of Nova Scotia*

Annual Reports of the Departments of Agriculture and Marketing, Education, Highways, Lands and Forests, Mines, Municipal Affairs (Municipal Statistics), Public Health, and Public Welfare; and of the Nova Scotia Liquor Commission and the Nova Scotia Power Commission. Also annual reports on Humane Institutions and Penal Institutions.

Department of Lands and Forests. *The Forest Resources of Nova Scotia.* 1958.

Department of Trade and Industry. *Directory of Manufactures, 1960.* Halifax, 1960.

Education Office. *The Education Act and Related Acts.* (Bulletin No. 1, 1956–7.) Halifax, 1956.

Johnson, Irene E. *Tourist Survey of Nova Scotia, 1960.* Nova Scotia Travel Bureau. Halifax, Department of Trade and Industry, 1960.

Legislature. 1961 Session, *Estimates,* Halifax: Queen's Printer, 1961.

Little, Arthur D., Inc. *A Statistical Analysis of Tourists Visiting Nova Scotia in 1956.* (A report to the Department of Trade and Industry, Government of Nova Scotia.) 1957. (Mimeographed.)

Public Accounts, for the fiscal year ended March 31, 1957. Halifax: Queen's Printer, 1958.

Public Accounts, for the fiscal year ended March 31, 1960. Halifax: Queen's Printer, 1960.

"Report of the Commission on the Larger Unit," *Journals of the House of Assembly,* 1940, Appendix 8.

Report of the Revaluation Commission for the Province of Nova Scotia, 1958. (Mimeographed.)

Report of the Royal Commission: Provincial Economic Inquiry. (Including "Complementary Report of Dr. Harold A. Innis.") 2 vols. Halifax: King's Printer, 1934.

Report of the Royal Commission on Public School Finance. Halifax: Queen's Printer, 1954.

Report of the Royal Commission on Rural Credit. Halifax, 1957.

Stanfield, Premier Robert L. *Speech on Second Reading: Hospital Tax Act.* April 29, 1958. Halifax, 1958.

Statutes of Nova Scotia. Various years.

A Submission on Dominion-Provincial Relations and the Fiscal Disabilities of Nova Scotia within the Canadian Confederation. (A brief submitted by Norman McL. Rogers to the Royal Commission: Provincial Economic Inquiry.) [Halifax: King's Printer], 1934.

5. *Other Government Publications*

City of Halifax. *Report of the Commission to Investigate the Taxation System in the City of Halifax.* 1957. (Mimeographed.)

State of New York. *Report of the New York State Commission on State Aid* to *Municipal Subdivisions.* Legislative Document No. 58, memorandum submitted by the State Tax Commission. Albany, 1936.

6. *Unpublished Material*

Alberg, A. O., Minister of Education, Province of Alberta. "Foundation Program of Public School Finance." Speech, March 24, 1961. (Mimeographed.)

Bird, R. M. "Growth and Structure of Nova Scotia's Economy" (A memorandum prepared for the Nova Scotia Department of Trade and Industry). Halifax, 1958. (Typewritten.)

Forsyth, L. A. "Memorandum in Connection with the Primary Iron and Steel Industry of Nova Scotia" (A submission to the Commission on Canada's Economic Prospects; Halifax, 1955). (Mimeographed.)

Government of New Brunswick. "The Case for National Adjustment Grants." Fredericton, undated. (Mimeographed.)

"Memorandum on Behalf of the Municipalities of Nova Scotia to the Government of the Province of Nova Scotia Respecting the Allocation of Powers, Duties and Revenues." 1947. (Mimeographed.)

Morse, Norman H. "Further Observations on the Economy of Nova Scotia." (A report for the Nova Scotia Research Foundation.) Wolfville, 1956. (Typewritten.)

—— "Preliminary Results of Research on the Economy of Nova Scotia." (A report for the Nova Scotia Research Foundation.) Wolfville, 1954. (Typewritten.)

Morse, N. H., and Watson, R. E. L. "A Report on a Preliminary Survey of Rural Conditions in Hants County, Nova Scotia." (With special reference to farmer organizations in the County.) Acadia University Institute, 1957. (Mimeographed.)

"Summary: Foundation Program Percentage Proportions," based on Academic School Year, 1957–1958. Supplied by Department of Education, Province of Nova Scotia.

7. *Other Sources*

Halifax Chronicle-Herald. Various issues.

Information supplied directly by federal and provincial government departments and by the Canadian Tax Foundation.

Interviews, mostly confidential.

Labour Gazette, various issues.

SOME OTHER RELEVANT WORKS NOT CITED

1. *Books and Pamphlets*

Adarkar, B. P. *The Principles and Problems of Federal Finance.* London: P. S. King and Sons, 1933.

Benson, G. C. S. *The New Centralization.* New York: Farrar and Rinehart, 1941.

Borts, George, and Stoltz, Merton P. *A Theoretical Framework for the Analysis of Regional Economic Problems with Applications to Rhode Island as an Example of a Mature Regional Economy.* (Mimeographed.)

Buck, A. E. *Financing Canadian Government.* Chicago: Public Administration Service, 1949.

Clark, Jane P. *The Rise of a New Federalism.* New York: Columbia University Press, 1938.

Crawford, K. Grant. *Provincial School Grants 1941–1961.* (Canadian Tax Papers, No. 26.) Toronto: Canadian Tax Foundation, 1962.

Gettys, Luella. *The Administration of Canadian Conditional Grants.* Chicago: Public Administration Service, 1938.

Goldenberg, H. C. *Municipal Finance in Canada.* (A study prepared for the Royal Commission on Dominion-Provincial Relations.) Ottawa: Queen's Printer, 1939.

Hanson, Eric. *Local Government in Alberta.* McClelland and Stewart Limited, 1956.

—— *Australian Commonwealth Grants Commission, a Quarter Century of Fiscal Judgement.* (Tax Papers, No. 20.) Toronto: Canadian Tax Foundation, 1960.

—— *Fiscal Needs of the Canadian Provinces.* Toronto: Canadian Tax Foundation, 1961.

Hicks, Ursula K., et al. *Federalism and Economic Growth in Underdeveloped Countries: a Symposium.* London: Allen and Unwin, 1961.

Innis, Mary Quayle. *An Economic History of Canada.* Toronto: Ryerson Press, 1935.

Keirstead, B. S. *Economic Effects of the War on the Maritime Provinces of Canada.* Halifax: Institute of Public Affairs, Dalhousie University, 1944. (Mimeographed.)

Lougheed, W. F., and MacKenzie, W. C. *Provincial Public Finance in Nova Scotia: An Introduction.* (Bulletin No. X of the Dalhousie Institute of Public Affairs.) Toronto: Thomas Nelson and Sons, 1940.

Phillips, Charles E. *The Development of Education in Canada.* Toronto: W. J. Gage Limited, 1957.

Saunders, S. A. *The Economic Welfare of the Maritime Provinces.* Wolfville, 1932.

Wolfe, J. N. *Taxation and Development in the Maritimes.* (Canadian Tax Papers, No. 16.) Toronto: Canadian Tax Foundation, 1959.

Wright, Frederick (editor of the *Municipal Review of Canada*). *Studies in Municipal Government.* (Symposium of articles appearing from 1915 to 1940.) Montreal, 1940.

2. Articles and Periodicals

Brown, H. P. "Some Aspects of Federal-State Financial Relations," *Federalism, An Australian Jubilee Study,* edited by Geoffrey Sawer. Melbourne: F. W. Cheshire (for the Australian National University), 1952.

Carrothers, W. A. "Problems of the Canadian Federation," *Canadian Journal of Economics and Political Science,* I (February, 1935).

Curtis, C. A. "The Changing Form of Municipal Government." *Canadian Tax Journal,* VI (September-October, 1958).

—— "Municipal Finance and Provincial-Federal Relations," *Canadian Journal of Economics and Political Science,* XVII (August, 1951).

Dehem, R., and Wolfe, J. N. "The Principles of Federal Finance and the

Canadian Case," *Canadian Journal of Economics and Political Science*, XXI (February, 1955).

Goldenberg, H. Carl. "Municipal Finances and Taxation," *Report of Proceedings of the Eleventh Annual Tax Conference*: convened by the Canadian Tax Foundation. Toronto: Canadian Tax Foundation, 1958.

Gordon, H. S. "An Economic Approach to the Optimum Utilization of Fishery Resources," *Journal of the Fisheries Research Board of Canada*, X (1953).

Graham, John F. "The Application of the Fiscal Equity Principle to Provincial-Municipal Relations," *Canadian Public Administration*, III (March, 1960).

—— "Economic Development of the Atlantic Provinces in a National Perspective," *Dalhousie Review*, 40 (spring, 1960).

Hardy, Eric. "Provincial-Municipal Relations: with Emphasis on the Financial Relations between Provinces and Local Governments," *Canadian Public Administration*, III (March, 1960).

Leland, S. E. "The Relations of Federal, State, and Local Finance," *Proceedings, National Tax Association*, XXIII (1930).

MacAllister, G. A. "Development of Local Government in Nova Scotia," *Public Affairs* (autumn, 1943).

Mackintosh, W. A. "Federal Finance," *Federalism, an Australian Jubilee Study*, edited by Geoffrey Sawer. Melbourne: F. W. Cheshire (for the Australian National University), 1952.

Mallory, J. R. "The Compact Theory of Confederation," *Dalhousie Review*, XXI (October, 1941).

Maxwell, J. A. "The Adjustment of Federal-Provincial Financial Relations," *Canadian Journal of Economics and Political Science*, II (August, 1936).

North, Douglas Cecil. "Location Theory and Regional Economic Growth," *Journal of Political Economy*, LXIII (June, 1955).

Rowat, D. C. Remarks in discussion of papers on provincial-municipal relations. Institute of Public Administration of Canada. *Proceedings of the Eleventh Annual Conference*, 1959. Toronto.

Samuelson, P. A. "The Pure Theory of Public Expenditures," *Review of Economics and Statistics* (November, 1954).

—— "Diagrammatic Exposition of a Pure Theory of Public Expenditure," *Review of Economics and Statistics* (November, 1955).

Somers, H. M. "Government Expenditures and Economic Welfare." *Revue de Science et de Législation Financères*, XLIII (1951).

Tiebout, C. M. "A Pure Theory of Local Expenditures," *Journal of Political Economy*, LXIV (October, 1956).

Waines, W. J. "Problems of Municipal Finance in the Prairie Provinces," *Canadian Journal of Economics and Political Science*, III (August, 1937).

Whalen, Hugh. "The Foundations of Local Self-Government," *Canadian Journal of Economics and Political Science*, XXVI (August, 1960).

3. *Government Publications*

Commission on Intergovernmental Relations. *Report to the President*. Washington, D.C.: U.S. Government Printing Office, 1955.

Government of Canada. *Report of the Royal Commission on Coal*. Ottawa: King's Printer, 1946.

—— Department of Trade and Commerce, Dominion Bureau of Statistics. *The Maritime Provinces in Their Relation to the National Economy of Canada*: a statistical study of their social and economic condition. Ottawa: King's Printer, 1948.

Government of New Brunswick. *Report of the Royal Commission on the Financing of Schools in New Brunswick*. Fredericton. 1955.

Government of Nova Scotia. *Report of the Royal Commission on Provincial Development and Rehabilitation*. 2 vols. Halifax: King's Printer, 1944.

—— *A Submission of its Claims with Respect to Maritime Disabilities within Confederation*: as presented to the Royal Commission on Maritime Claims. Halifax: King's Printer, 1926.

—— Department of Trade and Industry. *Nova Scotia, an Economic Profile*, 1959.

Johnson, Byron L. *The Principle of Equalization Applied to the Allocation of Grants-in-Aid*. (Bureau of Research and Statistics Memorandum No. 66.) Washington: Social Security Administration, 1947.

Phillipson, Sir Sydney, and Hicks, J. R. *Report of the Commission on Revenue Allocation* [in Nigeria]. Lagos: Government Printer, 1951.

State of New York. *Report of the Commission on Municipal Revenues and Reductions of Real Estate Taxes*. Albany, 1946.

—— *Report of the New York State Commission for the Revision of the Tax Laws*. (Legislative Document No. 77.) February, 1932.

Studenski, Paul. *Measurement of Variations in State Economic and Fiscal Capacity*. (Federal Security Agency, Social Security Board, Bureau of Research and Statistics, Memorandum No. 50.) Washington, 1943.

United States, Senate. *Federal, State and Local Government Fiscal Relations*. Sen. Doc. 69, 78th Cong., 1st Sess. Washington: Government Printing Office, 1943.

4. Unpublished Material

Bird, W. R. "History of the Highways of Nova Scotia," 1945. (Mimeographed.)

Government of Nova Scotia, Department of Trade and Industry. "Economic surveys of the communities of Glace Bay, Kentville and Antigonish." (Typewritten.)

Maxwell, J. A. "A Financial History of Nova Scotia, 1848–1899." Unpublished Ph.D. dissertation for Harvard University.

Morse, Norman H. "A Survey of Trends in the Economy of Nova Scotia." 2 vols. Acadia University, 1953. (Typewritten.)

Index*

*The reader will find it helpful to use the analytical table of contents and the list of tables in conjunction with this index, since, in accordance with the usual practice, items already listed there are not listed in the index, with a few exceptions.

Coal industry: loss of American markets, 18; subventions, 18–19, 127, 131; dependence of province on, 19–20, 147; dominates mining in Nova Scotia, 97–8; plight of, 126–32; closures, 128–31 *passim*; subventions proposed by Royal Commission, 129; criticism of public policy towards, 130–2; special problems of unemployment in, 138; decline of, 147–8. *See also* Royal Commission on Coal

Commission to Investigate the Taxation System in the City of Halifax, 215–17

Conditional grants: résumé of federal, 41–2; *vs.* unconditional grants, 189–94; in province's programme, 201–4; and fiscal equity criterion, 205; formula for general services, 242–3

Confederation: blamed for economic decline, 16, 20; a benefit to Nova Scotia, 21–2; distribution of powers in, 31–3

Cossor (Canada) Limited, 152

County Incorporation Act, 51, 54

Crawford, K. G., 245n

Cunard steamships, 17

DEBT, NOVA SCOTIAN: interest on, 44

Defence: importance to Halifax area, 11, 151–3; importance to Nova Scotia, 28

Democracy, importance of strong local government in maintaining, 256–60 *passim*

Department of Finance and Economics: its programme of voluntary economic planning, 141n

Differential fiscal pressure: in economic adjustment, 181

Dominion-Provincial Conference (1945), 36n

Dominion Steel and Coal Company (Dosco), 19, 127–31 *passim*, 134, 136, 156

Duncan Commission. *See* Royal Commission on Maritime Claims

ECONOMIC ADJUSTMENT: emigration and, 143–4, 149; sociological impediments to, 143–6, 255; and declining communities, 146–9; in coal industry, 148; and Scott-Buchanan debate, 153–70 *passim*; external and internal, 157–9; in primary industries, 158; and public services, 159–70; and differential fiscal pressure, 181; under imperfect competition, 181–2; proposals for, 254–6. *See also* allocation of resources; economic development

Economic decline, analysis of, 16–22

Economic development: reliance on interviews concerning, 6; regional disparities in, 33; possible avenues of, 139–42; likely to be slow, 141–2; importance of education to, 255. *See also* allocation of resources; economic adjustment

Economic growth of Nova Scotia compared with Canada, 22–30

Economic geography of Nova Scotia, 8–13

Economic history of Nova Scotia, 13–22

Education: general service, 57; provincial grants for, 60; history of finance of, 66–76; Commission on the Larger Unit, 67; and Regional and Rural High Schools, 69, 72; School Loan Fund, 69; increase in uniform tax burden for, 75–6n; revision of equalized valuation, 76; of labour force, 108; and allocation of resources, 161–5; in municipal budgets, 208; and economic improvement, 255

Foundation Program, 70–6, 91–2, 204, 206–8, 224–31 *passim*, 237, 256; adjustments in, 75–6

See also Pottier Commission

Education Acts: of 1864, 1865, and 1866, 66; of 1955, 74

Egalitarian postulate: explained, 183–7; degree satisfied in Nova Scotia, 219–22

Electric power, 98

Emigration: and population growth, 22–3; from farms, 114; and economic adjustment, 143–4, 149; and educational level, 155n; its small effect on resource use, 158

Equalized assessment, 234, 237, 242

Equalization: and fiscal equity, 200–1n; in provincial policies, 201–4; Rowat and, 235; for local services, 241; as it relates to individuals, 250–1. *See also* education; fiscal adjustment; fiscal equity; Pottier formula; Rowat, D. C.

Equitable treatment of unequals, 183–7

in Nova Scotia, 44–5; provincial-
municipal sharing of, 90–1. *See
also* individual taxes; revenue,
provincial
Differential: means of effecting fiscal
adjustment, 173n, 246–7
Municipal: description of, 173n,
211–14; possible new bases of,
218, 243; shared bases, 243–4
Tax collection arrangements (1962–3
to 1966–7), 39–41. *See also* federal transfers
Tax rental agreements: (1947–8 to
1951–2), 36–7; (1952–3 to
1956–7), 37, 41. *See also* federal
transfers
Tax-sharing arrangements (1957–8
to 1961–2): description of, 37–9,
41; stabilization payments, 38;
discussion of, 39; degree of equalization in, 43; implied principle of,
43. *See also* federal transfers.
Tidal power, 97n, 98
Topography of Nova Scotia, 8
Tourist industry: main attractions of,
11; weakness of, 132–3
Towns, declining, 158
Towns' Incorporation Act, 51, 54, 55
Transportation: facilities, 11–12; a
basic problem, 12–13; impediments to, 21; high cost of, 28;
large expenditure in Nova Scotia,
49; Royal Commission on, 101. *See
also* freight rates

Treaty of Paris (1763), 13
Tuberculosis care, 76, 77, 78, 91

UNCONDITIONAL GRANTS: federal, description of, 32–41; history of provincial, 87–91; *vs.* conditional
grants, 189–94; types of in Nova
Scotia, 201; present basis indefen-
sible, 208–9; and local services,
208–9, 224, 239–41, 242–3; for
streets, 209; Rowat in defence of,
234–5n
Unemployment Assistance Act, 42, 84–5
Unemployment insurance, 58, 124, 145,
167–9
United Empire Loyalists: effect on economic development, 14

VARIATIONS IN MUNICIPAL SERVICES, 195
Vertical equity, 183–7
Victoria General Hospital, 76, 83
Village Commissions, 54, 240–1
Village Service Act, 54

WELFARE: as a general service, 57–8;
responsibility for, 84–6; foundation
programme for, 242–3.
West Indies: early trade with, 14
White Commission (Royal Commission
on Financial Arrangements be-
tween the Dominion and the
Maritime Provinces), 35–6
Woodlots, 115
Wood-wind-water economy, 14, 16

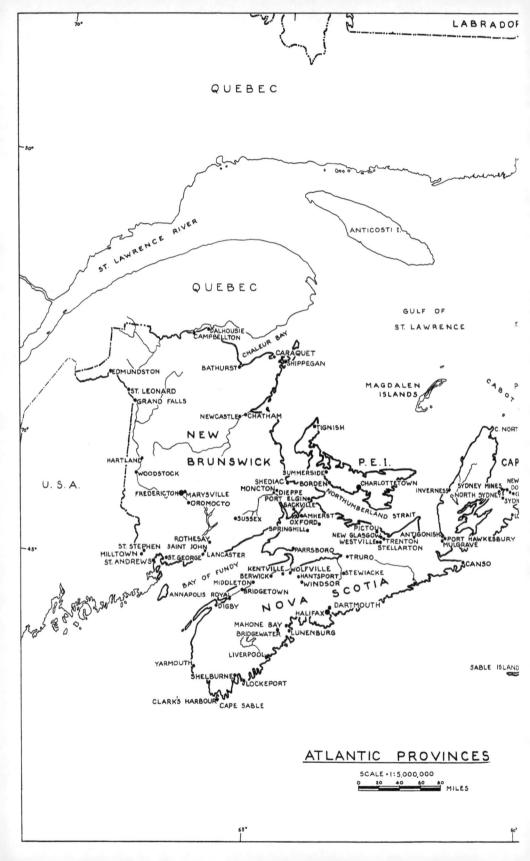

LABRADOR

QUEBEC

ST. LAWRENCE RIVER

QUEBEC

ANTICOSTI I.

GULF OF
ST. LAWRENCE

DALHOUSIE
CAMPBELLTON
CHALEUR BAY
CARAQUET
SHIPPEGAN
BATHURST

EDMUNDSTON

ST. LEONARD
GRAND FALLS

MAGDALEN
ISLANDS

CABOT

C. NORT

NEWCASTLE CHATHAM

TIGNISH

NEW

BRUNSWICK

P.E.I.

CAP

HARTLAND

WOODSTOCK

U.S.A.

SUMMERSIDE

BORDEN

CHARLOTTETOWN

INVERNESS

SYDNEY MINES

NORTH SYDNEY

NEW
DO

SYDN

SHEDIAC
MONCTON
DIEPPE
PORT ELGIN
SACKVILLE

FREDERICTON MARYSVILLE
OROMOCTO

NORTHUMBERLAND STRAIT

LC

SUSSEX

AMHERST
OXFORD
SPRINGHILL

PICTOU
NEW GLASGOW
WESTVILLE

ANTIGONISH

TRENTON
STELLARTON

PORT HAWKESBURY
MULGRAVE

ROTHESAY
ST. STEPHEN SAINT JOHN
MILLTOWN
ST. ANDREWS ST. GEORGE LANCASTER

PARRSBORO

TRURO

CANSO

KENTVILLE WOLFVILLE
BERWICK HANTSPORT
MIDDLETON WINDSOR
ANNAPOLIS ROYAL BRIDGETOWN

STEWIACKE

BAY OF FUNDY

NOVA SCOTIA

DIGBY

MAHONE BAY
BRIDGEWATER LUNENBURG

HALIFAX DARTMOUTH

LIVERPOOL

YARMOUTH

SHELBURNE
LOCKEPORT

SABLE ISLAND

CLARK'S HARBOUR CAPE SABLE

ATLANTIC PROVINCES

SCALE = 1:5,000,000

0   20   40   60   80

MILES

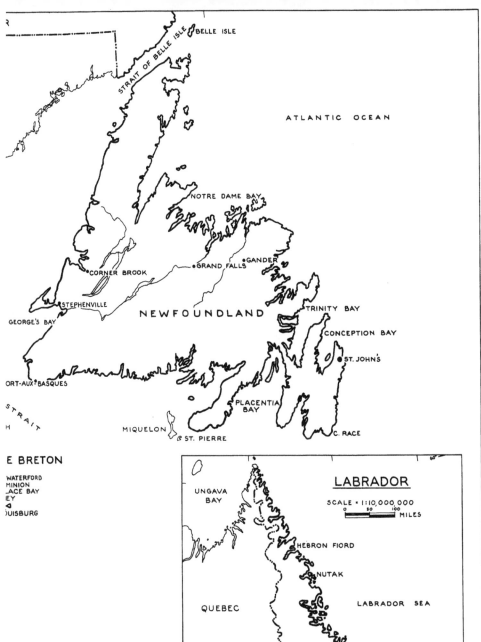

BELLE ISLE

STRAIT OF BELLE ISLE

ATLANTIC OCEAN

NOTRE DAME BAY

CORNER BROOK

GRAND FALLS

GANDER

STEPHENVILLE

GEORGE'S BAY

NEWFOUNDLAND

TRINITY BAY

CONCEPTION BAY

ST. JOHN'S

ORT-AUX-BASQUES

PLACENTIA BAY

C. RACE

STRAIT
H

MIQUELON

ST. PIERRE

E BRETON

WATERFORD
MINION
ACE BAY
EY
OUISBURG

UNGAVA BAY

LABRADOR

SCALE = 1:10,000,000

0   50   100

MILES

HEBRON FIORD

NUTAK

QUEBEC

LABRADOR SEA

HOPEDALE

INDIAN HARBOUR

ATLANTIC OCEAN

GRAND FALLS

GOOSE BAY

HAMILTON R.

QUEBEC

NFLD.

60°

55°

55°

65°

60°

55°